THE
ABUSE EXCUSE

THE
ABUSE EXCUSE

*And Other
Cop-outs, Sob Stories,
and Evasions of
Responsibility*

Alan M. Dershowitz

Little, Brown and Company
Boston   New York   Toronto   London

First Edition

ISBN 0-316-18135-8

Library of Congress Catalogue Card Number 94-77857

10   9   8   7   6   5   4   3   2

HAD

Published simultaneously in Canada by
Little, Brown & Company (Canada) Limited

Printed in the United States of America

*This book is dedicated to my first grandchild, Lori,
who always smiles and never makes excuses,
and to her parents, Jamin and Barbara,
who taught her almost everything she knows.*

ACKNOWLEDGMENTS

This book could not have been completed without the invaluable research assistance of Zachary McGee, the wonderful overall supervision of Gayle Muello, the important advice of my editor Fredrica Friedman, the support of my agent Helen Rees, and the loving input of my family members, especially Carolyn, Elon, Jamin, Adam, Rana, Marilyn, Nathan, and Claire. I am responsible for the contents, for which I make no excuses.

Contents

PART TWO
The "Everyone Does It" Excuse: Official
Corruption and Misconduct

Contents

PART THREE
The Political Correctness Excuse: Sexual Harassment, Censorship, Feminism, and Equality

Contents

THE
ABUSE EXCUSE

INTRODUCTION

THE "ABUSE EXCUSE" — the legal tactic by which criminal defendants claim a history of abuse as an excuse for violent retaliation — is quickly becoming a license to kill and maim. More and more defense lawyers are employing this tactic and more and more jurors are buying it. It is a dangerous trend, with serious and widespread implications for the safety and liberty of every American.

Among the recent excuses that have been accepted by at least some jurors have been "battered woman syndrome," "abused child syndrome," "rape trauma syndrome," and "urban survival syndrome." This has encouraged lawyers to try other abuse excuses, such as "black rage." For example, the defense lawyer for Colin Ferguson — the black man accused of killing white commuters on the Long Island Railroad — has acknowledged that his black rage variation on the insanity defense "is similar to the utilization of the battered woman's syndrome, the posttraumatic stress syndrome and the child abuse syndrome in other cases to negate criminal accountability."

On the surface, the abuse excuse affects only the few handfuls of defendants who raise it, and those who are most immediately impacted by an acquittal or reduced charge. But at a deeper level, the abuse excuse is a symptom of a general abdication of responsibility by individuals, families, groups, and even nations. Its widespread acceptance is dangerous to the very tenets of democracy, which presuppose personal accountability for choices and actions.[1] It also endangers our collective safety by legitimating a sense of vigilantism that reflects our frustration over the apparent inability of law enforcement to reduce the rampant violence that engulfs us.

At a time of ever-hardening attitudes toward crime and punishment, it may seem anomalous that so many jurors — indeed, so many Americans — appear to be sympathetic to the abuse excuse. But it is not anomalous at all, since the abuse excuse is a modern-day form of vigilantism — a recognition that since official law enforcement does not seem able to prevent or punish abuse, the victim should be entitled to take the law into his or her own hands.

In philosophical terms, the claim is that society has broken its "social contract" with the abused victim by not according him or her adequate protection. Because it has broken that social contract, the victim has been returned to a "state of nature" in which "might makes right" and the victim is entitled to invoke the law of the jungle — "kill or be killed." Indeed, these very terms were used in a recent Texas case in which one black youth killed two other blacks in a dangerous urban neighborhood. The result was a hung jury.

But vigilantism — whether it takes the old-fashioned form

---

1. "I see this trend as very disturbing. It brought down the Greek democratic experiment, it's that dangerous." Roger L. Conant, director of the American Alliance for Rights and Responsibilities, quoted in *American Bar Association Journal,* June 1994, p. 41.

of the lynch mob or the new-fashioned form of the abuse victim's killing her sleeping husband — threatens the very fabric of our democracy and sows the seeds of anarchy and autocracy. The abuse excuse is dangerous, therefore, both in its narrow manifestation as a legal defense and in its broader manifestation as an abrogation of societal responsibility.

The other characteristic shared by these defenses is that they are often "politically correct," thus reflecting current trends toward employing different criteria of culpability when judging disadvantaged groups. In effect, these abuse excuse defenses, by emphasizing historical discrimination suffered by particular groups, seek to introduce some degree of affirmative action into our criminal-justice system.

These abuse-excuse defenses are the daily fare of the proliferating menu of TV and radio talk shows. It is virtually impossible to flip the TV channels during the daytime hours without seeing a bevy of sobbing women and men justifying their failed lives by reference to some past abuse, real or imagined. Personal responsibility does not sell soap as well as sob stories. Jurors who watch this stuff begin to believe it, despite its status as junk science. The very fact that Sally Jessy and Montel repeat it as if it were gospel tends to legitimate it in the minds of some jurors. They are thus receptive to it in the courtroom, especially when the defendant is portrayed as sympathetic, and his dead victim is unsympathetic. William Kunstler is quick to point to recent public-opinion polls that show that "two-thirds of blacks and almost half the whites surveyed recognize the validity of our [black rage] theory of Mr. Ferguson's defense."

But neither public-opinion polls nor TV talk shows establish the empirical or normative validity of such abuse-excuse defenses. The basic fallacy underlying each of them is that the vast majority of people who have experienced abuses — whether it be sexual, racial, or anything else — do not commit violent crimes. Thus the abuse excuse neither explains nor justifies the violence. A history of abuse is not a psychological or a legal license to kill. It may, in some instances, be relevant at sentencing, but certainly not always.

Lest it be thought that the abuse excuse is credited only by radical defense lawyers, lay jurors, and talk-show-watching stay-at-homes, a quotation from the attorney general of the United States illustrates how pervasive this sort of thinking is becoming. In April 1993, Janet Reno was quoted as commenting on urban riots as follows: "An angry young man who lashes out in violence because he never had a childhood might do the right thing," and when the "right thing" is in contradiction with the law, "you try to get the law changed." I wonder if the angry young man's innocent victim agrees that the violence directed against his shop was the "right thing" and that the law protecting his property should be "changed."

The worst consequence of these abuse excuses is that they stigmatize all abuse victims with the violence of the very few who have used their victimization as a justification to kill or maim. The vast majority of abuse victims are neither prone to violence nor to making excuses. Moreover, abuse excuses legitimate a cycle of abuse and further abuse, since most abusers have themselves been victims of abuse. Thus, by taking the abuse excuse to its logical conclusion, virtually no abusers would ever be culpable.

The time is ripe for a critical assessment of the abuse excuse and other recent attempts by criminal defendants and others to deflect responsibility away from their crimes and onto other people, onto newly discovered — or created — "syndromes," and onto bizarre circumstances that they claim "caused" their violent actions. The time is also ripe for a somewhat broader evaluation of related excuses offered by politicians, groups, and even governments to justify such evils as corruption, repression, war, double standards, and intolerance. In the essays that follow, I explore a range of excuses — from the "abuse excuse," to the "everybody does it excuse," to the "political correctness excuse" — which raise both narrow issues of responsibility for criminal actions and broader concerns that go to the very heart of democratic theory.

First, a few words of explanation about how excuses in general, and the abuse excuse in particular, fit into the Anglo-American legal system.

With very few exceptions, all crimes require not only a criminal act such as killing, but also a criminal state of mind, such as intent or premeditation (advance planning). Even if both the act (called *actus reas*) and the state of mind (called *mens rea*) are present, the law also provides for defenses such as "official justification," "self-defense," and "insanity."

For example, the official state executioner who places the condemned man on the gurney and injects a lethal drug into his veins has killed that man with intent and premeditation. Yet he is, of course, entirely innocent of any crime, because he — like the policeman or the soldier who acts lawfully — has official justification for his actions.

So, too, the person who kills in self-defense is innocent of any crime, despite the fact that he intentionally took the life of the aggressor. The law expressly authorizes a person to use deadly force, if necessary, to prevent his imminent death or serious injury.

More controversially, if a mentally ill person kills his father because he hears voices commanding him to do so, he may be innocent of murder by reason of insanity.

In addition to complete defenses, the law also provides for an array of mitigating factors that may either reduce the charge — say, from murder to manslaughter — or reduce the sentence — say, from death to life imprisonment. These factors include being provoked, for example, by finding your spouse in bed with another person, or, as another example, making an unreasonable mistake, such as believing that an obviously unarmed person poses an imminent threat to your life.

Defenses and excuses have existed since the beginning of time. Virtually from the day they can speak, children seem endowed with a repertoire of excuses calculated to mitigate parental wrath. "I didn't mean it." "I couldn't help it." "He did it to me first." "All the kids do it." "You didn't tell me I couldn't do it." "You do it." "He made me do it." "Mary's mother lets her do it." "You let my older sister do it." "I saw it on TV." Whether these excuses are copied from parents, or whether there is some kind of built-in human "excuse" mechanism, it is beyond dispute that excuses are part of the earliest human vocabulary.

The first recorded excuses appear in the Bible near the very beginning of Genesis, when Adam blamed Eve and then Eve turned around and blamed the serpent for eating from the tree of knowledge. God rejected this "the serpent beguiled me" defense, but He was far more forgiving of Cain's "sibling jealousy syndrome" excuse. Cain killed his brother, Abel, after becoming "very wroth" when God accepted Abel's offering but not his. Instead of sentencing Cain to death, He required him to wander the earth. And when Cain whined about even this mitigated sentence ("my punishment is greater than I can bear"), God placed him in a protective program by warning anyone who slayed him that "vengeance shall be taken on him sevenfold." Abraham surely would have defended himself against the attempted murder or abuse of his child, Isaac, by invoking the "God made me do it" defense. A bit later we see a version of the rape trauma syndrome, when Jacob's sons killed not only the man who had raped their sister Dinah, but also all his friends and children because "they were in pain" over the rape. And the book of Exodus recounts a case of "defense of others" (a variation on self-defense) when Moses killed an Egyptian who was "smiting" a Hebrew. Pharaoh rejected Moses' defense and ordered him slain, whereupon Moses fled the jurisdiction.

In the millennia following the biblical age, the excuse of choice was "the Devil made me do it." As with most excuses, this one cut both ways: Sometimes it mitigated the crime, especially when the person claiming it was willing to be subjected to exorcism. But other times it aggravated the offense, as in the witchcraft trials conducted throughout Europe and even in the American colonies.

The earliest recorded cases in Anglo-American legal history include ancient accounts of what has come to be called the insanity defense. As Justice Felix Frankfurter put it:

> Ever since our ancestral common law emerged out
> of the darkness of its early barbaric days, it has been
> a postulate of Western civilization that the taking of
> life by the hand of an insane person is not murder.

In 1956, the philosopher J. L. Austin wrote an influential essay entitled "A Plea for Excuses," in which he analyzed a wide range of excuses and justifications that have been recognized throughout history. The law has traditionally distinguished among "justifications," "excuses," and "mitigations." A justification, such as self-defense, not only results in a complete *legal* exoneration, but generally also in a total *moral* exoneration. If an act is justified, it is the right thing to have done and to do in the future. It is praiseworthy, or at least not blameworthy. You are supposed to kill an aggressor in self-defense. The law prefers the life of the defender to that of the aggressor.

An "excuse," on the other hand, may be a complete legal defense, but it is not generally a moral exculpation. Killing someone by accident does not generally result in criminal liability (at least absent a high degree of negligence), but it surely is not praiseworthy. The act is indeed deserving of condemnation, though the actor is excused. We don't want him to do it again, though we will excuse him from criminal responsibility this time.

A mitigating factor does not constitute a legal defense, though it may reduce the degree of legal (and moral) responsibility. A defendant who is provoked into killing may have the charges reduced from murder to manslaughter or may have his sentence reduced, but he is not excused.

These distinctions are not always susceptible to neat categorization. Insanity, which sounds like a mitigating factor, may be a complete legal excuse. A mistake about self-defense may sound like an excuse, but if the mistake is a "reasonable" one, the law treats it as a justification. (If it is an unreasonable mistake, it may be a mitigation.) But at its core, the distinction among justifications, excuses, and mitigations is an important one that is becoming unfortunately blurred by some recent excuses. For example, the battered woman syndrome is generally introduced as part of self-defense, which is a complete justification. Yet many believe it should be regarded as a mitigating factor or, at most, as an excuse, since we do not want to encourage abused women (or children) to take the law into their own hands. We may want to excuse the conduct in extreme cases, but we surely don't want to justify it.

Another excuse, which is a variation on the abuse excuse, is the "crime of passion" mitigation. When a person kills or injures a loved one, or more commonly a former loved one who has spurned his love, the claim is that he acted out of passion and that this explanation should mitigate or excuse his punishment. "Texas self-defense" refers to the frequent acquittals in the Lone Star State of husbands who have killed their wives upon finding them in bed with another man. More often, a claim of "passion" is enough to reduce murder to manslaughter on the ground that the killer was provoked. Indeed, some recent abuse-excuse cases are really passion-excuse cases dressed up in the language of the day. Lorena Bobbitt's mutilation of her husband seemed as much to reflect her anger over his desire to leave her as her fear of his continued abuse.

Often passion defies understanding. When Judge Sol Wachtler — one of our most distinguished and respected appellate court judges — was accused of creating a fictitious character to stalk and frighten his former mistress, the legal community was shocked. When O. J. Simpson was accused of murdering his former wife,[2] his friends and fans couldn't believe that such a "nice person" was capable of such a brutal act. And the presumption of innocence requires that Simpson's plea of not guilty be credited unless the prosecution proves otherwise. But "nice" and "respected" people have engaged in crimes of passion since the beginning of history. At issue is not whether passion "explains" some crimes; it surely does. The question is whether or under what circumstances passion should excuse or mitigate a crime of violence.

Most of the abuse excuses that are criticized in this essay and those which follow are raised in an attempt to fit the defendant's conduct into self-defense, provocation, or insanity.

Consider, for example, the case of a frail woman with six children, including two infants, who has no independent means of support and who lives with her abusive and muscular husband in a rural area, with no phone, no available battered women's shelter, and a small police department that does not take domestic violence complaints very seriously.

Under traditional rules of self-defense, this woman would have the right to protect herself from being beaten up by her husband. So, if he came home drunk one night and started to punch and kick her in the head, she would be legally entitled

---

2. I have been asked to serve as a consultant to the Simpson defense.

to grab his gun and — if necessary to protect herself from imminent injury or death — shoot him. There would be no need in such a case to invoke the battered woman syndrome. Traditional rules of self-defense would justify her use of deadly force.

But let's vary the story just a bit. The husband beats her and then, in a drunken stupor, falls asleep on the floor, gun in his belt. As he is dropping off, he murmurs something about "finishing the job" when he wakes up.

If the woman lived alone, near a phone in an urban area, the law would require her to run away at that point and seek the law's protection, either through police intervention, a court order, or some other lawful means. But these options may not be realistically available to our original subject. The law may recognize, therefore, that from her actual perspective, the only prudent option is to disable her abuser. If she can do so without killing him, that is what the law requires, but if lethal force is the only safe option, she is entitled to employ it.

But what if she kills and then it turns out that she was mistaken — that her life was not really in danger? She still should be acquitted on self-defense grounds, if her decision was "reasonable" under the circumstances. Although the test of reasonableness is supposed to be an "objective" one, the jury is instructed to resolve doubts in favor of the woman who killed in what she believed was self-defense. As Oliver Wendell Holmes once put it: "Detached reflection cannot be demanded in the presence of an uplifted knife."

Where then does the battered woman syndrome fit into all of this? Before we can answer that question, we must have some idea of what the battered woman syndrome actually is, since there has been a great deal of misunderstanding about this controversial concept. A "syndrome" is a medical or psychological term referring to a group of symptoms or characteristics, all or most of which appear in common when the "syndrome" is present.[3] It helps the doctor or psychologist identify the cause, prognosis, and treatment for the condition or illness. For example, AIDS (acquired immune deficiency syndrome) is a medical syndrome that was first discovered in 1981 by a group of researchers who observed an unusually high occurrence of two rare forms of cancer among certain groups of individuals in the United States. The Centers for Disease Control defined AIDS as "a reliably diagnosed disease that is at least moderately indicative of an underlying cellular immunodeficiency in a person who has no known underlying cause of cellular immunodeficiency nor any other cause of reduced resistance reported to be associated with that disease." Persons afflicted with AIDS suffer a loss of the natural immunity that enables the human body to fight off certain infections and cancers; this loss of immunity often produces the following symptoms: swollen lymph nodes, weight loss, abnormal fatigue, night sweats, fever, and diarrhea. A person contracts AIDS after having been exposed to the human immunodeficiency virus (HIV), which may be contracted by engaging in sexual relations with an infected person, by coming into contact with tainted blood or other body fluids, or by sharing a contaminated hypodermic needle.

Another medical syndrome, which has an impact on not only an individual's physical condition but also his or her mental state as well is chronic fatigue syndrome (CFS). Chronic fatigue syndrome affects approximately 100,000 Americans, and is diagnosed after a person has exhibited the following symptoms for at least six months: fatigue severe enough to impair daily activities, fever or chills, sore throat, painful lymph nodes, muscle weakness, headaches, arthritis, photophobia,

---

3. *Barron's Medical Dictionary for the Non-Professional* defines syndrome as "a complex of signs and symptoms presenting a clinical picture of a disease or disorder."

depression, and sleep disturbance. Once diagnosed with chronic fatigue syndrome, doctors can implement a regimen of treatments designed to help patients better manage their illness. The list includes stress reduction, light exercise, diet emphasizing complex carbohydrates and vegetables, multivitamins, and other nutritional supplements like vitamin B_{12}, Kutapressin, and coenzyme Q_{10}.

The battered woman syndrome is a bit of a stretch from the paradigm of medically recognized syndromes. It was identified not by a medical doctor, but rather by a Denver psychologist named Lenore Walker, who coined the term "battered woman syndrome" in her book *The Battered Woman*. Dr. Walker, an adjunct professor of psychology at the University of Denver and a forensic psychologist, is currently serving as the executive director of the Domestic Violence Institute in Denver, Colorado. According to Dr. Walker, the battered woman syndrome arises from the cycle of abuse that women in these situations are forced to endure at the hands of their abusive spouses. The constant and unpredictable nature of this abuse gradually leads the woman to develop a condition that Lenore Walker calls "learned helplessness." Learned helplessness makes the woman feel that she has no control over her situation and that she is powerless to stop the abuse. Dr. Walker believes that battered woman syndrome and learned helplessness are both caused by spousal abuse and battering, terms that she defines broadly to include bullying and manipulation ("making women do things they otherwise wouldn't . . . by eroding their self-esteem").[4]

---

4. An extreme extension of the medical term "syndrome" is the recently created "legal abuse syndrome." In a book by that name, Karin Huffer, a social worker who coined the term, writes that victims of this disorder are "first, assaulted by crime, and secondly, by abuses of power and authority administered by the systems their tax dollars support to provide

14

The most significant point about the battered woman syndrome is what it does *not* include or explain, namely the *killing* of the abuser by the abused woman. The act of killing is *not* a symptom of the battered woman syndrome. Indeed, it is largely inconsistent with the characteristic symptoms of passivity. Very few women who fit the diagnosis of the battered woman syndrome kill their batterers.

Why then do legislators and judges permit defendants who *have* killed their batterers to introduce evidence of a syndrome that does not include or explain their act of killing — which is the only act that is on trial? The answer is somewhat complex, but important. The battered woman syndrome purports to explain not why the abused woman *killed* her batterer, but rather why she *did not* — and indeed *could not* — *leave* her batterer. If the jury believes that her psychological condition — the battered woman syndrome — precluded her from doing what other "normal" and "reasonable" women would have done, namely leaving, then they can begin to understand why she may have believed that her only realistic option was to kill. The unreasonable-*seeming* killing thus becomes "reasonable" to her, and the jury may acquit her on grounds of self-defense.

Some critics argue that in cases which would not amount to self-defense except for the battered woman syndrome, the jury should not be faced with a choice between total acquittal and conviction for murder. Instead, the jury should be instructed that if the defendant's condition caused her to act in a manner that would be "unreasonable" for a "normal" person, the conviction should be reduced from murder to, say, manslaughter. Other critics argue that the battered woman syndrome should be used to prove insanity, because an acquitted killer suffering from the battered woman syndrome is in

---

due process of law. . . . In short, they get a 'double whammy.'" See Karin Huffer, *Legal Abuse Syndrome* (1993).

15

need of psychiatric treatment. But today, the battered woman syndrome is used primarily to help prove self-defense, which is an absolute defense resulting in unconditional acquittal and freedom.

In some instances, the battered woman syndrome has been abused by defendants who clearly had options other than taking the law into their own hands. As one of the nation's leading experts in criminal law asked rhetorically: "Do any husbands get killed anymore who don't batter their wives?"[5] Any time a defense works, it is quickly abused by some who killed in cold blood. In other cases, the killing may not be calculated, but the killer may have resorted to lethal force when other options were available. Though we may be sympathetic with a childless, financially independent woman who is abused by her boyfriend or husband, a history of abuse does not justify killing the abuser, regardless of how unsympathetic he may be. The woman in that situation does have options, unpalatable as they may be. The law requires her to act on those options rather than kill her abuser. Using the battered woman syndrome in that sort of case is an example of what I call the "abuse excuse."

Although I have long been interested in the subject of defenses — especially the insanity defense — my concern over the abuse of the battered woman syndrome was first stimulated by the 1987 case of Stella Valenza, a twenty-four-year-old Queens, New York, woman who was brought to trial for hiring three thugs to murder her husband. The evidence showed that the paid assassins first tried to dispatch their prey by assaulting him with baseball bats. He survived the brutal attack and spent more than a week in the hospital.

Having failed with their Louisville Sluggers, the hired

---

5. Professor Yale Kamisar, quoted in *American Bar Association Journal*, June 1994, p. 41.

hoods upgraded their arsenal and went after him with guns. Miraculously, the victim again survived — this time after being struck in the head, leg, and hand by six bullets from a .25-caliber pistol.

Mrs. Valenza and her hired assassins were finally arrested while plotting yet a third assault on her husband's much-wounded body. They were charged with attempted murder, conspiracy to commit murder, and various weapons offenses. Mrs. Valenza, who was tried separately, admitted hiring the trio of bruisers to kill her husband. She claimed, however, that she was acting in "self-defense" because her husband had abused her.

The law does not, of course, recognize the hiring of hit men as proper self-defense. The law, properly, demands that an abused person seek protection from the police.

But despite the law, Mrs. Valenza was acquitted unanimously of all fourteen counts in the indictment by a vigilante jury, which took the law into its own hands.

She won her case by a familiar technique: She put the victim on trial. She testified that her husband had sexually abused and beaten her. Several jurors said they believed her account and acquitted her for that reason. If she was telling the truth, the net result is that two dangerous criminals were allowed to remain free: she and her husband.

The Valenza acquittal generated a series of talk show segments that encouraged abused women to take the law into their own hands. Oprah Winfrey's widely watched show was entitled "Is it Open Season for Wives to Kill Their Husbands?"

Several callers bragged about how they had shot, knifed, and scalded their abusive husbands. Audience members cheered as one woman explained why scalding a man with boiling grits is better than using just water: "Grits stick longer and leave more permanent scars."

There can be little doubt that in at least some cases in which women claim battered woman syndrome, they are offering after-the-fact rationalization for violence provoked by anger and frustration, rather than by the need to protect themselves against imminent and otherwise unpreventable danger.

There are a growing number of abuse excuses — and other excuses that are analogous — that have been raised or proposed. The list of "syndromes" which have been "discovered," "invented," "constructed," or "concocted" as excuses for crime is mind-boggling. A sampling follows:

Adopted child syndrome
American dream syndrome
Arbitrary abuse of power syndrome
Battered child syndrome
Battered woman syndrome
Black rage syndrome
Computer addiction
Distant father syndrome
Elderly abuse syndrome
"Everybody does it" defense
Failure-to-file syndrome
False memory syndrome
Fetal alcohol syndrome
Gangster syndrome
Holocaust survivor syndrome
Legal abuse syndrome
"The minister made me do it" defense
Multiple personality disorder
Parental alienation syndrome
Patient-therapist sex syndrome
"Pornography made me do it" defense
Posttraumatic stress disorder
Premenstrual stress syndrome
Rape trauma syndrome
Repressed (or recovered) memory syndrome

Ritual abuse (satanic cults) syndrome
Roid rage (violence caused by steroids)
Self-victimization syndrome
Sexual abuse syndrome
Sexually transmitted disease syndrome
Situational stress syndrome
Stockholm syndrome
Super Bowl Sunday syndrome
Sybil syndrome
"Television made me do it" defense
Tobacco deprivation syndrome
"Twinkies made me do it" defense
UFO survivor syndrome
Urban survival syndrome
Vietnam syndrome

Each of these syndromes and defenses shares in common a goal of deflecting responsibility from the person who committed the criminal act onto someone else who may have abused him or her or otherwise caused him or her to do it. Some of these excuses try to shift the blame to the abuser, others to a condition or circumstance. The likelihood of success increases if the finger of abuse can be pointed to the specific person whom the defendant killed or injured, allegedly to protect himself or herself.

One reason why the abuse excuse has become so popular lately is because it is often a vigilante defense that places the victim — who is usually dead and incapable of defending himself — on trial. If the dead victim can be painted in an unflattering light and the live defendant can be seen sympathetically, the jury may be persuaded that "he had it coming" and that his killer should not be held culpable.

"The victim had it coming" is not, of course, a valid legal defense. Thus, defense lawyers try to dress up the abuse excuse as a variation on self-defense. Self-defense, however, generally requires the killer to have reasonably feared that his or her life was in "imminent" danger from the person killed. In many abuse-excuse cases, on the other hand, the person killed or maimed was either asleep or did not, for other reasons, pose any "imminent" danger. Nonetheless, defense lawyers are raising self-defense claims in questionable cases and some judges are allowing defendants to argue self-defense — or some variant — even in the absence of evidence that they were in imminent danger when they attacked their alleged abuser. These judges prefer to leave the issue to the common sense of the jury rather than risk appellate reversal for taking an issue away from the jury in a close case. And some juries simply take the law into their own hands and acquit, despite the absence of a factual or legal basis for the defense. Once a jury has acquitted — no matter how baselessly — that is the end of the matter, since the constitutional protection against double jeopardy precludes attack on a jury acquittal.

Sometimes, the alleged abuse occurred years earlier, during childhood, and the long repressed "memory" was only recently "recovered" with the help — or prodding — of a therapist who specialized in "recovered memories." The recovered memory syndrome is quite controversial among therapists and has given rise to several lawsuits. There is, of course, no statute of limitations on the use of the abuse excuse. The killing can occur decades after the abuse stopped and the killer can still claim that it was caused by the abuse. In other situations, the alleged abuse began a long time ago but continues to the present day.

At bottom, the subtle message of these abuse-excuse defenses is that the *real* criminal is the dead victim and the defendant performed a public good by dispatching him. Thus, the abuse excuse places the *victim* of the killing or maiming on trial — generally in absentia — and if the defense lawyer can persuade the jury that he or she "had it coming," there is a chance that the jury will disregard the established rules of self-defense and take the law into its own hands by acquitting the defendant or reducing the charges.

The murder trial of the Menendez brothers for the cold-blooded shooting of their parents is a paradigm of the abusive and successful employment of the abuse excuse. Indeed, it was this case which led me to coin the term in a column about the Menendez and Bobbitt cases.[6]

It is certainly possible — and in my view highly likely — that the Menendez brothers concocted out of whole cloth the entire story of sexual abuse by their father. The fact that while confiding their carefully planned killing to a trusted psychologist, they never even mentioned the alleged history of the abuse is strong evidence of its falsity. So is the fact that Erik chose to attend UCLA, which is near the Menendez home, rather than Berkeley, which is hundreds of miles away — at a time when he claimed to be trying to escape the ongoing abuse.

But even assuming that the story of abuse was entirely true, how does that justify, excuse, or even mitigate the culpability of Lyle and Erik Menendez for their carefully planned execution of both their parents and their lengthy cover-up of the killings? Their lawyers claimed self-defense, despite the ease with which the brothers could have left home, moved to another part of the country or the world, and escaped the alleged sexual abuse. Even if they believed that their father *and mother* would hunt them down and kill them, they could have sought police protection. Instead, they decided to take the law into their own hands, shopped for weapons, plotted a "perfect" double murder, executed a cover-up, and — perhaps — contrived an abuse-excuse defense in the event they were caught.

------

6. See Stephanie Goldberg, "Fault Lines," *American Bar Association Journal,* June 1994, p. 40.

Despite what appeared to many knowledgeable observers of the criminal justice system to be an open-and-shut case of first-degree murder,[7] and despite the trial judge's refusal to instruct the juries — they were tried together but to separate juries — that they could acquit the defendants on grounds of self-defense,[8] each Menendez brother *won* a hung jury based on the abuse excuse. I use the word "won" advisedly, since in most criminal cases a hung jury is a clear victory for the defendant, giving the defense considerable leverage in negotiating a favorable plea bargain. In the Menendez cases this was a spectacular victory, since the evidence of guilt — both factual and legal — appeared so overwhelming.

If the defense had managed to persuade only a handful of jurors in each of the Menendez cases, observers might attribute this to the vagaries of jury selection or to the uniquely quirky character of California juries. But public-opinion polls and other measures of public attitudes strongly suggest that a large proportion of Americans throughout the nation bought the Menendez brothers' abuse excuse.

Why, in an age of ever-toughening attitudes toward law and order, could so many Americans be so sympathetic to two such cold-blooded parricides? The answer, I believe, lies in a number of factors, some more specific to the Menendez cases, others of an historical nature, and still others more general to the time in which we live. Ironically, although abuse excuses

---

7. Professor Yale Kamisar, who has been teaching criminal law for more than thirty-five years, says that if he "had given the facts of the Menendez case to his students in an exam 10 years ago, it would have seemed like a joke." *American Bar Association Journal*, June 1994, p. 41.

8. The judge did instruct the jury that it could find "imperfect self-defense" — an *unreasonable* belief that their lives were in imminent danger. Such a finding would have reduced the charge from murder to manslaughter. See *Los Angeles Times*, December 6, 1993. But the jury could not agree even as to such a finding.

are *defenses* to crime, at another level they are also manifestations of our deep need to control our environment — to take the law into our own hands. They argue that since official law enforcement is incapable of protecting victims of abuse, these victims are entitled to engage in vigilante justice.

At the narrowest level, the prosecution in the Menendez cases made a serious tactical blunder — at least in retrospect. Had it tried the brothers *first* for the murder of their mother *only*, it would have been more difficult for the brothers to mount a sympathetic abuse excuse for killing *her.* She, after all, did not herself abuse the boys, even according to their highly questionable account. By putting the brothers on trial for killing both their mother and father, the prosecution made it easier for them to counter by putting their dead and defenseless father on trial for abusing them. And José Menendez was the perfect victim to place on trial. Whether or not he was guilty of the specific crime of sex abuse — and he was not there to defend himself against somewhat vague accusations of this very private crime — he was surely guilty of being an overbearing and overambitious parent. In the minds of several jurors and many observers of this widely watched trial, José Menendez "had it coming."

In contrast to the single-dimensional portrait of evil painted of José Menendez by the lawyers for the Menendez brothers, his killers were painted in a far more sympathetic and multi-dimensional light. Jurors cried more openly when Erik and Lyle described their lives with José than when photographs of the bullet-riddled bodies of the Menendez parents were passed around. In the midst of this after-the-fact attempt by the brothers to pin the blame for the killings on their father, Kitty Menendez got lost. Did she, too, "have it coming"? Did she pose an imminent threat to the brothers' lives? Why did she have to be killed as she was filling out college application forms for her younger son and eating strawberries?

Instead of focusing on the legal issues — primary among which was whether an alleged history of abuse can justify or mitigate a carefully planned "preventive" execution — the trial degenerated into an emotional blame-a-thon between two spoiled young men and their dead father and mother.

The murder of parents by children has fascinated chroniclers throughout human history. From biblical times through Sophocles, Shakespeare, Dostoyevsky, and Freud, we have been repelled and intrigued by sons and daughters who have taken life from those who gave them life. Nearly a century before a California jury refused to convict the Menendez brothers of their admitted killings, a Massachusetts jury acquitted Lizzie Borden of axing her parents to death. Controversy still rages around that verdict.

There is actually a California criminal lawyer who "specializes in defending children who kill their parents."[9] This lawyer, Paul Mones, acknowledges that "children who kill their abusers usually do so when the adult is sleeping or walking in the front door." He argues that although these killings "look like premeditated murder," these children really believe that they must strike first. The problem is that the law does not agree. For very good reasons, it does not allow "preventive" executions, except where there is no alternative. When an alleged abuser is asleep, there are almost always alternatives. And the law requires an abuse victim to try those alternatives — ranging from running away, to calling the police, to obtaining a court order — before resorting to lethal self-help.

For those who argue that the abuse *caused* the retaliation or preventive killings, the data poses an insuperable empirical obstacle. The fact is that very few abuse victims resort to lethal force. As Mones himself acknowledges, "parricides occur only

---

9. *American Bar Association Journal*, May 1992.

in a small percentage of seriously abusive households." Indeed, he estimates that there are only about three hundred parricides a year in the United States. The amount of abuse is thousands of times that number, and abuse is not a factor in all the cases. Nor is there any correlation between the severity, frequency, or type of abuse and the deadliness of the response. It follows, therefore, that something *other than*, or at least in addition to, the abuse explains the relatively rare parricides. Put another way, there is no abuse *"syndrome"* that includes as one of its "symptoms" parricide — or indeed any kind of "cide." As demonstrated previously, even the battered woman syndrome — the best documented and most widely accepted of the abuse excuses — does not explain the *killing* of the batterer by the batteree, since very few battered women kill their batterers.

What we are left with is a history of victimization that may or may not be a *contributing factor* — among many others — to the act of killing or maiming committed by the abuse victim. How much of a factor it may be in any given situation will vary from case to case and may be beyond the ken of current science to determine. It should be up to the law to decide — as a matter of policy — how much weight to ascribe to this very partial causative factor, both in general and in any particular case.

The battered woman syndrome and the rape trauma syndrome have many factors in common with the abused child syndrome. Among other things, they treat women like children. But there is at least one important difference. Since the battered woman syndrome and the rape trauma syndrome almost always involve a *female* abuse victim who killed or maimed a *male* abuser, a political dimension is added to these cases, which often degenerate into "men-versus-women," "we against them" show trials. The Bobbitt trials were a case in point.

In theory, it is difficult to imagine a clearer case of culpable criminal mayhem. Lorena Bobbitt willfully cut off her husband's penis while he was asleep. She claimed that he had raped her, though he was acquitted of that charge. Even if it were true, she had easily available options short of mayhem. She could simply have left him. There were no children. There were not even economic ties, since she held a good job. He had not threatened to harm her if she left. Indeed, he seemed anxious to be rid of her. She reported his alleged misconduct, but refused to take the next step toward securing legal relief. Instead, she struck with a knife.

Women throughout the world — not all but many — rallied to her "cause" and cheered her on. Her lawyers raised a defense of "temporary insanity," which combined elements of self-defense, rape trauma syndrome, and battered woman syndrome. She was acquitted by reason of insanity, sent to a mental hospital for observation, and quickly released when — as expected — the doctors found that there was nothing really wrong with her. The "insanity" defense had been a cover for the real defense of "the sexist son-of-a-bitch had it coming." The same feminists who rail against putting the victim on trial in rape cases cheered the tactic of putting John Wayne Bobbitt on trial in this case. (Nor did some feminists have much hesitation in putting Paula Jones's prior sexual history on trial after she filed a lawsuit against President Clinton.)

And John Wayne Bobbitt was also the perfect victim to put on trial. He made a terrible impression, both in and out of court. He was arrogant, unrepentant, sexist, and insensitive. He exploited his injury commercially on television and in magazines. His trial testimony was repeatedly contradicted by more believable witnesses. He was an utterly unsympathetic character. Lorena Bobbitt, on the other hand, made a very sympathetic impression. She cried, appeared remorseful, and created an impression of honesty. In the end, the jury decided that they liked Lorena better than John. And who can blame them for that! But a criminal trial should not be a popularity contest. The Bobbitt jury was hoodwinked into believing an "insanity" defense that had little medical basis, as evidenced by Bobbitt's quick release from the mental hospital. Bobbitt was an angry, vengeful woman who chose to exact revenge rather than exercise the option of leaving her abusive husband.

The tactic of putting the dead or maimed victim on trial and getting the jury to identify with the defendant can be dangerous. Recall the early days of the civil rights movement, when white juries in the Deep South routinely acquitted white sheriffs, Klansmen, and other assorted killers for murdering both black and white civil rights workers "who had it coming." Everyone loves vigilante justice when the vigilantes are on "our side," but they hate it when the vigilantes are on "their side."

That is why — as a *civil libertarian* and as a *defense attorney* — I am so concerned about the excesses of the abuse excuse. Taken to its current and projected extremes, it is a lawless invitation to vigilantism, both on the part of abuse victims and on the part of jurors who sympathize more with them than with those whom they have killed or maimed. It threatens to increase the cycle of violence, not only by women but also against women. It endangers civil liberties by substituting vigilante justice — which is an oxymoron — for courtroom justice, and the rule of man (and woman) for the rule of law. It endangers legitimate defenses — such as insanity based on mental illness, self-defense when there is no recourse, and diminished capacity — by expanding them to the point where a swing of the pendulum is inevitable. Charles P. Ewing, a psychologist and law professor, points to a jury trial following the Menendez and Bobbitt cases in which the jury deadlocked in a clear-cut battered woman syndrome case. He attributes this to a backlash caused by the media barrage in the Menendez and Bobbitt cases.[10]

In light of this reality, it might be expected that civil libertarians, feminists, and defense attorneys would share my concern about the abuses of the abuse excuse. Some do, but others have virtually accused me of treason for criticizing the extremes to which the abuse excuse has been taken.

A prominent criminal-defense lawyer wrote an entire article in the *California Criminal Defense Practice Reporter* castigating me for "bashing juries that don't convict and bad-mouthing the lawyers" who raise the abuse excuse.[11] I plead guilty to the former but not to the latter. No one should criticize any defense lawyer who honestly and ethically raises an available defense. What I am criticizing is the easy availability of the defense in cases like Menendez and Bobbitt and the foolish jurors who fall for the sob stories told by the lawyers. I strongly believe that these defenses do great damage to civil liberties by encouraging vigilante justice. That is why I believe they are popular in an age in which most Americans want to see us get tough on crime. Abuse-excuse defenses play right into the hands of those who do not trust our legal system to do justice. Lorena Bobbitt is a female version of "Dirty Harry," who is certainly no hero to civil libertarians.[12]

---

10. *American Bar Association Journal,* June 1994, p. 42.

11. Leslie Abramson, a defense lawyer in the Erik Menendez case, went even further, saying that "Alan Dershowitz used to be a criminal defense lawyer . . . maybe he was kidnapped by space aliens. And they brainwashed him." It must have been a very large spaceship, since almost every criminal law professor and practitioner I know has been critical of the Menendez hung jury.

12. Two former law students of mine expressed "outrage" at my trivialization of the abuse excuse, arguing that "battered women who kill their abusive partners use the same self-defense laws as all other defendants." They must have missed my class on self-defense. Nowhere in the civilized world do self-defense laws justify the killing or maiming of a

Abusive defenses such as those employed by the Menendez brothers and Lorena Bobbitt also undercut the credibility of legitimate defenses in appropriate cases. Finally, they stigmatize entire groups of people — women, blacks, and others — who share characteristics in common with the criminals but who do not commit similar crimes.

That is why I criticize the abuse excuse *as a* civil libertarian, *as a* defense lawyer, and *as an* egalitarian. That is why I criticized vigilante defenses used by Southern lawyers in defense of Klan members who killed civil rights workers. Being a civil libertarian and a defense lawyer does not obligate me to favor *every* defense to crime, regardless of whether it hurts or helps civil liberties. The abuse excuse hurts civil liberties by undercutting personal responsibility and encouraging lawlessness.

Civil liberties cannot thrive in an age of lawlessness. Anyone concerned about the rule of law should be appalled at those who, for example, applauded Ellie Nesler for murdering a defendant in a courtroom while his hands were shackled.[13] She said she did it to stop him from abusing other children, as he allegedly had abused one of her children several years earlier. But her act of vigilantism denied her victim his day in court. No civil libertarian or defense lawyer can approve that kind of lawlessness. It is the most basic violation of due process.

Moreover, accepting abuse as an excuse for violence does nothing to break the cycle of abuse. We are told that most abusive

---

sleeping spouse by a woman who has the option of either leaving or calling the police. Only the abuse excuse — a special and unjustified *extension* of self-defense laws — claims that a history of abuse licenses the woman to take the law into her own hands. My critics argue that their goal is "to get judges and juries to apply the self-defense laws *equally* and without bias to battered women and children." That is my goal as well, and it will be accomplished only if *all* citizens are denied the right to kill their *sleeping* past abusers in "self-defense." *San Francisco Examiner,* January 25, 1994, p. A-18.

13. See *People v. Nesler* (Sonora County Superior Court, No. 20634F).

parents, husbands, boyfriends, and others were *themselves* victims of abuse by others. Taken to its illogical extreme, the abuse excuse would justify — or at least mitigate — the conduct of the *abuser* as well as victim. To be sure, the abuser is not abusing the same person or persons who abused him. But many of those who advocate the abuse excuse do not limit the history of abuse, which is deemed to excuse, solely to the actions of the particular abuser who was killed or maimed; they argue that the woman who killed should be able to introduce evidence of abuse by *other* men in her life. Under that approach, virtually no one — except the *original* abuser in history — should be held responsible for his or her actions. The cycle of abuse-violence-abuse is thus perpetuated by the abuse excuse. The big losers will be the most vulnerable people in our society — those who most need the protection of our criminal laws. The aged, young children, mothers on welfare, the handicapped will all suffer if criminal responsibility is compromised by the abuse excuse.

Another serious problem with the abuse excuse — and other excuses that are gender- or race-specific — is that it sends a dangerous double message of irresponsibility, especially about women. After all, if women who have been abused are *not responsible* for their violence, then does it not follow that such women are *ir*responsible and thus untrustworthy? Such a generalization — if accepted — would contribute a major setback for abused women, and for women in general. It would confirm the sexist stereotype of the woman out of control. Such a generalization would also be an insult to the thousands of abused women who obey the law — who have *not* engaged in violence.

The truth is that the vast majority of women (and men) who have been abused are entirely capable of controlling their behavior and complying with the law. They should not be tainted by the violence of the infinitesimal proportion of women who choose to use their history of abuse as an excuse for violence or a license to commit crimes.

This point can be illustrated even more powerfully if one considers another currently voguish defense that is a cousin to the abuse excuse, namely, the premenstrual syndrome defense. When a prominent Virginia surgeon won acquittal on charges of drunken driving and assaultive behavior on the ground that she was suffering from PMS, that victory constituted a significant setback for the women's movement. It confirmed the sexist stereotype of the woman unable to control her raging hormones. It stigmatized all women with PMS who do not drive drunk or engage in assaultive behavior during the premenstrual part of their cycle. And it endangers the careers of all female surgeons and other women in positions of responsibility — certainly all those with PMS — who now have been given a judicial license to be out of control during several days each month. Anyone who believes that the successful invocation of the PMS defense is a victory in the long run for women is fooling himself or herself.

Indeed, it was this danger of stereotyping that led me to refuse to represent a Holocaust survivor several years ago who wanted me to raise the "Holocaust survivor syndrome" as an excuse for his defrauding of the government. His psychiatrist pointed to some literature suggesting that several Holocaust survivors who had engaged in illegal conduct had done so because of a deep-seated distrust of government that grew out of their experiences during the war. These people had managed to survive by breaking the rules in Germany, Poland, and other countries occupied by the Nazis, and they continued to break the rules when the war ended.

Despite my deep sympathy for anyone who experienced the Holocaust, I had a strong visceral negative reaction to the Holocaust survivor syndrome excuse. I grew up with many Holocaust survivors who did not break the rules, once they came to America. It would be an insult to the integrity of these brave men and women who had learned to live within the rules of law to stigmatize all — or even most — survivors as incapable of playing by the rules of the nation that gave them a home. The Holocaust survivor syndrome excuse also raised the danger of anti-Semitic stereotyping, by seeming to confirm bigoted generalizations about Jews as "Shylocks," tax cheats, and financial frauds.

The same can be said for excuses that are race-specific, such as "black rage" or "urban survival syndrome." By generalizing about blacks as a group or even blacks who live in dangerous urban neighborhoods, advocates of these abuse excuses are sending a double message: If all, or even most, blacks who live in dangerous neighborhoods are affiliated with urban survival syndrome, then would it not follow that all, or most, such blacks are *dangerous?* Any such racist conclusion would reinforce existing stereotypes and would be an insult to the millions of blacks who do not use their "rage" as an excuse for violence or their urban situation as a license to kill.

On May 16, 1994, CNBC devoted an hour to the abuse excuse, focusing particularly on black rage. One of the panelists was attorney William Kunstler, who is raising black rage in support of an insanity defense for Colin Ferguson, the man accused of killing six commuters on the Long Island Railroad. I asked Kunstler whether he would be willing to raise a "white rage" defense on behalf of a skinhead who killed blacks as a result of his "rage." He said no, because only blacks have legitimate rage, whereas white rage is racism. I suggested that by allowing a defense of black rage, the courts would, in effect, be considering a black defendant's racism as a *mitigating* factor, rather than as an *aggravating* factor in a racially motivated crime. Kunstler's reply was that blacks are not capable of racism, since they have no power. But Colin Ferguson had all the power he needed when he stood over cowering commuters and selected who among them would live and who would die on the basis of their race.

Another panelist, a black activist lawyer named Colin Moore, took the abuse excuse to its illogical conclusion by arguing that "racism is in itself a form of insanity." Under that view, all racially motivated crimes — ranging from Klan lynchings to interethnic gang shootings — would be legally "excused" on the grounds of insanity. As I said in response to Moore: "Every racist white in the South has an insanity defense. Everybody who is a racist now has an abuse excuse. Is no one responsible?" Nor could the acquitted defendants be confined in mental hospitals, because no reputable psychiatrists would claim to be able to treat racism as a mental illness.

A number of callers to the show, who identified themselves as African Americans, were appalled at Kunstler's black rage defense, precisely because it stigmatized *them*, along with *all* blacks, as prone to violence and lawlessness on the basis of their collective rage.

All of these "political" syndromes — which pit one group against another — perpetuate images of victimization, powerlessness, and inability to exercise self-control. They send dangerous messages both to the stereotyped groups and to those who stereotype them.

I am confident, moreover, that if the black rage defense were to succeed, we would see white skinheads invoking "white rage" in defense of white-against-black racist killings. Rage is simply not a valid excuse for violence against members of a different race. Indeed, when rage is based on race, we have a word for it: racism. And racism — no matter how dressed up in psychiatric or psychological garb — should never be allowed to mitigate a crime, even if it helps to explain it.

In addition to the dangers of stereotyping, arguments in favor of abuse excuses often convey dangerous misinformation. For example, on February 4, 1994, I was on a special ninety-minute *Nightline* "Town Meeting" devoted to the subject "Is abuse an excuse?" The program was stimulated by an article I had written about the abuse excuse. Much of the discussion focused on the battered woman syndrome. In the course of the discussion, TV talk show hostess Sally Jessy Raphaël tossed out "a fact" that is the common fare of daytime TV talk shows. I had argued that Lorena Bobbitt should have left home rather than cut off her husband's penis. Sally Jessy Raphaël responded: "Alan, now you know yourself that *a woman is 75 percent more likely to be killed if she leaves than if she stays.*" The panel's expert on the battered woman syndrome, Lenore Walker, jumped in quickly: "That's correct."

Now think of what a message that "fact" sends to women who are being battered: *Don't* leave home; *stay* in the place where you are being battered; if you leave you are *much more* likely to be killed; if you kill your abuser, you will be better off than if you leave him.

The problem is that the underlying "fact" is simply false, though it is widely cited by battered-women experts and advocates. On the *Nightline* show, I characterized it as "statistic-babble" that sends a false and terrible message. After I returned to Cambridge, I asked my research staff to find out how this false and dangerous fact had made its way onto the talk-show circuit. The story is a fascinating one, which I believe should caution us against ever accepting uncritically those "facts" that are used by advocates to make political points.

Sally Jessy Raphaël attributed the 75 percent statistic to the New York State Coalition Against Domestic Violence, which claimed that the 75 percent statistic, which is cited on a "fact sheet" that the organization uses, comes from Barbara Hart, a domestic-violence expert.

When we told Hart that the *Nightline* "fact" had been traced to her, she was "furious," insisting that the 75 percent statistic is "absolutely false": "I repudiate that piece of information entirely." Hart said that her research is frequently misrepresented — this is not the first time she has heard the false 75 percent statistic being tossed around on the talk-show circuit. She added that in the arena of sexual violence, numbers are often misconstrued and quoted out of context: "The *way* the statistics are reported is flawed. Even if the study is empirically correct — and it often is not — its social significance is often interpreted poorly by others." She was especially angry at those who "twisted my work and spread that bullshit statistic."

Since Sally Jessy Raphaël's statistic was false, I wrote to Lenore Walker, the expert on the battered woman syndrome who had said that it was "correct." Walker wrote back: "Sally Jessy Raphaël did state that 75 percent of all women who left were *in danger.*" However, that is not what Raphaël stated on *Nightline.* She said that a woman is 75 percent *more likely* to be killed if she leaves than if she stays. In any event, Walker denied that she had confirmed Raphaël's statistic. She wrote: "I don't know where she got that number. I did support the fact that women were in greater danger of being more seriously hurt or killed when they left." According to Walker, this "fact" is documented by Boston psychologist Angela Browne. Browne, however, *does not* support the "fact" that women are in "greater danger of being more seriously hurt or killed" if they leave their abusers:

> To separate from an individual who has threatened to harm you if you go increases — at least in the short run — the very risk from which you are trying to escape. . . . Some estimates suggest that at least 50 percent of women who leave their abusers are followed and harassed or further attacked by them.[14]

---

14. Angela Browne, *When Battered Women Kill* (New York: The Free Press, 1987), p. 110.

Browne leaves unanswered the critical question of what happens in the long run.

Moreover, if we subcite Browne's text, we run into even greater difficulties. There appears to be *no basis* for Browne's "at least 50 percent" estimate, which she attributes to Donna M. Moore's book, *Battered Women*.[15] Moore, however, does not indicate any survey or study that would support Browne's 50 percent estimate, referring her readers to a pamphlet published by the Michigan Women's Commission entitled *Domestic Assault: A Report on Family Violence in Michigan*.[16]

This obscure pamphlet doesn't even mention statistics comparing the risks of leaving to the risks of staying. In fact, the Michigan Women's Commission's report is primarily a compilation of anecdotal case studies. These case studies *do* illustrate that some batterers become increasingly violent when their wives leave home. However, the Michigan report *does not* support Browne's contention that "at least 50 percent of women who leave their abusers are followed and harassed." Nor does the report support Walker's point that women are in "greater danger" of being seriously hurt or killed if they leave.

Ultimately, there is no scientific research showing that women who leave their abusers are in greater danger than women who remain at home. The 75 percent statistic, heralded on the talk-show circuit, is pure fabrication. Moreover, it is a fabrication that, if believed, can harm both women and men. It is almost always better and safer for battered women to leave their batterers and seek help and shelter. Many of

15. Donna M. Moore, *Battered Women* (Beverly Hills: Sage Publications, 1979).

16. Nancy K. Hammond, *Domestic Assault: A Report on Family Violence in Michigan: Based on testimony taken at public hearings*, September–October 1976. Prepared by Nancy Hammond under the direction of the Hearings Report Committee, Lansing, Michigan, Michigan Women's Commission, 1977.

those who kill are convicted and sentenced to prison. Even those who kill and win acquittal would often have been better off leaving. Killing a batterer may be a cathartic experience for some, and a subject of heroism to others, but for most sensitive people, it leaves lifelong scars.

None of the foregoing is intended to deny the reality of suffering, rage, and abuse that exists in the world. My daily mail is witness to the pain and frustration that many people genuinely feel. Hundreds of victims write or call me every year, and their grief is palpable. But to recognize, understand, and even sympathize with these real feelings is not necessarily to justify or excuse violent crime that may have been stimulated, at least in part, by the abuses suffered at the hand of the victim or others, or by "syndromes" or other conditions. To understand is not necessarily to forgive. If it were, then we would be moving further and further away from holding individuals responsible for their conduct as science provides more insight into human behavior, especially violence. It is true that today we understand more about the causes of violence and crime than ever before, but there is also apparently no significant decrease in crime as our knowledge increases. Our growing understanding of the causes of violent crime does not necessarily decrease either its incidence or the moral culpability of its perpetrators, though some apparently believe it does.

Lisa B. Kemler, who successfully defended Lorena Bobbitt, offered a defense lawyer's variation on the "naturalistic fallacy": "The more we learn about how and why we act in a certain way, unless we rule out everything as psychobabble, the more we're able to offer viable defenses." The "naturalistic fallacy" is a famous flaw in logic that makes the mistake of confusing the empirical realities of nature with the moral implications to be drawn from these realities. Nature *informs* morality, but it does not determine it. For example, the relationship between male homosexuality and AIDS may be relevant in assessing life choices (just as the relationship between heterosexuality and pregnancy may be relevant). But it surely does not "prove" the "immorality" of male homosexuality, as some religious fundamentalists argue. Just as it is fallacy to condemn because of nature, it is also a fallacy to *excuse* because of nature. Nature may well inform our decision on whether to condemn or excuse, but it should not determine it.

Lisa B. Kemler is wrong, therefore, in assuming that the "more we learn about how and why we act," the *better* it should be for criminal defendants. Much of what we learn may simply not be determinative of, or even relevant to, the moral decisions we must make about culpability. Some may be relevant but *disadvantageous* to defendants. Some may be advantageous. But we cannot simply assume that the more we learn, the more willing we will or should be as a society to allow this knowledge to be used as an excuse.

Kemler was correct in one respect: when she raised the question of whether some new knowledge is "psychobabble." Much of it is, and we must not be seduced by the jargon of experts, particularly "experts" who are really advocates for a particular political position or worldview. New knowledge must prove its worth, first empirically and then morally, before a society is prepared to rely on it for important policy judgments.

Moreover, knowledge, when misused, can be a dangerous double-edged sword. The more we learn about the causes of violence, the more we may be tempted to try to prevent violence by intrusive means incompatible with civil liberties. For example, several years ago some defense lawyers pointed to new information about the genetic disposition toward violence of men with XYY chromosomal abnormality. This led others to argue for the preventive detention of all such violence-prone men. It turned out that the predisposition argument was largely psychobabble, and few scientists give it much weight today. But even if it had turned out to be true, this knowledge would not automatically convert into a moral imperative. We would still have to decide what to do with the knowledge — whether to allow it to be used as a mitigating factor showing a lesser degree of culpability or an aggravating factor showing a higher degree of dangerousness.

The same would be true of the various abuse excuses discussed in this book. If people who suffer from these syndromes are, in fact, less able to control their violence, that knowledge too would be a double-edged sword that might harm more sufferers than it helps. We cannot afford simple-minded, knee-jerk responses to new knowledge, especially in such volatile areas. We must think about both the short- and long-term implications of the policy choices presented by the new knowledge — after we decide whether it is knowledge at all.

Nor does the acceptance of abuse excuses really do anything constructive about addressing the very real and terrible problem of abuse. Our society must confront that issue directly, by creating more accessible shelters for battered women, abused children, and the abused and battered elderly. The police and the courts must be required to give high priority to what is now all too frequently ignored or denigrated as "family" or "domestic" disputes. These are real crimes.

But one wrong does not justify another. Allowing victims of abuse to invoke an abuse excuse, while doing nothing to prevent the underlying abuse, is little more than symbolism on the cheap. We *appear* to be recognizing the problem of abuse, while doing nothing to break the cycle of violence. Indeed, encouraging victims of abuse to kill and then to raise the abuse excuse, instead of society's spending money and devoting significant societal resources to preventing abuse, allows us to pretend we are confronting the problem, while perpetuating the very cycle it is supposed to break.

The law should do more to facilitate the separation of the abuser from the abused — by removing the abuser and preventing recurrence of the abuse. Taking the law into one's own hands should be a last resort, not a preferred solution. The abuse excuse, coupled with phony rhetoric and statistics about the futility and danger of leaving, sends precisely the wrong message. It is little more than a rhetorical, "feel-good," cheap, short-term nonsolution to a complex and pressing societal problem that deserves real solutions, high priority, and significant allocation of resources.

Acceptance of the abuse excuse also encourages criminals to believe that they can get away with their acts of violence, since everyone has something in his or her background that might mitigate culpability. When a German judge freed Guenter Parche, the thirty-five-year-old unemployed machinist who stabbed tennis star Monica Seles, that absurd decision sent a loud message throughout the world. Parche admitted that he stalked and stabbed Seles in order to enhance the tennis prospects of his fellow German, Steffi Graf. Despite this calculated act, the judge imposed a suspended sentence, which let Parche walk out of the courtroom a free man, because the judge found that he had a "highly abnormal personality."

I can easily imagine the reaction of Tonya Harding and her claque to that sentence as they contemplated her upcoming competition with Nancy Kerrigan.

Even in cases of terrorism and neo-Nazi violence, German judges have been soft on criminals with psychological excuses. This, too, sends a message of encouragement to such criminals, many of whom do have histories of psychological disturbance.

Yet another problem, illustrated by the German cases as well as the infamous Dan White case in San Francisco, is that these highly questionable excuses are more likely to succeed when the victim is disliked. In the German cases, the victims were all foreigners and the perpetrators were locals. In the Dan White case, one of the victims was Harvey Milk, the controversial leader of the city's gay population. Many observers wondered whether White's "Twinkie defense" — he ate too much sugar because of junk food — would have worked as well had his victim not been gay.

Perhaps the most profound danger posed by the proliferation of abuse and other excuses is that it may be a symptom of a national abdication of personal responsibility. For every bad act, there seems to be a made-to-order excuse. Not all of them are even psychological. When politicians are accused of misconduct, their frequent answer is "That's the way it's always done," or "That's the way it's done in Arkansas," or "The press is picking on me," or "My political enemies are trying to criminalize policy differences." Part Two of this book includes a series of essays on governmental corruption and the various excuses that have been offered in defense of business-as-usual. These excuses, like the abuse excuses in Part One, are an attempt to deflect personal accountability — in this instance from the person accused of corruption onto "the system" or some other institutional scapegoat.

Even in the area of international conflict, a version of the abuse excuse is prevalent. Nations and groups seek to justify their actions by references to the abuses they and their people have suffered. Palestinian terrorists blame their terrorism against innocent civilians on the abuse they have suffered. Jewish extremists justify Baruch Goldstein's killing rampage by reference to Palestinian terrorism, and the cycle of violence persists. This, of course, is an ancient phenomenon that has recurred throughout history. Each nation or group "begins" its story at the point where it has been the victim. The story then continues with accounts of revenge for past wrongs and prophylactic actions necessary to prevent recurrence of old abuses. I address some of the issues raised by this international abuse excuse in Part One.

In Part Three, I turn to yet another series of excuses —

offered in this case by some radical leftists, feminists, minorities, and others who perceive themselves as victims of long-term abuse by "the system." They offer their abuse as an excuse for demanding censorship, special rules, and double standards for judging their victimization and the appropriate societal responses to it.

All these excuses taken together — the abuse excuses, the international excuses, the corruption excuses, and the political correctness excuses — encourage a sense of helplessness, which leads to an unbroken cycle of abuse, counterabuse, excuse, and violence.

This cycle is dangerous to the psyche of a nation, a group, or a person. It encourages scapegoating, such as that preached by the Reverend Farrakhan, David Duke, and their ilk. It discourages the acceptance of responsibility, which is the essential first step to breaking the cycle. Indeed, the diminishing sense of personal, familial, and group accountability — of which these excuses are one important symptom — lies at the root of many of our most pressing concerns. It is almost as if we have collectively thrown up our hands in desperation over our inability to solve the problems of crime, poverty, equality, peace, and the breakdown of family. "We are not responsible" is the cry of frustration. This kind of attitude is inconsistent with democracy and an invitation to lawlessness and then tyranny, as we search for autocratic, quick-fix solutions to complex social problems. In order to regain control over our destiny, we must first reassert responsibility for our choices and actions. In the essays that follow, this point will be illustrated and elaborated, along with other points about related — some more closely, others more distantly — legal and political issues. The time has come to declare a moratorium on the excesses of the abuse excuse and its correlates, and to insist on more personal accountability for our actions.

PART ONE

Abuse Excuses, Cop-outs, Sob Stories,
and Other Evasions of
Responsibility

THE ABUSE EXCUSE

CRIMINAL DEFENSE lawyers throughout the country eagerly watch the unfolding legal sagas of the Menendez brothers and Lorena and John Wayne Bobbitt. These cases are among the most recent manifestations of the current rage among defense lawyers: I call it the "abuse excuse."

It all began with the so-called battered woman syndrome, which has proven surprisingly successful in some cases. In these cases, the woman has killed her alleged abuser — often while he is asleep — and defends on the ground that the pattern of abuse made it psychologically impossible for her to leave or call the police. The not-too-subtle hidden message underlying this legal approach is to ask the jury to find that the abuser "had it coming." The basic thrust of this "he asked for it" defense is to put the victim on trial.

It is likely to be far more effective, of course, if the victims happen to be dead, as in the Menendez case. Dead victims cannot defend themselves against charges of abuse, however far-fetched these charges may be. Nor is the jury likely to be sympathetic to dead defendants whose testimony they do not hear and whose faces they do not see, except in photographs and on grisly medical charts. Lorena Bobbitt has a somewhat more difficult task since her victim is alive, and he has testified — though not very convincingly — in opposition to her corroborated claims of abuse.

Perhaps one of the reasons why the abuse excuse is so successful is that many jurors can identify with someone who has been abused. Tales of abuse fill the airwaves and dominate our popular culture from Roseanne Arnold to the Jackson family. Such claims are difficult to prove, but they are also difficult to deny. The real question facing the courts these days is whether abuse — even if proved conclusively — should excuse violent conduct such as murder and mayhem.

Clever defense lawyers attempt to fit the abuse excuse into existing law. For example, in the Bobbitt case, Lorena Bobbitt's attorney, Lisa B. Kemler, tried a combination of sexual abuse, self-defense, and insanity. As she argued to the jurors: "What we have is Lorena Bobbitt's life juxtaposed against John Wayne Bobbitt's penis. . . . In her mind, it was his penis from which she could not escape. At the end of this case, you will come to one conclusion. And that is that a life is more valuable than a penis." Despite this emotional and somewhat sexist harangue, Ms. Kemler had difficulty explaining why Lorena Bobbitt had to choose between her own death and her husband's dismemberment when her husband had already indicated that he was leaving and seeking a divorce. But it is precisely the function of the abuse excuse to muddle logical thinking and to substitute emotional empathy.

In the Menendez case as well, logic points unerringly to a murder verdict, since there was no immediate threat of death and the two adult children — if actually abused — could simply have left home. The judge recognized that the Menendezes' story, even if true, did not justify the carefully planned murder of both their parents. Accordingly, he refused to give the self-defense instruction and told the jurors that they must convict of at least involuntary manslaughter. But the defense has attempted to muddle the jurors' thinking with highly emotional evidence of abuse, in hopes of either a deadlocked jury or an act of jury nullification.

In a particularly clever ploy, defense attorney Leslie Abramson repeatedly challenged the judge's authority, thus conveying a subtle invitation to the jurors to do likewise: namely, to defy the judge's instructions and refuse to convict the brothers of any crime, despite the undisputed fact that they had killed and then had lied about it to the police.

Whatever the ultimate outcomes of these highly publicized cases, two clear messages have been sent. The first has been sent to victims of abuse: namely, that the legal system may excuse you if you take the law into your own hands instead of either leaving or reporting the abuse. This unfortunate message has been underlined by the outpourings of public support for abuse victims who kill or maim.

The second message has been directed to criminal-defense lawyers: namely, when neither the law nor the facts are on your client's side, argue abuse. It may get you an acquittal, a reduced charge, or a hung jury.

The popularity of the abuse excuse poses real dangers to our safety and to the integrity of our legal system. It is far too easy for a desperate criminal to concoct a false history of abuse, for a disturbed criminal to imagine such a history, or for a sleazy lawyer to manufacture such a defense. The time has come to place limits on testimony about excuses that are so subject to abuses.

January 1994

The Menendez juries were unable to reach verdicts and the cases are scheduled to be retried.

No Justice in Vigilantism

DANIEL MARK DRIVER will never receive the fair trial to which he was entitled under our constitution. He was denied that fundamental right, because Ellie Nesler — whose son he was accused of abusing at a summer church camp several years ago — took the law into her own hands and gunned Driver down in the courtroom. Now Ellie Nesler is seeking a fair trial. Hopefully, Daniel Mark Driver does not have an angry friend or relative who is gunning for Ellie Nesler. If he did, the cycle of vigilante violence could continue endlessly — as it does in Sicily and in the former Yugoslavia.

The need for vengeance is older than recorded history. Aggrieved people took "the law" into their own hands even before there *was* a law. Indeed, one of the reasons the criminal law came into being was to channel personal vengeance into a more formal societal system of justice. *"Lex Talionis"* — the law of retaliation — may sound like an oxymoron, since "law" and "retaliation" may seem incompatible. But retaliation is an important part of every just legal system. Retaliation is not all there is to a system of justice, since prevention, rehabilitation, and treatment are also important. But vengeance too has its claims, so long as it is administered by society and is proportional to the harm, culpability, and danger of the offense and offender. The Bible's demand for "eye for eye," "tooth for tooth," and "hand for hand" is a primitive description of the need for proportionality in the law. "No more than an eye for an eye" is the way the Talmud interprets that influential but oft-misunderstood verse.

Ellie Nesler violated every rule of justice, *Lex Talionis,* and "eye for eye." She denied the legal system — which represents all of us — the chance to do justice. She became judge, jury, and executioner. She imposed the death penalty for a crime that traditionally carries a prison sentence of several years and that cannot — under our Constitution — be punished by death.

And now Ellie Nesler has become something of a hero, a female version of Bernard Goetz. Lawyers, including Melvin Belli, are clamoring to defend her. But what she did was far worse than what Goetz did. Bernard Goetz — the so-called subway vigilante — shot his assailants while they were in the act of trying to rob him. Goetz believed he was in danger from the gang of young hoods who surrounded him. In my view, Goetz overreacted and used his illegal weapon promiscuously, but at least he had the excuse of arguing that the law was not there to protect him.

Ellie Nesler, on the other hand, shot Daniel Mark Driver in the back when he was unarmed and in the custody of the police.

Nesler enjoys a presumption of innocence, though she hardly denies that she killed Driver in plain view of dozens of witnesses. But so too did Driver enjoy a presumption of innocence. For all we know, he may not even have molested Nesler's son. Erroneous charges of child molestation are not unheard of — as evidenced by recent acquittals and appellate reversals in several such cases. But Nesler decided to kill Driver on the basis of what she believed was a "smirk" by which he meant to say, "I've done it before and I'll do it again." Nesler's sister justified the act by saying: "It was that . . . smirk." Columnist Patrick Buchanan also seemed to be justifying Nesler's lethal act when he wrote: "Danny Driver smirked once too often." But a psychological report on Driver stated that he tended to smile when he was nervous. The fatal smirk may have been nothing more than a nervous gesture. The report also indicated that Driver had a good potential for rehabilitation.

Ellie Nesler will get the fair trial she denied Daniel Mark Driver. Her lawyer will try to put the victim on trial. Some who complain when rape defendants put their alleged victims on trial will applaud that tactic in this case. A sympathetic jury may acquit or a judge may give a lenient sentence.

Either of those results would send a message to other potential vigilantes that crime pays, provided you pick your victim well. But even more dangerous messages have already been sent: that the cowardly act of shooting a confined man in the back will be turned by some into an act of courage, and that vigilante injustice is seen by many as American justice. Buchanan quotes a local citizen as saying that people are saying that Ellie "deserves a medal and they want to be on the jury so they can let her go." It seems like too many Americans, including Buchanan, are watching too many bad vigilante movies and reading too few good books — including the Bible — which preach justice for all.

April 1993

Ellie Nesler was found guilty of involuntary manslaughter. She was sentenced in January 1994 to ten years in prison, six years for the manslaughter charge and four years for the gun charge. Shortly after beginning her sentence, Ms. Nesler was diagnosed with breast cancer. Her physicians have given her a 50/50 chance of living until her first parole hearing.

THE PMS DEFENSE FEMINIST SETBACK

THE TROOPER stopped the swerving BMW on Thanksgiving night and noticed a strong odor of alcohol on the breath of the woman who was driving her children home from a dinner party. When the trooper asked the driver how much she had to drink, the driver identified herself as "a doctor" and told the trooper that it was none of his "damn business."

The trooper then asked her to place her hands on top of her head, but instead she tried to kick him in the groin. According to the trooper, she then began to yell: "You son of a [expletive]; you [expletive] can't do this to me; I'm a doctor. I hope you [expletive] get shot and come into my hospital so I can refuse to treat you, or if any other trooper gets shot, I will also refuse to treat them."

After being arrested, the doctor was asked to take a Breathalyzer test, whereupon she kicked the machine. When she finally agreed to take the test, she failed it. She was then charged with drunken driving.

The doctor's defense was that she was afflicted with premenstrual syndrome (PMS). Her lawyer argued that women absorb alcohol more quickly during their premenstrual cycle and that women with PMS become more irritable and hostile than other people.

The Virginia judge apparently agreed with this argument and acquitted the woman. It is the first known instance of a PMS acquittal in this country and may serve as a precedent for future cases. The doctor and her lawyer were ecstatic over their victory.

Lest anyone believe that this acquittal was a victory for women, for feminism, or for those women who are affected with PMS, just consider the implications of excusing women with PMS from criminal responsibility.

This woman is an orthopedic surgeon, who presumably performs delicate surgery all through the month. Does she now have to notify each of her patients that her PMS may make her irresponsible during several days each month? Will she abuse nurses and kick the medical machinery in the midst of a surgical procedure? Should there be special rules limiting the amount of alcohol women with PMS are allowed to drink during the premenstrual part of their cycle? Must women with PMS display a surgeon general's warning during this time alerting all persons who come in contact with them that their PMS may cause irritability, hostility, or drunkenness? May employers now refuse to hire women with PMS for certain jobs? May they require all women to submit to medical tests designed to uncover latent or hidden PMS?

Any defense of criminal irresponsibility is — as Dostoyevsky once put it — "a knife that cuts both ways." It may excuse in one case, but it causes suspicion and prejudice in other cases. For example, when we excuse the mentally ill from responsibility for their criminal actions, we stigmatize all mentally ill people as irresponsible and incapable of controlling themselves. Nor is suspicion and prejudice against women who suffer from PMS warranted by the empirical data. Though some women who are irritable and hostile during the premenstrual period of their cycle may well suffer from PMS, the vast majority of women who suffer from PMS do not behave the outrageous way the surgeon in this case did. Her PMS did not cause her unlawful and rude behavior. Her actions were caused by her entire background, personality, and circumstances. She is obviously an elitist and deprecating person during the entire month, or else she would not have said what she did to the trooper. PMS alone does not change Dr. Jekyll into Mr. Hyde. She admitted that she had several drinks before she drove that night, and surely her PMS is not responsible for that behavior.

We live in an age when everybody tries to blame someone or something for their failures. Several years ago there was the "Twinkie defense." And then there was the "TV made me do it" excuse. Now it's raging hormones. This well-educated doctor should have realized that during the premenstrual part of her cycle, she behaves differently, and she should have taken precautions against breaking the law. Surely her PMS did not come on suddenly without previous manifestations. Her acquittal sends a doubly dangerous message. First, that our hormones are beyond our control and that we are not responsible for how they manifest themselves. And second, that women with premenstrual problems are somehow less reliable and less predictable than other people. Neither is true.

The PMS defense is a setback for feminism, especially when used in a case like the surgeon's. She ought to take responsibility for her own actions. And if her hormones are indeed beyond her control, her patients should be made aware of that dangerous reality. She can't have it both ways.

June 1991

DID VIRGINIA WIFE ACT IN SELF-DEFENSE?

L ORENA AND JOHN WAYNE BOBBITT were far from an ideal young married couple. The twenty-six-year-old man and his twenty-four-year-old wife fought continuously. Both called the police on several occasions over the course of their rocky marriage.

On June 21, 1992, Lorena Bobbitt requested a restraining order against her husband, but when she was told she had to appear before a judge, she opted not to.

Then, two days later, Lorena took the law into her own hands, in a dramatic and forceful way that has captured the imagination of the world. While John was fast asleep on his back, Lorena went into the kitchen, got a knife, and cut off John's penis.

Following that act of mayhem, Lorena got into her car and fled, taking the severed penis with her — inadvertently, she now says. When she discovered that the penis was with her, she tossed it out the car window and onto the highway.

After an extensive search — talk about a needle in a hay-stack! — the penis was found and reattached to John. It will take about a year before it can be determined whether it will work properly.

Now, in defense of the mutilation of her husband, Lorena claims that he had raped her twice previously. She does not explain why she did not call the police immediately after either of the alleged rapes and before she engaged in self-help.

She knew how to dial 911, as evidenced by the fact that she had done it previously on several occasions. She was in no immediate danger from her sleeping husband. She could simply have left the house and filed a rape report. There were no children who would be left behind if she went to the police.

She acknowledges that she acted out of rage and revenge: "I was the victim of repeated emotional, physical and sexual assaults. Everyone has a limit, and this was mine."

She testified that following the second rape, she went to the kitchen for a glass of water and "saw the knife. I took it. I went to the bedroom. I pulled the sheets off him and I cut him." Not surprisingly, Lorena is defending on grounds of "temporary insanity."

Her lawyer is also talking about a kind of after-the-fact "self-defense": "Moments after the last rape, he was cut. That's about as fundamental a self-defense plea as you can ask for."

Not quite! The law does not recognize self-defense "moments after" the alleged crime, especially when the person who is being defended against is sound asleep. Nor does the law recognize "temporary insanity" without proof of mental illness. Rage alone will not do, or else virtually all violence would be excused if provoked by past actions.

Despite her virtual admission that she is guilty of a heinous crime punishable by twenty years in prison, Lorena Bobbitt is being treated as something of a hero and a celebrity by some. As one woman put it: "Every woman I've talked to about this says, 'Way to go.'" Lorena has hired an agent to handle her book and movie offers and to book her on talk shows. Jokes abound, most of them unprintable. And the city in which the crime occurred is referred to by locals as the place where men now sleep on their stomachs.

But what Lorena Bobbitt did is no joke. It is part of a growing justification for vigilante violence by those who claim they cannot receive justice from the legal system. The widespread support she is receiving will only serve to encourage others to take the law into their own hands when they have been victimized, or — worse — to concoct false stories of victimization as a cover for their own unprovoked violence.

It is one thing for a battered woman with children who cannot leave without considerable risks to strike a preemptive blow against her assailant. It is quite another thing for a healthy twenty-four-year-old childless woman who can easily report a rape to exact revenge after the fact.

When Lorena did report the rape, John was immediately charged and brought to trial, proving that she did, in fact, have a lawful alternative. She is also now obtaining a divorce.

John's lawyer denies that his client raped Lorena, claiming that "this was all contrived to strike back at him after he said he was going to leave her."

After four hours of deliberating, a jury of nine women and three men acquitted John Bobbitt of rape charges.

"The proof just didn't exist for the majority of us," William Vogt, a member of that jury, said later.

This acquittal will pose an additional hurdle for Lorena to overcome at her upcoming trial for mayhem. But it is surely possible that a sympathetic jury may acquit her as well. Such are the vagaries of trial by jury in emotionally laden cases like this one.

November 1993

After his acquittal on marital sexual assault charges, John Wayne Bobbitt was arrested and charged with one count of domestic battery against his new fiancée. Lorena Bobbitt was acquitted by reason of insanity, served forty-five days in a psychiatric hospital, and was released in late February 1994.

The Minister Made Me Do It

YET ANOTHER HIGH-PROFILE trial is now under way, in which yet another defendant seeks to justify violence on the basis of yet another excuse. Like the Bobbitt case, this defendant claims loss of memory as to the moment of violence and temporary insanity. Like the Bobbitt trial, this defendant, too, has legions of supporters who stand outside the courthouse waving banners of support.

But unlike Bobbitt, no feminists are praising what this defendant is accused of doing. He is standing trial for murdering a doctor who performed abortions.

The defendant in this Florida case is Michael F. Griffin, who initially admitted shooting Dr. David Gunn a year ago outside a Pensacola abortion clinic. Now, according to his lawyer, Griffin doesn't remember whether he fired the fatal shots or whether his delusions "may have induced him to say he had some culpability when he may not have or did not have." But whether or not Griffin pulled the trigger, the real culprit, say his lawyers, is Reverend John Burt, a lay minister who was leading a nonviolent anti-abortion demonstration at the time of the shooting. By using this creative variation on the "devil made me do it" defense, Griffin's lawyers are hoping to avoid the life sentence that prosecutors are seeking. (Although the judge has precluded an insanity defense, Griffin's lawyers will still be able to argue this undue-influence variation.) While disclaiming responsibility for the shooting, Reverend Burt is hoping that Griffin is either acquitted or receives a reduced sentence because his act saved the lives of fetuses.

But Eleanor Smeal, president of the Feminist Majority Foundation, opposes any mercy: She wants a first-degree murder conviction in order to deter anti-abortion violence. She is joined by a Florida spokeswoman for the National Organization for Women, who argues that if Griffin's defense were to succeed, it would be a "very, very dangerous precedent." She worries that "people are going to be blaming gangster rap and violent movies." Of course, some people — including radical feminist Catharine MacKinnon — are already blaming pornography and other speech for rape and violence against women.

Some abortion activists, on the other hand, are pleased with Griffin's "the minister made me do it" excuse. The vice-president of the National Abortion and Reproductive Rights Action League argues that this defense helps make its point that "the escalating rhetoric of the anti-choice movement has created a climate for violence and what their members view as a justification for violence." The same can, of course, be said about some of the radical feminist rhetoric justifying what Lorena Bobbitt did to her husband.

There can be little doubt, as a matter of empirical truth, that a climate of violence can contribute to acts of violence by marginal individuals. But that should neither justify censorship of otherwise constitutionally protected speech, nor provide an excuse for those who engage in the violence. Our First Amendment is based on the premise that there is an important legal and political distinction between speech and actions. The government may not — except under the narrowest of circumstances — abridge freedom of speech or expression. But it has broad powers to regulate conduct, especially violent conduct. In general, it must wait until advocacy ripens into unlawful action before it imposes punishment.

Potential victims of violence sometimes find it difficult to understand why the government does not act on the old saying "an ounce of prevention is worth a pound of cure." The answer lies in our history. When governments were empowered to punish dangerous speech on the theory that it would lead to violence, they overused their powers to ban unpopular and controversial expressions, and liberty suffered in the process. The temptation to censor is overwhelming and pervasive. If given the power, many feminists would censor anti-abortion advocates, and many anti-abortion activists would censor feminists.

The American way is to let all sides advocate their positions, and to prosecute and punish vigorously those who engage in violence, without permitting the excuse that the "speech made me do it." An important corollary of freedom of speech is individual responsibility for one's actions.

The time has come to take these principles seriously, lest we weaken both freedom of speech and individual responsibility. If we allow violent criminals to defend their actions by claiming that someone else's speech made them do it, the next step will be to censor that speech. Already there are calls by some pro-abortion radicals for censorship of certain anti-abortion rhetoric. That would be a terrible mistake. But it would also be a terrible mistake to allow those who engage in violence to blame it on the devil, the minister, or anyone else. The marketplace of ideas imposes on every consumer of speech the obligation to choose carefully and to take responsibility for his or her own choices and actions.

March 1994

On March 5, 1994, a Florida jury took less than three hours to find Michael Griffin guilty of first-degree murder in the shooting death of Dr. David Gunn. Griffin was sentenced to life imprisonment, the mandatory sentence in Florida for first-degree murder where the death penalty is not sought.

Tonya's Abuse Excuse

I
N WHAT CAN ONLY be characterized as a blatantly sexist plea bargain, Tonya Harding has been spared prison, despite the prosecutor's expressed belief that she was directly involved in the plot to maim her skating competitor Nancy Kerrigan. Her male counterparts are facing prison terms for their roles in the assault, but Harding has been permitted to pay a fine and undergo psychiatric evaluation, apparently on the ground that she had been abused by her former husband several years earlier. This is yet a new wrinkle on the abuse excuse, which has resulted in a "temporary insanity" acquittal for Lorena Bobbitt, and hung juries for the Menendez brothers.

If Tonya Harding was directly involved in the conspiracy to injure her rival, she belongs in prison. There is simply no excuse — abuse or other — for an athlete to participate in a coordinated attack on a fellow athlete that could have ended her career and left her crippled for life. This was a carefully planned crime motivated by greed, desire for fame, and career opportunities. It is precisely the type of calculated crime that requires substantial deterrence. The message of this plea bargain is that those who have the most to gain from the violence of others will get the most lenient sentences, so long as they can get those others to do their dirty work and then be able to claim some variation of the abuse excuse.

Imagine if this were an organized crime hit that went awry and the Capo who ordered it received probation while the gangsters who carried it out went to prison. Ordinarily, it is the "soldiers" or the "mules" who get favorable plea bargains in exchange for helping to put the boss in prison. Here, the primary beneficiary of the crime — known in advance to her, according to prosecutors — got the best deal.

This unusual plea bargain also reinforces sexist stereotypes about the passive role of women and the dominance of men. Tonya Harding is a smart, tough, calculating professional who carefully weighed the costs and benefits of her actions. If she decided to take the risk of injuring her rival, as the prosecutor says the evidence shows, then she had to realize the costs of getting caught. Those costs should include imprisonment.

To be sure, her competitive career may now be over as a result of her forced resignation from the Figure Skating Association, but she can still participate in ice shows and other lucrative commercial ventures. The very terms of the plea bargain, under which she has admitted only that she hindered an investigation, gives her deniability as to any acts directly relating to ice skating, thus making it possible for her to continue to earn money as a skater.

Indeed, the entire plea bargain smacks of a crass commercial deal. The prosecutor obtained $160,000 for his constituents, and Harding gave up some commercial opportunities while retaining others. It sends a terrible message to an already cynical public.

Finally, the public has a right to know precisely what the evidence of Harding's involvement actually is. How strong was the case against her? Were the notes allegedly found in the trash authentic? If so, do they prove that she actively participated in the plot against Kerrigan?

If the evidence was as strong as the prosecutor has implied, why did he agree to a weak deal that avoided Harding's imprisonment? If he believes Jeff Gillooly's testimony that Harding was centrally involved — indeed, that it was her idea! — how could he have accepted this plea to hindering the investigation? If he believes that Gillooly is lying, will we see a perjury prosecution against him? Does the prosecutor now believe Harding, despite the fact that he believes she had lied at least twice to law-enforcement authorities: first by originally denying any knowledge of the crime and then by denying any prior knowledge? Does he buy into her abuse excuse?

This sweetheart deal will leave an uncomfortable feeling among those who follow our criminal justice system. Too many questions remain unanswered. Did the local favorite receive a home court advantage from prosecutors who care more about looking good to their constituents than about doing justice? Will the entire story ever come out? Why would Harding have hindered the investigation unless the investigation would prove her complicity?

Tonya Harding's freedom from imprisonment will be difficult to explain to poorer defendants who are daily sent to prison for far less serious crimes. Equal justice requires that equally culpable defendants be punished equivalently, regardless of gender. Under that principle, some prison time is the only just sentence for a woman who was involved in a plot to gain a competitive advantage over a rival by the use of violence. Tonya Harding appears to have gotten away with mayhem.

March 1994

Shawn Eckhardt pleaded guilty to racketeering. Shane Stant and Derrick Smith both agreed to plead guilty to conspiracy to commit assault. They will each serve eighteen months in jail but received no fines. On June 30, 1994, the United States Figure Skating Association stripped Harding of her national championship and banned her from the association for life.

AA Made Me Confess

I F THERE WERE AN ENTRY in the *Guiness Book of Records* for the longest list of excuses for a double murder, Paul Cox would surely be the titleholder to that dubious claim to fame. On New Year's morning of 1989, Cox broke into the bedroom of a married couple, both medical doctors, and slashed them to death. The brutal murder remained unsolved until Cox confessed his crime to several fellow members of Alcoholics Anonymous. Now he is on trial for double murder, and the parade of excuses has begun.

First, he says he thought the couple were his parents, because they were sleeping in the bedroom of the home in which he and his parents used to live. Second, he claims that a psychologist once told him that he had "patricidal and matricidal tendencies." Third, he was in a "drunken stupor." Fourth, he was "temporarily insane" — "he really snapped." And fifth, he had to confess to his fellow AA members because he was "obligated" to follow the rules of AA in order to recover.

Cox is receiving some support for his last excuse. Several experts agree with Adele Waller, a lawyer who specializes in legal claims of confidentiality. She argues that since AA does so much good, confessions to a fellow recovering alcoholic — like confessions to a priest or a psychiatrist — should not be admissible at a trial. "It doesn't seem right. It's like he's being punished for recovering."

Maybe it's more like he's being punished for killing two people in cold blood! The question is not what he is being punished for — that is all too clear. The question is whether he should be excused from a deserved punishment because the evidence of his guilt originated in conversations that should be recognized as legally confidential.

The conversations at issue here were informal "bull sessions" after the conclusion of the more formal meetings. Moreover, an important tenet of AA is that alcoholics must be responsible for their drunken actions. It would seem inconsistent with that principle for an AA member to hide behind a shield of confidentiality and thereby evade responsibility.

Nor are Cox's other excuses particularly compelling. If "patricidal and matricidal tendencies" were a valid excuse, then no one could be convicted of murdering their parents. This excuse is worthy of Leslie Abramson, the brassy Menendez lawyer, who gave new meaning to the classic definition of chutzpah: killing one's parents and then demanding mercy on the ground one is an orphan.

Finally, we get to the "drunken stupor–temporary insanity" excuse. If a New Year's drinking binge that ended up in a car crash and a double murder were ever to be recognized as a valid "excuse," AA might just as well go out of business. Since high levels of alcohol consumption are directly associated with the most serious of crimes — from rape to murder to vehicular homicide — surely a drunken stupor ought not be recognized as an excuse. If anything, it should be an aggravating factor in sentencing.

Paul Cox knew he was killing two innocent people during

his New Year's rampage. That he may have believed them to be his parents is monumentally irrelevant to his legal culpability. He knew what he was doing when he confessed his crime to fellow AA members. That he made the confession as part of an effort at recovery should not immunize him from responsibility for his actions. Paul Cox's excuses for his horrible deed just don't work.

The broader issue of whether communications made to fellow alcoholics should be recognized by the law as confidential is troubling. Had Cox confessed during a formal therapy session, his confession might well be excluded from evidence by the "patient-therapist" privilege. In this case he confessed to fellow "patients" in the absence of a therapist, and the trial judge has ruled that these patients can be compelled to testify about what he told them. If Cox is convicted, the judge's ruling may well be raised on appeal.

Whichever way the courts ultimately decide this issue, it is imperative that AA — and other self-help groups — now advise its participants whether, and under what circumstances, their statements can be used against them in court. The law is unclear outside the context of traditional one-on-one, patient-therapist communications. For example, can a fellow patient in a formal group therapy session conducted by a licensed therapist be compelled to disclose what another patient confided to the group? Perhaps not, but there is little law on that subject.

It may seem untherapeutic to start an AA meeting with a "Miranda warning," but it is far more damaging — both therapeutically and constitutionally — for a recovering alcoholic to learn later on that what he assumed he said in confidence can now send him to prison.

June 1994

THE URBAN SURVIVAL EXCUSE

T HE MOST RECENT ENTRY into the growing catalogue of abuse excuses has been given the catchy title "urban survival syndrome." This new defense was contrived by a Fort Worth, Texas, lawyer who is representing a young black man accused of murdering two other black youths.

In a creative attempt to bolster an otherwise weak self-defense case, the lawyer coined a medical-sounding term. It apparently worked, at least to the extent of producing a hung jury in a case that would probably have resulted in a conviction had traditional self-defense alone been raised.

There is, of course, no such medically recognized syndrome as "urban survival." Rather, the catchphrase is simply a way of trying to medicalize a social and political problem. The problem is real enough. In some urban ghettos, black-on-black murder is the leading cause of death among young men. Many of those who were brought up in such dangerous neighborhoods probably do live by the motto "Kill or be killed." The question raised by the urban survival syndrome defense is whether that motto should be elevated to a rule of law.

The facts giving rise to this question are largely undisputed. Eighteen-year-old Daimian Osby shot and killed Marcus Brooks, age eighteen, and his older cousin, Willie Brooks, age twenty-eight. The victims were unarmed at the time of the shootings, but the defense claims that a gun was found in the cousins' truck, that they had pointed a shotgun at Osby a week earlier, and that they jumped him in a parking lot just moments before the shootings. The prosecution argued that Osby had the option of running away. The defense countered that since the neighborhood was a "jungle," the applicable rule is "Kill or be killed."

Even the traditional rules of self-defense recognize the importance of context in deciding whether a defendant "reasonably believed" that he was in imminent danger. What is reasonable in one context may be unreasonable in another. For example, an elderly, weak woman living in an isolated rural setting without a phone might be more reasonable in shooting an unarmed assailant than would a strong young man living next door to a police station. But the rule of law is always the same: The defendant must reasonably believe that he must kill to prevent his own imminent death.

The urban survival syndrome borrows heavily from other recent attempts to broaden traditional self-defense by recognizing "syndromes." Battered woman syndrome has been, perhaps, the most successful. But others, such as the rape trauma syndrome, the Vietnam trauma syndrome, and the Holocaust survival syndrome, have also been raised, with occasional success. Each of these syndromes seeks to explain behavior that seems unreasonable outside of the context of the defendant's experiences.

In the Osby case, urban survival syndrome seeks to explain why the defendant shot his unarmed assailants instead of trying to run away. But not all explanations, even if compelling, should become lawful justifications. In claiming that he is entitled to be acquitted on the basis of urban survival syndrome self-defense, Osby is asking the jury for a complete vindication, since self-defense is always a complete justification for otherwise criminal conduct. It is not merely an excuse, like the insanity defense, or a mitigating factor, like provocation.

It would be wrong for the law to justify what Daimian Osby did, even if we understand it better because of urban survival syndrome. Accepting this defense would send a terrible message to the black community — namely, that we accept as a legal reality the claim that in certain inner-city areas the law of the jungle should apply. If we were to justify this kill-or-be-killed mentality, the ultimate losers would be inner-city blacks. Instead of trying to break this cycle of violence, our legal system would be legitimizing it. This double standard of justice would truly deny the equal protection of the laws to an entire community, and the denial would be based on race.

Moreover, acceptance of this urban survival syndrome defense would stigmatize an entire community unjustly. The reality is that most young black men in the inner cities do not live by the law of the jungle. They obey the law of society even in the face of pervasive violence. These law-abiding citizens, not those lawbreakers with excuses, should set the standard of reasonableness for a valid claim of self-defense.

Eleven jurors in the Osby case apparently agreed, and there is likely to be a retrial. But the one holdout may encourage other creative lawyers to come up with even more novel "syndromes."

April 1994

Adopted Child Syndrome

ADOPTED CHILDREN of the world beware. A new variation on the abuse-excuse defense is about to stigmatize and demonize you. Your friends and neighbors will soon be looking at you warily, wondering whether you are afflicted with "adopted child syndrome" and thus pose a danger of violence.

This newest entry into the competition over which defense lawyers can come up with the most bizarre "syndrome" is from Jeremy Rifkin's lawyer, Martin Elfman. Jeremy Rifkin has admitted to murdering seventeen women, mostly prostitutes. His abuse excuse for this serial killing rampage: "I was rejected by [my] biological mother." Rifkin apparently believes that his biological mother, who gave him up for adoption as an infant, may have been a prostitute. And, according to his lawyer, this explains why "he sought refuge in the world of prostitutes." Fair enough, but why did he have to kill them? Simple! "He strangled women to ease his suffering!"

If this kind of psychobabble were not becoming so prevalent in our courts of law, it would be a very sick joke — or perhaps an hour-long sob story on Sally Jessy Raphaël. But adopted child syndrome — and its dozens of variations — is now the defense of choice in a growing number of murder cases.

Nor are defense lawyers alone in their creativity. Psychologists and other professionals are lending their credibility to this parade of pathetic excuses. Dr. David Kirschner, a psychologist and director of a psychotherapy clinic in Baltimore, will be testifying on Rifkin's behalf. Dr. Kirschner has already assisted in the defense of ten adopted children who have been charged with murder. Indeed, it was he who invented the name "adopted child syndrome," a claim to fame of which he is apparently quite proud.

This "syndrome" includes the following symptoms: "pathological lying, learning problems, running away, sexual promiscuity, an absence of normal guilt and anxiety, and extreme antisocial behavior." These sound to me like some of the same characteristics shared by many, if not most, criminals and antisocial people. I doubt that a scientifically valid double-blind experiment could distinguish which people with these general symptoms were, in fact, adopted and which were not. That is probably why the adopted child syndrome is not recognized by most psychologists or psychiatrists as a mental disorder.

But the important point is that the vast majority of adopted children do not kill. Indeed, I doubt that adoptees, as a group, have a higher rate of murder or other serious crimes than non-adoptees. Even Dr. Kirschner acknowledges that only "a small sub-group of adoptees commit violent crimes," and almost none become serial killers like Rifkin. Thus, the fact of adoption — or, as Rifkin's lawyer likes to put it, of "rejection" by one's biological mother — neither explains nor justifies Rifkin's murderous actions. Indeed, his adoption seems monumentally irrelevant to any assessment of his culpability.

Dr. Thomas Gutheil, one of the nation's leading authorities on forensic psychiatry, argues that using this "syndrome" to raise an insanity defense "is meaningless noise." He is correct in calling it "noise," but unfortunately, it is not "meaningless." In addition to sometimes carrying the day in court, these new syndromes send terrible mixed messages about the millions of adoptive children who do not become serial killers.

These excuses du jour also send a dangerous message about personal responsibility. In this age of "blame everyone but yourself" sob stories, few people seem ready to take responsibility for their own actions. The quest for a scapegoat — in this case Rifkin's biological mother, who he believes was a prostitute — is a lame attempt to deflect attention away from personal culpability for criminal behavior and onto either the victims — in this case his mother's fellow prostitutes — or some newly concocted "syndrome."

It probably won't work in the Rifkin case, because the defendant is not as "sympathetic" a character as Lorena Bobbitt or the Menendez brothers. But the abuse excuse does sometimes succeed in deflecting responsibility away from the defendant, especially in cases where the defendant is sympathetic and his victims are not.

The time has come for judges to insist on scientific validation before they allow jurors to be exposed to junk-science syndromes that explain little and excuse even less. For a syndrome to be a valid explanation of an act — say, murder — it would have to include, as one of its characteristic symptoms, the act in question. Few, if any, of the current abuse-excuse syndromes meet that fundamental test. Even the battered woman syndrome — which has been most widely accepted by courts — does not include the killing of the abuser as one of its characteristic symptoms. The courts should be wary of made-to-order syndromes, like the adoptive child syndrome, which do not meet the most basic scientific criteria.

May 1994

THE "I READ A BOOK" EXCUSE

T HERE IS A NEW and dangerous wrinkle on the proliferating use of the abuse excuse, and this one poses a direct challenge to the First Amendment. Kimberly Mark is suing the author of a book she read, claiming that the book falsely induced her to believe that she had been molested. The book — *The Courage to Heal Workbook* by Laura Davis — is a popular self-help workbook for alleged victims of sexual abuse. It grows out of the controversial "recovered memory movement," which encourages people to remember long-forgotten incidents of having been abused.

In one sense, this bizarre lawsuit is poetic justice, since these kinds of self-help books promote the abuse excuse by turning everyone into alleged "victims" of abuse, real or imagined. After reading the book, Kimberly Mark says she came to believe that she has four hundred personalities and that she had suffered Satanic ritual abuse at the hands of her father and others. Now she says that none of this really occurred and that reading the book produced emotional damage to *her* by causing her to accuse innocent people of abusing her. No mention is made of the emotional damage done to those she falsely accused.

This is a perfect example of what the cycle of excuses inevitably leads to: everyone blaming someone else for their crimes and problems. Kimberly Mark first blames her father for abusing her. Then when she realizes that her allegation is false, she immediately turns the finger of blame to the author of a book she read. I wonder if she has ever looked at *herself* in the mirror and acknowledged her *own* responsibility.

The Courage to Heal Workbook does encourage people to dredge up their repressed memories of abuse, to believe them even when in doubt, and to confront the alleged abuser. It does not encourage reflective self-doubt, and it clearly errs on the side of believing vague memories of even the most bizarre ritual abuse. It is, in my view, a dangerous and polemical book, which may do more harm than good, especially to vulnerable readers who are searching for scapegoats on whom to shift the blame for their personal failures.

It is not surprising, therefore, that these same vulnerable readers would try to shift the blame away from themselves for falsely accusing parents of abuse and onto the author of the book. But under our First Amendment, writers cannot be held legally responsible for how their readers act in response to their books. If the First Amendment were to permit such legal responsibility to be imposed on authors, there would have to be an immediate cessation of all sales of the writings of Karl Marx, of the Bible, and of murder mysteries in which the killer escapes justice. Our First Amendment imposes responsibility on the *readers* for their actions, not on the writers for their *ideas*.

Indeed, according to Kimberly Mark's lawyer, it was another publication that made Ms. Mark doubt that she had ever been abused. After reading *The Courage to Heal Workbook*, Kimberly Mark read an article in *Time* magazine that raised questions about the "recovered memory movement." Without the protection of the First Amendment, the author of *The Courage to Heal Workbook* could sue *Time* magazine and other critics for defaming her book, her movement, and herself. But under our First Amendment, no such suits are permitted. Instead, the marketplace of ideas must remain open to controversy about such hotly disputed issues as recovered memory. And the marketplace is working effectively, as evidenced by Kimberly Mark's rejection of one publication's ideas on the basis of ideas contained in another publication.

Implicit within the First Amendment's theory of the marketplace of ideas is the personal responsibility of the consumer of each idea for how it is used. Thus, the author of *Final Exit* — a bestseller self-"help" book about suicide — is not legally responsible if a reader commits suicide.

A recent case did hold a therapist liable for malpractice in encouraging a patient to believe that she had been raped by her father, and Ms. Mark's lawyer is seeking to use that verdict as precedent for his lawsuit. But therapists have a one-on-one relationship with their patients. They are supposed to fit the therapy to the particular needs of their individual patients. Books are written for all potential readers, and the authors cannot know who will read them and how each of their readers may misuse the ideas contained in their pages. Authors cannot be required to purge their books of all ideas that are capable of being misused by the most vulnerable readers.

"It wasn't my fault, because I read a book" must be rejected as an excuse. Let the marketplace judge books, and let the buyer beware of books like *The Courage to Heal Workbook*, which encourages readers to blame others for their problems.

May 1994

D.A. Predicts Juice Excuse[*]

NOW THAT O. J. SIMPSON is in custody — following his highway pursuit and surrender — prosecutors and defense attorneys are turning their attention to what Simpson's defense will be. There are basically two options.

The first is the complete defense of "I didn't do it." In his "farewell" letter, Simpson proclaimed that "I have nothing to do with Nicole's murder." His second lawyer also confirmed his alibi defense by telling the media that Simpson was at home at the time of the killings. The prosecutor's case will rely largely on forensic and circumstantial evidence — matching blood, items found in Simpson's home, and his "flight" from justice as suggestive of consciousness of guilt. Unless the state can prove beyond a reasonable doubt that Simpson was at the scene of the crime at the time of the killings, there will be no need to proceed to any other possible defenses or mitigations.

---

*This analysis was offered before I was asked to consult with the Simpson defense, and it reflects my views at that time, when my information was based entirely on media reports.

But Simpson's lawyer may already be preparing for option two: a defense of "I did it, but . . ." The "but" can be anything from "I did it while I was temporarily insane," to "I did it but I was provoked," to "I did it in self-defense." In his letter, Simpson may have begun to lay the groundwork for a variation on the "abuse excuse," namely, the claim that he, like some women who kill their abusive husbands, was a battered spouse. Lest this seem far-fetched, look again at Simpson's letter: "At times I have felt like a battered husband or boyfriend. . . ." The prosecutor, Gil Garcetti, is already preparing to counter an abuse-excuse defense. He speculated that Simpson may eventually admit that he did the act but raise "a Menendez-type defense." The abuse excuse was successful in at least three recent cases — the Menendez brothers and Daimian Osby obtained hung juries in open-and-shut cases of murder, and Lorena Bobbitt was acquitted by reason of insanity in a clearcut case of mayhem. The media focus on these cases has created an environment in which people accused of violence automatically respond by reference to their own perceived abuse. Particularly in California, the land of unpredictable jury verdicts, the abuse excuse seems to be a defense of choice, at least in cases where the act cannot plausibly be denied. Because of his strength and wealth, O. J. Simpson is not the most obvious candidate for an abuse-excuse defense. But a jury may well be sympathetic to this folk hero who received cheers even while he remained a fugitive from justice. His lawyers may hope that a jury may be looking for a legal hook on which to hang a compassionate verdict. It is their job to present the jury with such a hook, if one is legally and ethically available.

Several such hooks seem likely to be explored. Insanity is a full defense, and even before Simpson's "flight," his lawyer was searching for forensic psychiatrists who could testify as to Simpson's mental condition. His bizarre actions on Friday, followed by his deep depression and suicide threats, may well support an insanity defense. But his long history of rational conduct will require explanation.

A successful plea of self-defense would also result in an outright acquittal, but the circumstances — at least as the prosecutors have recounted them — do not seem to support this claim. California law does permit a plea of "imperfect self-defense," under which a defendant can get a murder charge reduced to manslaughter if he honestly, but unreasonably, believed that his life was in danger. Either of these may be possible if it were to turn out that Nicole's friend attacked Simpson, and the football star then flew into an uncontrollable rage. As of this writing, no murder weapon has been found. If a weapon is found and it belongs to Simpson, that fact would make self-defense less likely. If, on the other hand, the weapon belonged to either of the victims, it would strengthen his case.

Another possible mitigating factor would be "provocation." If Simpson were provoked by the sight of his former wife with another man, a jury could reduce the charges, or refuse to impose the death penalty. Crimes of passion have always been viewed more sympathetically than crimes motivated by financial or other considerations.

It is too early to know for certain which tack the defense will take in this still unfolding legal and personal drama. Much will depend on the nature of the evidence, both factual and expert. It may well be that this is a case where one of the classic defenses fits. One conclusion is, however, obvious: Unless a plea bargain is arranged, or unless the DNA tests exclude Simpson, this promises to be the most closely watched trial in history, since O. J. Simpson is probably the most famous American ever charged with murder.

June 1994

Black Rage Defense

I T WAS ONLY A MATTER of time before the abuse excuse was taken to its illogical conclusion and extended to cover an entire race of "abused" people. Radical lawyer William Kunstler recently announced that he would defend a black client accused of murdering six passengers on a Long Island train on the ground that he was insane as the result of "black rage."

Kunstler said that Colin Ferguson's shooting spree was caused by the anger that many black Americans feel as the result of centuries of unjust treatment. "If you treat people as second-class citizens, they're going to snap," declared Kunstler's law partner. Though the lawyers conceded that racial injustice alone might not justify an acquittal, they claimed that it was the "catalyst" that pushed Mr. Ferguson over the edge into insanity.

Kunstler has used racial defenses previously. Several years ago, he defended a black man named Larry Davis, who had participated in a shootout with several policemen during an arrest and was charged with attempted murder. Kunstler claimed that Davis was acting in self-defense. Some blacks rallied to Davis's defense, seeing him as an "avenging angel" and a "folk hero." Kunstler played this race card and persuaded a largely minority jury that Davis was protecting himself from a police conspiracy to kill him. Kunstler is preparing to play the race card once again by raising the "black rage" defense before what he hopes will be a racially sympathetic jury.

It is unlikely that this racial gambit will succeed, regardless of the composition of the jurors, since the "black rage" variation on the abuse-excuse defense is an insult to millions of law-abiding black Americans. The vast majority of African Americans who never break the law have not used the mistreatment they have suffered as an excuse to mistreat others. Crime is not a function of group characteristics: It is an individual phenomenon that must be treated on an individual basis.

Indeed, it is the essence of racism to make the kind of group "rage" and group "abuse" arguments that Kunstler is now raising. It will reaffirm racist fears among too many Americans that violent crime is a "black problem." If black rage produces violent crime, or even if it is a "catalyst" for it, then racists will be quick to justify their fear of blacks as a group.

Moreover, if blacks as a group have more "rage" than others, and are thus more inclined toward violence, some racists will argue for longer sentences for black recidivists, earlier and harsher police intrusion against black suspects, and other forms of "preventive" intervention in black neighborhoods. This is especially troubling since Kunstler points to centuries of past abuse as the precipitator of crime, and nothing can be done to change history. The black rage argument that Kunstler plans to use is a dangerous invitation to the kind of stereotyping that has long characterized such groups as the Ku Klux Klan and the Nation of Islam. It has no place in the courtrooms of America.

In addition to being a racist defense, it is also without any basis in fact. There is no evidence to support the notion that groups that have been victimized by injustice turn to rage and violence. That has not been true of Holocaust survivors, of Cambodian refugees, of Soviet dissidents, or of a majority of black Americans. According to Kunstler's "social science," what explains the absence of criminality among so many who have been subjected to so much injustice? The search for the particular causes of Colin Ferguson's rage must begin by looking at him, at his own life experiences as a person, and at his prior history. But even if this search were to produce an explanation for Ferguson's murderous actions, no explanation — regardless of how convincing — necessarily requires exculpation. "To understand is not to forgive," says an old and wise proverb. The black rage defense neither explains nor excuses the cold-blooded murder of six innocent train commuters. A history of racial victimization is not a license to kill at random.

It is precisely this kind of abuse of legitimate defenses that is leading to a backlash. Last week, the Supreme Court let stand a ruling permitting the states to abolish the insanity defense, as three have now done. Insanity and other traditional defenses serve an important function in our system of law enforcement, by distinguishing between culpable and nonculpable harm-doers. When these defenses are abused, as they recently have been by the expansion of the abuse excuse to include political defenses, the pendulum will swing in the opposite direction. Neither extreme will serve the interests of justice.

April 1994

TRIAL BY THREAT OF MOB VIOLENCE

I N THE BAD OLD DAYS of the common law, some English judges would threaten to punish jurors who did not return verdicts that the judges believed were just. The enactment of our Sixth Amendment was designed to assure jury independence from both the government and the mob. Jurors are supposed to render verdicts on the basis of the evidence before them, not on the basis of fear of reprisal — either from the government or from the mob in the streets.

Yet many Americans believe that fear of mob violence may have influenced the verdicts rendered by the jury in the case involving two black men who were accused of beating the white truck driver Reginald Denny. We will never know for sure whether these verdicts were tainted by fear, because jurors need not explain or justify their verdicts. Even when individual jurors do give interviews, they tend to put the most positive light on their own decision-making process. But there is cause for concern, both from the nature of the verdicts themselves and from a report delivered to the judge by the jury forewoman just hours before the final judgment was rendered.

The verdicts themselves defy common sense, just as did the original verdict that precipitated the riots in which these defendants participated. In both instances, the violence itself — the *actus reas* of the crime, in the technical terms of the criminal law — was captured on videotape. If there are two vivid symbols that characterize the racial violence of the early 1990s, they are surely the videotaped image of the Los Angeles police repeatedly beating a helpless Rodney King and the videotaped image of Damian Williams rearing back, hurling a brick at the head of Reginald Denny, and then doing a victory dance as if he had just scored a touchdown.

Yet in both cases, the original jurors saw these videotapes differently from the vast majority of Americans who watched them on TV. In the Rodney King beating case, a second jury — selected from a more heterogeneous jury pool — eventually convicted. In the Reginald Denny beating case, the only jury — at least for now — has apparently concluded that despite the videotaped evidence of the *act*, the defendants lacked the *intent* necessary to convict them of crimes more serious than misdemeanor assault for one defendant and felony mayhem for another.

It is clear to experienced observers of the criminal justice system that these merciful verdicts would not have been rendered in the ordinary case in which the eyes of the world and the threats of the mob were not a factor. Jurors ordinarily *presume* the intent of the actor from the nature of the acts. Intent, after all, cannot be seen. Only the act can be observed. Intent must be inferred from the surrounding action.

Had Reginald Denny been killed by the force of Williams's brick — as he almost was — few would deny that the killing was intended. It is more difficult to prove the intent required for *attempted* murder than it is to prove the intent required for murder itself, because the defendant can argue that if he really wanted to kill, he would have hit the victim harder. But in this case, the videotape shows sufficient force to kill. It was only luck — both for Denny and Williams — and excellent medical care that made the difference between life and death. Jurors are typically more hard-nosed in assessing the intent of criminal defendants whose acts are clearly criminal in nature. That is why experienced observers are focusing on the message delivered to the judge by the forewoman concerning the fear at least one juror expressed for her safety and that of her family. The judge responded to this fear by issuing a boilerplate instruction telling the jurors that "you must not be influenced by public opinion or public feeling" and that you should "apply the law regardless of consequences." Not much solace for jurors who feared that if they voted to "apply the law," the consequence might well be general riots and specific reprisal against them and their families.

Juries simply cannot function in a climate of intimidation. In the Denny case, the consequence may have been the conviction for less-serious crimes than the facts and the law warranted. In other cases, the consequence of mob intimidation may be the conviction of the innocent.

Nor is there any simple solution to mob intimidation. *Judges* may be *more* subject to external influences than are jurors. Changes of venue carry their own risks, as the first Rodney King verdict illustrated. The jury continues to be the worst system for doing justice — except for all the others.

October 1993

FARRAKHAN'S SCAPEGOATING EXCUSE

LOUIS FARRAKHAN'S RECENT "criticism" of Khalid Abdul Muhammad's bigoted words at Kean College was accompanied by a defense of the "truths" his senior aide spoke. Farrakhan pointed specifically to one such "truth," namely "that 75 percent of the slaves owned in the South were owned by Jewish slaveholders." That would indeed be a remarkable statistic, if it were true, since Jews constituted less than one-fifth of one percent of the population before the Civil War. The Farrakhan statistic is, of course, totally made up. Jews owned considerably less than one percent of the slaves. Yet this phony 75 percent figure has become a staple of the bigoted rhetoric of the Nation of Islam. Why would Farrakhan and his "information ministers" want to exaggerate the Jewish ownership of slaves by more than a hundredfold?

The answer to that question is as old as the history of classic anti-Semitism. Farrakhan's purpose is to single out and scapegoat Jews for all the problems — historical and contemporary — faced by African Americans. That is why it has also become a staple of the Nation of Islam's rhetoric that Jewish doctors deliberately injected the AIDS virus into black babies as part of some genocidal master plan. That is why classic anti-Semitic forgeries, such as *The Protocols of the Elders of Zion*, are on sale at Nation of Islam bookstores, along with copies of *The Secret Relationship Between Blacks and Jews* and *The Jewish Onslaught*. And that is why a brand-new newspaper, published by the Nation of Islam, is being widely circulated around college campuses: It is called *Blacks and JewsNews*, and it is an anti-Semitic screed that would have made Joseph Goebbels proud.

These speeches and publications are part of a well-orchestrated campaign by the Nation of Islam to focus black anger and frustration on the historic target of scapegoating, namely "the Jews."

Several columnists have criticized Jewish leaders for "overreacting" to the bigoted words of Khalid Muhammad "before 100 students at Kean College." That misses the point. According to the respected *Chronicle of Higher Education*, Khalid Muhammad is very popular among many black college students, who refer to him as "the new Malcolm X." He often speaks at two or three colleges in a single day, drawing "more than 1,000 to a single speech." His anti-Semitic and other bigoted statements are cheered by many black students and faculty members.

Nor are Farrakhan and his Nation of Islam trivial figures in the black community. If they were, the Congressional Caucus would not have established a "sacred covenant" with them — a covenant that it has now broken following Farrakhan's refusal to disavow the content of Khalid Muhammad's notorious speech. The NAACP, on the other hand, has stated that it is "satisfied" with Farrakhan's press conference and is "prepared to believe Minister Farrakhan's statement that he is neither anti-Semitic nor racist. . . ." When asked about Farrakhan's claim that Jews owned 75 percent of the slaves, the NAACP's director of communications said that Farrakhan "may have exaggerated the historical fact [but] that is a matter for academics to debate." He concluded that Farrakhan's possible exaggeration "should not be a yardstick upon which he or anyone else should be condemned as anti-Semitic." I respectfully disagree. Exaggerating the role of a small number of individual Jews by more than a hundredfold in order to scapegoat "the Jews" for the horrors of slavery is a proper yardstick by which to measure and condemn for anti-Semitism.

Some defenders of the NAACP's soft line on Farrakhan point to the fact that the Nation of Islam does some good in its fight against drugs and its emphasis on black pride. But that is precisely why its pervasive scapegoating of the Jews is so dangerous. Its "good" works give its "bad" speech credibility within elements of the black community. If it did no good, few would be listening to its divisive message of hate. For bigotry to succeed, the negative message must be attached to something positive. Bigotry alone rarely has an audience. In Germany, the message of the Nazi party was twofold: German pride must be restored, and the Jews are to blame for most of Germany's problems. In the pre–civil rights South, the message of the Ku Klux Klan was also twofold: White Protestant pride and economic power must be restored, and the blacks, Jews, and Catholics were to blame for most of the problems.

It should neither be surprising nor excusing that the Nation of Islam has learned from past bigots that for its scapegoating message to be heard, it must be accompanied by a positive program. Let the NAACP take over the positive work now being done by the Nation of Islam. But if it is to retain its soul, it cannot make a pact with the devil.

February 1994

No Excuse for Flogging

NOBODY HAS EVER accused President Bill Clinton of being soft on crime — nobody in this country, at least. But now an international crisis is brewing because our president — who favors the death penalty, three-strikes-and-you're-out, and a general toughening of criminal penalties here at home — has publicly protested a sentence recently imposed by the government of Singapore on an eighteen-year-old American. Michael Fay pleaded guilty to spray-painting eighteen cars and other assorted acts of vandalism, while living in Singapore with his mother. The teenager was sentenced to be flogged six strokes with a rattan cane. The Dayton, Ohio, native was also sentenced to serve four months in prison and to pay a $2,230 fine. But it is the six lashes that have generated the presidential protest.

Before President Clinton persists in this criticism of another country's punishment policies, he would be wise to check on American law and practices, lest he himself be criticized for double-standard hypocrisy and for preaching what we ourselves do not practice.

A brief submitted to our own Supreme Court as recently as 1989 cited data compiled by the United States Department of Education showing that "30,000 American school children are physically injured every year by teachers in public schools because of the infliction of corporal punishment." In that case, two children — age five and six — were each swatted across their buttocks five times by a wooden paddle. Their crime: "snickering." Doctors who examined the children observed physical injuries, which led them to conclude that the paddling was "too hard," and child welfare workers characterized the beatings as "child abuse." The children missed a week of school and were terrified of returning to their abusive teacher. But the Texas authorities pointed to legislation that authorized any corporal punishment "short of deadly force," and the Supreme Court let stand a lower court ruling that children do not have a constitutional right not to be subjected to harsh physical punishments.

Many states, including the state that used to be governed by Bill Clinton, still authorize corporal punishment for students, though several others have now outlawed it. Paddling is still rampant in many parts of our nation. Nat Hentoff, an expert in children's rights, says that "the majority of kids who are whacked repeatedly are poor, black, and Hispanic."

Ironically, convicted adult criminals are no longer subject to corporal punishment — at least in theory. The last state to abolish it was Delaware in 1972. Thus, if Michael Fay had been convicted of vandalism in an American court, he could not be hit with a paddle. But if a teacher suspected his younger sister of "snickering," she could be paddled severely, so long as the beating did not reach the level of deadly force. Current Arkansas law is typical of this situation. It makes it a misdemeanor for a prison guard to inflict corporal punishment, but it expressly authorizes "any teacher or school principal" to employ "corporal punishment" for "good cause." Despite state laws prohibiting corporal punishment by prison guards, beatings are still commonplace in many American prisons.

The flogging to which Michael Fay has been sentenced in Singapore is more severe than most paddlings administered to schoolchildren in this country. Flogging in Singapore is administered by an officially trained martial-arts flogger. He is to strike the offender's buttocks six times with a half-inch-thick rattan cane moistened in water. The pain is occasionally so severe that some prisoners go into shock during the procedure. And the lashes leave permanent scars.

There can be little doubt that this sort of corporal punishment could have a significant deterrent effect on some potential vandals. And the scars would be a constant reminder of what awaits the offender if he were to recidivate. Some law-and-order Americans are certain to agree with Singapore officials who argue that swift and severe punishment — including flogging — has contributed to preventing that small nation from experiencing the fate of many American cities where vandalism, and worse, is rampant.

The real issue is whether we, as a nation, are in a position to preach to other nations about the severity and proportionality of punishments imposed in an effort to stem crime. We inflict among the most severe punishments of any civilized nation and we have among the highest crime rates. Our statutes authorize far longer sentences for far less serious crimes than do statutes of other nations. And the average duration of our sentences are likely to rise dramatically with the introduction of three-strikes-and-you're-out, mandatory minimum sentences, and other recent get-tough innovations.

Before we preach proportionality in punishment to other countries, we should begin to practice it ourselves. A good beginning would be for President Clinton to advocate nationally what he did not do while he was governor of Arkansas: Outlaw all corporal punishment in our schools.

March 1994

Michael Fay received a reduced sentence of four lashes in May 1994 and has completed his four-month sentence and left Singapore.

THE AGE EXCUSE

I F CRAIG PRICE HAD BEEN two and a half weeks older, and if he had murdered the Heaton family in Oklahoma — or in one of several other states which authorize the imposition of capital punishment on sixteen-year-olds — he almost certainly would have been sentenced to death for his crimes. After all, he deliberately butchered thirty-nine-year-old Joan Heaton and her two daughters, Jennifer, ten, and Melissa, eight. Nor had this been his first killing. Two years earlier, he had murdered another woman. All of his victims were neighbors in the Buttonwoods section of Warwick, Rhode Island. He also had a record of assaults, burglaries, and other assorted crimes.

Craig Price, who was known as "Iron Man" to his football teammates, would have been a paradigmatic candidate for the death penalty. Except for his age, he fit the profile of those murderers who tend to receive the ultimate sentence. He is black and his victims were white, and it is ten times more likely in our still-all-too-racist criminal justice system that a black man who kills white victims will be sentenced to death than a white man who kills blacks. His victims included children. They were local and came from good families. These are the kinds of factors that incline a sentencing judge or jury toward the death penalty.

Moreover, Craig had shown no remorse when he was apprehended and confessed to the killings. "There is nothing there, no emotion whatsoever," observed the arresting officer. "You look at him and say: 'Is he a psychopath?'" After pleading guilty to the four murders, Craig Price smiled and told his friends, "Later, when I get out, I'm going to smoke a bomber" — referring to a large marijuana cigarette.

Craig's friends won't have to wait too long for him to get out. Under Rhode Island law, "later" means five years for Craig Price — one and a quarter years in a training school for each human being he killed. By 1994, Craig and his friends will be smoking their bomber, and Craig's neighbors will have to get extra security for their homes.

Because Price was two and a half weeks short of his sixteenth birthday, the 240-pound youth had to be treated as a juvenile under Rhode Island law. And the maximum sentence for a juvenile, regardless of his crime or the number of his victims, is confinement in a training school until he turns twenty-one. When he reaches that birthday, he must be released, regardless of whether he has been rehabilitated or merely turned into an even more dangerous adult criminal.

Had Price reached his sixteenth birthday at the time he murdered the Heaton family, he could have received three consecutive terms of life imprisonment. (Rhode Island does not impose the death penalty.) But the fact that he was two and one-half weeks short of legal adulthood makes all the difference, under Rhode Island law, between a relatively short term in a juvenile facility and spending the rest of one's natural life behind bars. In some states, a few weeks could make the difference between life and death.

Ironically, the Rhode Island legislature had considered and tabled legislation earlier in the year, which would have allowed juveniles charged with murder to be tried as adults.

The disparity in punishments illustrated in the Price case is not limited to Rhode Island or even to juveniles. Approximately 2,200 convicted murderers are now awaiting execution on the death rows of our states. Following a judicially imposed moratorium on — and near judicial abolition of — capital punishment between 1967 and 1976, approximately 120 death sentences have been carried out. But during that same thirteen-year period, more than one-quarter million homicides have been committed. A significant percentage of these killings could easily have been charged as first-degree murders (either premeditated or committed during the course of a felony). And the vast majority of those crimes were committed in states that authorize capital punishment. Thus, only an infinitesimal percentage of killers eligible for the death penalty are actually executed.

What happens to the rest of these convicted killers? A considerable number of murderers plea-bargain their way not only out of the death penalty, but also out of long prison terms. Others who receive theoretically long prison terms get out on parole after a relatively short time. Indeed, the average time spent in prison by a person convicted of homicide but not sentenced to death is four years. Even when we consider only those homicides that resulted in a murder conviction, the average is about eight years.

This disparity fuels the argument in favor of retaining, or even expanding, capital punishment. If the only realistic alternatives are the death penalty or a few years in prison, then the case for the safer and more protective ultimate punishment takes on an understandable persuasiveness. That is why — among other reasons — opponents of the death penalty should be outraged whenever a Craig Price, or an older murderer, receives an unjustly short term of confinement. While we do not need capital punishment to protect us from murderers, we do need longer prison terms for murderers who pose a risk of recidivism. But even putting aside practical arguments about protection, simple justice rebels at the idea of an admitted serial killer — whether sixteen or sixty years old — serving only a little more than a year for each human life he deliberately snuffed out.

February 1990

Craig Price will be released on October 11, 1994. Warwick, Rhode Island, community groups have taken out national advertisements to warn people about this imminent event, and Price may be charged with assaults committed while incarcerated.

Preventive Confinement

W HAT SHOULD SOCIETY be allowed to do with a convicted sex offender who has completed his prison term, but who brags to his cellmates that he intends to continue to commit predatory sex crimes when he is released?

Several years ago, the State of Washington released a former convict named Earl Shriner, after he had served a term for a violent sex crime against a child and after he had boasted that he would commit additional crimes against children. True to his word, he then sexually assaulted a seven-year-old boy and cut off his penis.

The outrage that followed Shriner's predicted mayhem resulted in the passage of a new law in Washington, a law that several additional states are now considering. Under this so-called sexual predator law, a prosecutor may seek to detain a sexual offender even after he has completed his sentence if they can persuade a jury that the offender has a "mental abnormality" that causes him "to lose control" over his "sexual impulses."

Since the law's enactment, all fifteen people charged with being "sexual predators" have been found guilty by juries.

None has been released, and none is likely to be released for a long time.

Consider, for example, the case of Vance Cunningham, who was convicted of raping two prostitutes who refused to have sex with him because he did not have any money. He served his four years. Before he was released, he was examined by a prison psychologist, who concluded that he was neither dangerous nor mentally ill. Indeed, while in prison, Cunningham had earned his high school equivalency diploma. Upon his release he got a job as a mechanic on a fishing boat and started dating women, apparently without incident. Notwithstanding his perfect record for five months, the Washington sex police picked up the twenty-six-year-old ex-con on the fishing boat and charged him with being a sexual predator.

The prosecutor tried to persuade the prison psychologist to change her diagnosis so that Cunningham could be classified as mentally abnormal. She refused. Undaunted, the prosecutor simply hired another psychologist, showed him Cunningham's paper record — which included one juvenile conviction and one other adult conviction for sex crimes — and the newly hired psychologist concluded, without even interviewing Cunningham, that he was mentally abnormal. A jury concurred by a vote of eleven to one, and Cunningham was committed for "treatment." But there is no treatment available, since there is no such recognized psychiatric category as "sexual predator." Indeed, none of the people on the review committee that decides which ex-cons should be recommended for detention is even a mental-health professional. Nor is there any valid evidence that even psychologists, like the one who certified Cunningham to be a sexual predator, have any ability to predict which prior offenders will commit new sex crimes. As one expert, who cited studies showing that such predictions are wrong twice as often as they are right, put it: "You'd do better if you flipped a coin."

The Washington law is now being challenged by the ACLU before that state's highest court. The ACLU and other critics of the sexual predator law believe it is nothing other than "preventive detention," which is generally repugnant to our basic rights. But recent judicial trends favor preventive detention laws, as long as they purport to be nonpunitive in nature. Thus, denial of bail to juveniles has been upheld. Detention of the mentally ill has long been permitted. And most recently, the Supreme Court even upheld a law denying bail to adults who are charged with certain crimes and are deemed dangerous.

The author of the Washington statute admits that locking up people like Vance Cunningham, after he had completed his sentence, "wouldn't have been fair" — "*if* we were punishing" him. But he denies that Cunningham is being punished. Rather, he is being confined "for purposes of public safety and treatment." The fact that there is no treatment and that the Washington State Psychiatric Association denies that being a "sexual predator" is a "mental illness" does not seem to faze the law's author.

It is true, of course, that Cunningham is being confined "for purposes of public safety." But so are most violent criminals who are serving their sentences. And if confinement against one's will as a sexual predator is not "punishment," then it is difficult to know what that term means. In the Germany of the 1930s and 1940s, even "therapeutic execution" of the sick, the handicapped, and the unfit was not called punishment. It was called treatment for purposes of public safety. I would have thought that matters had improved over the past half century, but Washington's sexual predator law is a throwback to a dark period in our history.

December 1992

On August 9, 1993, the Washington Supreme Court voted 6–3 in favor of upholding that state's controversial sexual predator statute.

"THREE STRIKES" IS
NO ANSWER FOR CRIME

WHEN PRESIDENT CLINTON in his State of the Union message led the chorus of politicians who favor a three-strikes-and-you're-out approach to crime, he character-ized the plan as both "tough" and "smart." It is neither. It is bumper-sticker criminology that will actually increase crime, while wasting the taxpayers' millions of dollars.

The main impact of mandating life sentences for all three-time losers will be to raise the average age of our prison pop-ulation. Since all three-time losers must remain in prison until they die, and since the average life expectancy of prisoners actually exceeds that for nonprisoners, we can expect to have to provide expensive prison cells for many sixty-, seventy- and eighty-year-old criminals. And every prison cell occupied by an octogenarian is a cell that is not available for the confine-ment of a twenty-year-old. No matter how many new prisons we build — at enormous expense to the taxpayer — there will never be enough room for all violent offenders. Cases involving younger offenders will have to be plea-bargained because the cells that would otherwise be available will be occupied by aging three-time losers.

The problem with this approach is that old criminals, even three-time losers, are for the most part less violent than younger ones. The high-violence age range tends to be between the middle teen years and the middle thirties. That does not mean, of course, that there are no fifty-year-old violent criminals. It does mean, however, that the crime curve drops sharply by the middle thirties and that any system of mandatory life terms will necessarily include a great many prisoners who would be less violent than their younger counterparts.

Another reason why three-strikes-and-you're-out will increase crime is that jurors will be less likely to convict three-time losers when they learn — as they inevitably will — that a guilty verdict will mean an automatic life sentence. Already there is evidence that jurors allow sentencing considerations to enter into their verdicts, even though they are not supposed to. When the word gets out that a guilty verdict may mean life imprisonment, we will see more Menendez-type hung juries and Bobbitt-type acquittals.

Three-strikes-and-you're-out will also distort our already confused plea-bargaining system, by giving two-time losers no choice but to go to trial, thereby increasing the chances of acquittals or hung juries for the most dangerous offenders.

Finally, if the net is cast widely, as the proposed laws provide, it will catch thousands of relatively minor three-time losers, who have been convicted of widely separated, borderline crimes. This has been the experience with most multiple offender sentencing statutes that have been tried unsuccessfully by several states over the past half century. That is why most professional criminologists — conservatives, liberals, and nonideologues — are against mandatory life sentences for three- or even four-time offenders.

Three-strikes-and-you're-out is only the most recent manifestation of an approach that has confounded any possibility of realistic solutions to our serious crime problem. That approach focuses on punishments at the extremes. While we debate the death penalty and mandatory life imprisonment, we neglect the reality that most vicious killers serve less than ten years in prison and many armed robbers receive probation. It is also ironic that at a time when the public is demanding extreme sentences, many also seem willing to excuse killers and maimers who claim they were abused. We are both too hard and too soft on criminals. That is a symptom of the irrationality of our attitudes toward crime.

If we are to reduce crime, we must stop sloganeering and start thinking. What is needed are realistic sentences that reflect both the seriousness of the crime for which the defendant has been convicted and a scientific assessment of the nature and likelihood of his recidivism.

February 1994

SUPER SUNDAY SYNDROME

S O NOW IT'S FOOTBALL that causes violence against women — especially on Super Bowl Sunday! Last year it was pornography.* A century ago the villain was demon rum. Maybe next year it will be dirty jokes, or slackened church attendance, or listening to Pat Buchanan.

Violence against women is a serious problem throughout the world. Its causes are as complex and varied as human nature itself. But there are zealots who are using the tragedy of battered women to promote their own ideological agendas and personal preferences.

On the eve of Super Bowl Sunday, several self-proclaimed women's advocates declared that there was a direct relationship between men watching the Super Bowl and men beating up their wives or women friends. Characterizing Super Bowl Sunday as a "day of dread" for women, these zealots issued

---

* In *Shiro v. Clark,* 693 F.2d 962 (1992), a man convicted of rape and murder tried to argue that the pornography made him do it, but the courts rejected his argument.

the following warning to women who were at risk: "Don't remain alone with him during the game." They cited "data," which they claimed supported the conclusion that Super Bowl Sunday was "the biggest day of the year for violence against women."

The data included a study of the relationship between football and violence against women that purported to show a 40 percent increase in such violence after games won by the Washington Redskins. The *Boston Globe* reported that women's shelters and hotlines are "flooded with more calls from victims [on Super Bowl Sunday] than any day of the year."

It was a frightening story and it was highlighted all over the nation, on television, in the newspapers, and on radio talk shows. There was only one problem: It is entirely false! There is absolutely no reliable data to support any relationship between men watching football and beating women. Nor is there any data confirming the hyperbolic claim that Super Bowl Sunday is any more dangerous for women than any other day.

For example, an author of the study cited in support of the 40 percent increase said, "That's not what we found at all." The psychologist who was quoted as saying that shelters "get the most . . . complaints of domestic violence [on] Super Bowl Sunday" denied that conclusion: "I never said that. I don't know that to be true." The *Boston Globe* reporter who said that hotlines are flooded with "more calls" on Super Bowl Sunday "than any day of the year" acknowledged that she never saw any report supporting that conclusion, but instead relied on a hearsay account provided her by an advocacy group, which could not back it up. "You think maybe we have one of these myth things here?" asked the alleged authority on whom the advocacy group was relying.

There are many "myth things" out there when it comes to data that purports to support the agendas of zealots. Another such myth is the alleged link between pornography and violence against women. There is absolutely no reliable data that supports any connection between watching a sexually explicit movie and beating or raping women. There may be some connection between watching *violent* films and committing violence, or between watching *sexist* films and having sexist attitudes, but there is no documented connection between watching *sexual* films and committing violence. Yet the myth persists. Indeed, it is deliberately disseminated by those whose agenda is to censor sexually explicit material *because they don't like it.* They arbitrarily define pornography to fit precisely into the category of images they most despise, and then set out to prove — by pseudoscience — that pornography, so defined, causes rape.

The time has come to stop pandering to zealots who misuse social science to serve their own personal likes and dislikes. They must be exposed for the dangerous charlatans they are. Nor are their good intentions or the importance of preventing violence an excuse for sounding false alarms. Let's try to find out what really are the actual causes of violence against women, rather than trying to prove that activities that are disliked by some feminist zealots — whether it be watching football or sexually explicit films — cause violence. Every dollar wasted on pseudoscientific agenda-driven advocacy "research" is a dollar that could be better spent on real research that might actually help prevent violence against women. The problem with real scientific research — at least for zealots — is that a genuine scientific researcher cannot be told which way his or her conclusions should come out. The zealots will be afraid that some of their pet myths may be debunked and that neither the old devil porn nor the new devil football will be shown to cause violence against women.

As one social scientist, who was misquoted by the zealots about Super Bowl Sunday, put it: "I hate this. I've devoted fourteen years of my life trying to bring to the public's attention the very serious problem of battered women. And when people make crazy statements like this, the credibility of the whole cause can go right out the window." Let's not allow a few irresponsible zealots to destroy the credibility of an important and serious concern.

February 1993

WRONG RIGHTS

A NOVEL AND DANGEROUS "vocabulary of rights" is being constructed as part of an attempted end-run around the Constitution. "Victim rights," the "right to be protected from pornography," "fetus rights," the "right not to be exposed to secular humanism" are all manifestations of this new right-wing head-fake, which is calculated to deceive the listener into believing that an invocation of governmental *power* is really an exercise of individual *rights.*

Rights — especially constitutional rights — exist in relation to governments. The Bill of Rights (and the post-Civil War amendments, which applied most of its provisions to the states) was designed to limit governmental powers by assuring that certain individual rights could not be taken away by government officials. In the context of criminal prosecutions, it was the criminal *defendant* who was given the right to be free from unreasonable searches, self-incrimination, double jeopardy, cruel and unusual punishment, excessive bail, and other governmental infringements.

There is no provision granting "victim rights" in the Constitution, for a very good and simple reason: It is not the government that is seeking to deny the victim any legitimate claim. The victim was assaulted by a *private* citizen. The government is on the side of the victim, and is seeking to punish the defendant. The government is using its power in the interests of the victim and against the defendant, and so the Bill of Rights seeks to strike a balance by granting the defendant certain rights.

That is the way the system is supposed to work, in theory. But in practice, the government does not always work in the interest of victims, especially when the victims are themselves poor, unpopular, or powerless. Even middle-class victims are often neglected, inconvenienced, or abused. Understandably, therefore, some victims have banded together to form lobbies, seeking for themselves a greater role in the criminal justice system.

And these groups have become the darlings of prosecutors and politicians. How can any decent citizen resist the emotional importunings of victims? Prosecutors no longer claim to be representing the impersonal government (the same one that takes your hard-earned money and doesn't answer your letters). Now they are champions of the victims — a group with which every citizen whose home has been burgled or whose pocketbook snatched can identify! No longer is the policeman denying a suspect his rights by engaging in a questionable search or interrogation. He is helping the victim vindicate his or her rights to retrieve stolen property and bring a perpetrator to justice.

Legislatures have also jumped on the "victim rights" bandwagon. More than half of our states have enacted "victim rights" laws. Most of these enactments contain the old wine of law-and-order legislation relabeled with the new code words "victim rights." Some contain few or no real protections for victims. They simply take rights away from defendants in the name of victims. Others do improve the situations of victims and witnesses by eliminating inconveniences and requiring that the interests of those important participants be taken into account by those who administer the criminal justice system.

Among the most controversial provisions is the right of the victim — or the victim's representative — to appear before the sentencing judge and the parole board and to present a "witness-impact statement." What this means is that the sentencing authorities are told and shown — with emotional and dramatic force — how the crime actually affected, and continues to affect, the victim. It helps to humanize the process somewhat, by pitting the person called "defendant" against the person called "victim." But this very humanization carries with it considerable costs. It invites inevitable class and race biases. When the victim is someone with whom the sentencing authorities can identify, they are apt to see the crime as more serious and deserving of harsher punishment than when the victim is poor, homeless, unemployed, or a member of an unpopular group. It has long been true that the nature of the victim has had a demonstrable impact on the severity of the punishment, but the increasing visibility of the victim in the criminal justice process threatens to exacerbate this discrimination. The concept of "victim rights" is clearly a knife that cuts both ways.

The Supreme Court recently ruled — by a 5–4 vote — that in the context of life-or-death sentencing decisions, the victim-impact statement cuts too deeply against a defendant's constitutional rights and has the potential for inflaming the jury in favor of imposing capital punishment. Justice Lewis Powell, writing for the majority, also pointed out that the degree of suffering experienced by the victims and survivors "may be wholly unrelated to the blameworthiness of a particular defendant."

Notwithstanding the Supreme Court's rebuke of the victim's impact statement in capital cases, the rhetoric of rights is likely to persist in other contexts. "Victims of pornography" will continue to parade through the streets demanding their "right" to have the government remove offending material from the bookshelves. Graphic photographs of "victims of abortion" have become common fare at demonstrations in front of abortion clinics. Religious fundamentalists are declaring themselves "victims of secularism" (or secular humanism, as Judge Brevard Hand called it when he performed an act of legal hocus-pocus by including nonreligion under the rubric of a religious establishment within the meaning of the First Amendment).

Those right-wingers who are using this new rhetoric of governmental rights in an effort to undercut individual rights are misusing words in a deliberately confusing manner. The concept of rights in relation to governmental powers is too important a part of our national history to be obscured in the name of a faddish rhetoric that ill suits our national character.

October 1987

The Michael Jackson Feeding Frenzy

OW SHOULD THE PUBLIC and the media treat unproved allegations of the sort that have been made against pop star Michael Jackson? Whether these allegations are eventually proved, disproved, or remain unproved, the stigma of an accusation always lingers. A recent poll shows that while most of his teenage fans disbelieve the charges, they no longer admire Jackson as much as they used to. This is especially true when the accusation fits the stereotype of the accused. Everyone knows that Michael Jackson enjoys the company of children. That is perfectly normal — indeed, commendable. But it makes him an easy target for false charges of pedophilia.

On the other hand, every allegation of child molestation must be carefully investigated, since it is a very serious crime. Jackson's lawyers have been cooperating with the Los Angeles police, and thus far no hard corroborative evidence has resulted from searches of Jackson's homes.

In the end, this may turn out to be yet another case of

the uncorroborated word of the accuser against the uncorroborated word of the accused. To complicate matters even further, there is the counterallegation of extortion made by Jackson's investigator against his accuser's father. This allegation appears to have some degree of corroboration from audiotapes on which the father of the alleged victim reportedly threatens, "There is going to be a massacre if I don't get what I want. . . . I have the evidence [against Jackson] . . . you'll hear it on tape recordings." As of this writing, however, the father has produced no tape recordings to substantiate the allegation of sexual wrongdoing by Jackson.

It is theoretically possible — though unlikely — that *two* crimes may have occurred: first, that there was sexual misconduct by Jackson; and second, that there was an extortionate demand by the victim's father. The media seem to be assuming that if extortion can be proved, that would necessarily establish Jackson's innocence. What is true is that if extortion can be proved, it will be virtually impossible to secure a conviction against Jackson. It will make it unlikely, but not impossible, that Jackson is guilty. But extortion is sometimes attempted against guilty celebrities.

What makes it extremely unlikely that this is what occurred here is the reality that guilty celebrities generally pay off the extortionist, though even this rule of thumb has exceptions. Sometimes the guilty refuse to pay. Sometimes the innocent do pay.

In the end, we may never know precisely what has occurred, even in this highly publicized case, which is being scrutinized by police, social welfare, and media investigators. Nor is it certain that the truth — if it were to emerge — would fall into the category of black or white. It is possible in this kind of case for the alleged sexual conduct at issue to fall into a gray area where it is unclear whether boundaries were crossed or whether, if crossed, the conduct passed into the territory of criminal violation, as distinguished from socially inappropriate behavior. It is also possible for the alleged extortionate conduct to fall into a gray area in which legitimate, if questionable, economic demands were being made. Thus, it is entirely possible that following an extensive investigation, no criminal charges will be filed against anyone.

At the moment, all this falls into the category of hypothetics and speculation, where it may well remain. We are constantly reminded of the fact that child molestation and rape are the most *underreported* serious felonies in our nation. And that is true. But we are rarely told of the equally true — and equally disturbing — reality that child molestation and rape are also the most *falsely reported* serious felonies. The rate of unfounded allegations in these emotionally laden and often murky areas is more than double the rate of unfounded allegations for other serious crimes.

What is absolutely clear — and what should never be forgotten in the midst of this feeding frenzy — is that we live in this nation under a powerful presumption of innocence. That presumption should guide not only law-enforcement officials, but the media and the public as well. It applies to celebrities no less than ordinary people, despite our collective obsession with gleefully watching the high and mighty fall from their lofty perches. Despite his celebrity status, Michael Jackson is a vulnerable — indeed, somewhat fragile — young man who has brought great joy to millions. For that he is entitled to no more justice or fairness than the most obscure among us. But he is certainly entitled to no less. He is also entitled to a modicum of privacy, despite his very public persona. Let the investigation unfold, and let us all withhold final judgment until all the facts are in. And unless they point conclusively to guilt — either as to Jackson or his alleged ex-

tortionist — let us learn to live with the presumption of innocence.

September 1993

*While an out-of-court settlement was reached in the civil case,
Michael Jackson is still under investigation by the Los Angeles Police
Department.*

THE LESSONS OF
THE WOODY ALLEN CASE

OLIVER WENDELL HOLMES once said that "great cases like hard cases make bad law." It is also true that highly publicized cases sometimes teach important lessons to the public. There is an intensely important lesson for all potential litigants to learn from the custody suit brought by Woody Allen against Mia Farrow and decided last week in Farrow's favor by Judge Elliott Wilk in New York. That lesson is that litigation, like radical surgery, should almost always be a *last*, not a first, resort.

In August 1992, Mia Farrow called me and told me about the sordid situation with her former lover. She asked me if I would call Woody Allen, whom I know casually, and try to resolve the problem. I could not call Woody directly, since he was represented by a lawyer, but I did call his lawyer in an effort to resolve the issues without the need for public litigation, which would obviously have a deleterious impact on the children. We agreed to have a meeting between Woody's lawyers and Mia's lawyers, at which I would try to orchestrate a compromise that would be acceptable to Mia, on whose behalf I was acting, and also to Woody.

At the meeting, Mia's lawyers offered a series of recommendations, focusing primarily on visitation by Woody. Naturally, there were also discussions of financial issues — payment for therapy, education, broken contracts, etc. It was a conventional settlement discussion, typical in matrimonial cases. It seemed to us that substantial progress was being made by both sides, and the meeting ended with an agreement that Woody's lawyers would call Mia's lawyers the next day with a response to the proposals made at the meeting.

But unbeknownst to Mia's lawyers, including me, *while* the settlement meeting was going on, Woody filed a preemptive lawsuit seeking sole custody of their one biological and two jointly adopted children. He then convened a press conference at which he disclosed that he was being accused of molesting his adopted daughter and his biological son (there was never any allegation regarding his son, and that issue quickly disappeared).

By filing the lawsuit and convening the press conference, Woody Allen ended the settlement discussions and made the public litigation a virtual certainty. The next several months were a living hell for Mia Farrow and her family, as the media had a field day probing into every nook and cranny of her life. It was no picnic for Woody Allen either, and it is still unclear why he took the public path, rather than continuing to try to resolve the issues discreetly behind the scenes.

In his press conference, Woody tried to portray the settlement meeting as extortion, despite the fact that it was a conventional settlement discussion, entirely typical of such cases. At the trial itself, his lawyers attempted to paint it in a negative light, but the judge disagreed, characterizing it as an ordinary "meeting of the lawyers at which settlement discussions were taking place."

The end result of Woody's lawsuit is now known throughout the world. It was an unequivocal defeat for him and a potential disaster for his career. He ended up far worse off than he would have in any reasonable settlement. The judge declared him to be a person with "no parenting skills," who knew almost nothing about his children's lives, who had "never considered the consequences of his behavior with Soon-Yi," whose behavior toward his own adopted daughter, Dylan, "was grossly inappropriate," and who is "self-absorbed, untrustworthy and insensitive." The judge ruled that Woody would not be able to see Dylan, except "within a therapeutic context," that he could see his own biological son, Satchel, only with "appropriate professional supervision," and that he "will not require this fifteen-year-old child [Moses] to visit with his father if he does not wish to do so."

The judge went out of his way to declare Woody's lawsuit for sole custody to be "frivolous" and of "no merit," and he ordered Woody to "bear the entire financial burden of this litigation."

All in all, it was an unmitigated disaster for Woody Allen and his lawyers and a total victory for Mia Farrow and her lawyers.

Woody Allen must now be kicking himself for not continuing the settlement discussions that he cut off by filing his frivolous lawsuit. Indeed, following his defeat, *he* offered to sit down for settlement discussions. But it is too late to undo the damage to him, to the children, and to Mia that resulted from his taking the case public in the first place.

I suspect that Woody Allen's next movie may be about the virtues of alternative dispute resolution — settling cases without the need for public litigation. The opening line might well be a quotation from Learned Hand, one of the most respected judges in American history: "I must say that as a litigant I should dread a lawsuit beyond almost anything else short of sickness and death."

June 1993

On May 12, 1994, a New York State Appeals Court voted to uphold a lower court ruling that gave the three children of Woody Allen and Mia Farrow to their mother and severely limited his rights to visit them. The judges cited Mr. Allen's continued relationship with Soon-Yi Previn, Ms. Farrow's oldest adopted child, as one of the most important factors in their decision. The appeals court also directed Allen to pay Ms. Farrow's legal fees.

Can a Judge Be Judged Fairly?

W HEN A HIGH-RANKING member of the judiciary — especially a respected and popular judge — is arrested for a serious crime, the entire judicial system is placed on trial. The world waits to see whether judges can judge other judges fairly and equally. Never in recent memory has so distinguished a judge as Chief Judge Sol Wachtler of the New York Court of Appeals been arrested for so serious a crime — extortion, by threatening to kidnap a young child.

If Sol Wachtler were an ordinary defendant — say, a respected businessman — and if the allegations were proved to be true, the defendant would be facing a federal guideline sentence of anywhere from fifty-seven to seventy-two months. That is so because extortion is one of the most serious federal crimes and, under the guidelines, extra time is automatically added for threatening to endanger an especially vulnerable victim and for demanding more than $10,000. Even without these aggravating factors, simple extortion carries a mandatory prison term of twenty-seven months. Probation is not an option.

Despite these generally applicable rules, we are hearing understandable demands for special consideration because of Judge Wachtler's distinguished background. His lawyer, a former prosecutor who put many white-collar criminals behind bars, has already asked for special justice for his judicial client: "I believe that no right- and fair-thinking person, considering all the facts and circumstances, will ever believe that Judge Sol Wachtler should do 12 seconds in any jail-type setting." On the basis of what I know about the facts and circumstances, I agree with that sympathetic and understanding assessment. But I would also agree with that assessment for hundreds of other one-time perpetrators of crimes of passion who have led distinguished and worthy lives. Yet, under the harsh and unforgiving federal guidelines that now govern all federal sentencing for crimes committed after November 1, 1987, hundreds of decent people like Judge Sol Wachtler are serving heavy prison terms.

Two conclusions seem clear: the first is that no judge, regardless of his or her judicial record, can be treated more leniently by fellow judges than would similarly situated nonjudicial defendants be treated in comparable cases. I do not subscribe to the "leaning-over-backwards" theory, under which a sentencing judge must treat a judicial defendant more harshly in order to underline the appearance of equal justice. But more compassionate justice for a judicial defendant would be indefensible.

The second conclusion is that in order to assure that no special justice is accorded a judicial defendant, the underlying facts of this case must be made available to the public. Secret deals should never be acceptable in criminal cases, and certainly not in cases involving judicial figures. The public is entitled to evaluate whether special compassion is being accorded a judicial defendant.

The challenge to the judicial system — prosecutors, judges,

probation officers — is to be certain that Judge Wachtler is treated exactly as he would be if he were not a judge. Under today's harsh sentencing laws, that means he will almost certainly have to go to jail — unless, of course, he was insane or seriously incapacitated mentally.

It is always a tragedy to see a great judge have to go to jail, and Judge Wachtler was indeed a great judge — and a judge whose expansive view of civil liberties I deeply admired. As with many talented defendants, it is especially tragic to see their abilities locked behind prison gates, rather than being creatively harnessed as part of a community service punishment to help solve the many problems of our cities and towns. But the response to this human tragedy and waste of talent cannot take the form of special justice for a well-liked judge. It must take the form of generic change in today's harsh and mandatory sentencing laws — change that would allow judges to temper justice with mercy in all cases, not just in cases involving judicial colleagues with whom they can readily identify.

If, in the end, the facts were to prove that Judge Wachtler is guilty of extortion, and if he were to escape the imprisonment that other convicted extortionists routinely receive, that would be conclusive evidence that the promise of the sentencing guidelines — equal justice for all — has not been kept. Perhaps the Wachtler case will generate widespread interest in more creative and compassionate approaches to justice than the current lock-'em-all-up-and-throw-away-the-key mentality — which, ironically, Wachtler himself campaigned on during his initial run for judicial office — that is reflected in the federal sentencing laws.

Anyone who concludes that Sol Wachtler does not deserve to go to prison — as I do — is making the more general case against the harsh mandatory sentences characteristic of the federal guidelines.

If Judge Wachtler's lawyers had their way, the case would

probably be resolved by a quiet plea bargain and a probationary sentence involving private psychiatric care. Perhaps the alleged victim would prefer such a discreet resolution as well. But this is not a private dispute between two parties. It is a criminal case, which must be resolved under laws of general applications. If Sol Wachtler is to escape mandatory imprisonment for his alleged conduct because he was insane or seriously incapacitated, then the medical facts may be subject to public evaluation.

November 1992

On September 9, 1993, Sol Wachtler was sentenced to a prison term of fifteen months, probation of two years, a fine of $30,000, and restitution of $30,500.

"Provocation" Excuse Fuels Violence

FTER RASHAD BAZ was arrested on fifteen counts of attempted murder for shooting four Jewish Chasidim in a van, he told police that his shooting rampage had been "provoked" by the driver of the van, who had tried to cut him off near the approach to the Brooklyn Bridge. Whether this is true or not, the fact that anyone accused of so grievous an assault would even think that his conduct should be excused — or mitigated — by a traffic dispute demonstrates how far we have gone in accepting, and indeed encouraging, "provocation" as an excuse for even the worst acts of mayhem.

In Israel, friends and supporters of Dr. Baruch Goldstein — who murdered dozens of Palestinians at prayer — claim that he, too, was "provoked," not by anything as trivial as a traffic incident, but rather by the repeated terrorist acts directed against his fellow Jews by Palestinian extremists.

From the former Yugoslavia, we hear a constant refrain of provocation, counterprovocation, and retaliation for the violence allegedly provoked by earlier violence.

The shootings in Israel, New York, and Bosnia may seem

to have little direct relationship to what went on in the Virginia, California, and Florida courtrooms in which Lorena Bobbitt, the Menendez brothers, and Michael Griffin have been tried. But there is an insidious and dangerous relationship. An atmosphere of excusing violence by distraught people who claim they were "provoked" is spreading like a contagious disease. Excuses have become the staple of daytime TV talk shows. Viewers come away from this steady diet of woeful tales with a sense of entitlement based on their own victimization — real, imagined, or exaggerated. Court TV brings the abuse excuse from the courtroom into the living room. I was provoked to sever my husband's penis by his past violence toward me, claims Lorena Bobbitt. We were provoked to kill our parents by our father's sexual abuse of us, say the Menendez brothers. I was provoked to kill an abortion doctor by those awful anti-abortion pictures, says Michael Griffin. I was provoked to shoot the Chasidic children by their driver cutting me off. I was provoked to murder Palestinians at prayer by the terrorist acts of other Palestinians.

How many of these alleged "provocations" were actually the operative causes is open to debate. Despite the jury's insanity acquittal, it certainly seems plausible that Lorena Bobbitt's act was motivated as much by rage over her husband's decision to leave her as over her fear that he would stay and continue to assault her. Despite the hung juries, it seems plausible that the Menendez brothers were motivated by cold cash rather than hot passion. One of those arrested along with Rashad Baz told police that Baz had been robbed by a black man and that this experience had provoked him into carrying guns and ranting about killing blacks. He also told police that Baz had become enraged by Goldstein's actions in Hebron the previous Friday. And friends of Dr. Goldstein have said that he had been talking about killing Arabs for a long time.

But even if all or some of these horrible acts were, in fact, "provoked" by the earlier acts of others, that might only explain the resulting barbarities. It would not necessarily excuse them. To understand an action is not necessarily to forgive it. Moreover, these alleged provocations do not offer a complete explanation for anything. After all, most women who are mistreated by their husbands do not resort to the kitchen knife. Few abused children murder their parents. Almost no one who is cut off in traffic responds by shooting thirty rounds into the offending vehicle. And very few Israelis have responded to terrorism by violence.

There are other factors — unique to the individuals — that explain why they, as distinguished from the many others who were at least equally provoked, resorted to violence. These other factors are what distinguish criminals from the rest of us. Yet by focusing on the "provocations," we diminish the moral importance of the other factors that differentiate criminals from law-abiding citizens who are also provoked but do not respond with lawlessness.

Unless we insist on holding violent law-evaders responsible for their actions, we will never break the cycle of violence. Most violent criminals were "provoked" by something. Surely that should not excuse their violence. Most abusers were themselves abused. If the abuse excuse were ever to become widely accepted, the greatest beneficiaries would be men who abuse women and children and who claim that they, in turn, were abused. Victimization must not be allowed to become a moral or legal license to engage in vigilantism. The law must make it crystal clear that we expect our citizens to respond to provocation by invoking the law, not taking it into our own hands.

March 1994

Rashad Baz was arrested on March 2, 1994, and held without bail after being charged with fifteen counts of attempted murder. One of his victims has since died from the injuries suffered during the shooting. Mr. Baz's trial is pending.

WHAT THE ZEALOTS DON'T SAY

RECENT HEADLINES ABOUT violence committed by religious zealots once again raise the elusive and politically charged question of what factors cause people to become violent. Throughout history, charlatans have claimed to know with single-minded certainty the precise causes of society's evils.

One of the favorite pseudoscientific gambits employed by censorial feminists and fundamentalists in their effort to "prove" that pornography "causes" crimes of violence against women is to show that some violent criminals were exposed to pornography before they committed their crimes. A particular favorite was the deathbed "confession" of serial killer Ted Bundy, who — in a transparent last-minute effort to save himself from execution — tried to blame his violent propensities on pornography. "The porn made me do it!" seems to be the excuse du jour. The speeches and law school classes of Catharine MacKinnon — high priestess of radical-feminist censors — are riddled with similar anecdotal evidence, purporting to "prove" that pornography uniquely causes violence.

There can be little doubt that some people who enjoy pornography also commit violent crimes. But it is also true that millions of people who enjoy pornography do *not* engage in violence. By deliberately ignoring the important reality that the vast majority of pornography consumers are nonviolent, advocates of censorship create a false correlation between pornography and violence.

The falsity of this correlation can be illustrated by looking at the recent headlines about religious zealots. Those who planted the deadly explosives at the World Trade Center, those who engaged in the lethal shootout with federal officials in Waco, the man who killed the abortion doctor in Pensacola, and those who have planted bombs in Bombay and Cairo all have one thing in common: They were religious zealots who studied their "Bibles" and acted in the name of their "God." Indeed, every year there are many murders and other crimes of violence committed by readers of religious literature. But as with readers of pornography, the vast majority of Bible readers are nonviolent.

No reasonable scholar would ever argue that reading the Bible "causes" violence, despite the indisputable fact that some people who engage in violence do read the Bible. The obvious answer to that anecdotal connection is the indisputable fact that so many people who read the Bible are not "caused" thereby to commit crimes. During the heyday of Soviet-mandated atheism, there were some Communist pseudoscientists who purported to prove that the Bible did, in fact, cause crime and other evils, but no respectable social scientists took that junk-science seriously. It was obviously an agenda-driven bit of contrived research designed to achieve the propaganda goals of the Soviet government. As a *New York Times* editorial recently put it: "To blame religion [for the current violence] is like blaming oxygen for pyromania." It went on to point out that radical politics, not mainstream religion, is what causes this violence.

Similar distinctions must be drawn regarding pornography. It may well be that extremely violent portrayals — which are part of *some* pornography — may contribute to an atmosphere of violence. But not all pornography is violent. And not all violence is pornographic. And there is no evidence that explicitly sexual portrayals that are nonviolent contribute to violence. We should not confuse pornography with violence, any more than we should confuse the Bible with some of its violent portions.

If the radical-feminist claim is that portrayals of violence cause violence, then let those who advocate censorship in the name of preventing violence be clear about what they are proposing. But let us not confuse sex — even explicit sex — with violence.

Agenda-driven polemicists always claim that their pet peeves are the "real" causes of all evils — whether it be "demon rum," "devil porn," "permissiveness," "godless communism," or "mongrelization of the races." There is an old story from Germany in the 1930s that illustrates this point. Hitler is holding one of his anti-Semitic rallies at Nuremberg and haranguing the crowd with his favorite rhetorical question: "Who is causing all of Germany's problems?" Suddenly a lone voice responds: "The bicycle riders!" Hitler turns to him angrily and asks, "Why the bicycle riders?" to which the voice replies: "Why the Jews?"

It is easy to claim to have proved that any particular devil caused any particular evil, since causation is so complicated and multifaceted. But any proponent of such simple-minded theories of causation must answer the obvious question: If "X" is supposed to cause "Y," then why do so many people who have done "X" not do "Y"?

Neither those who claim that the Bible causes violence nor those who claim that pornography causes rape can answer that question. And until and unless they do, we should not take seriously their self-serving calls for censorship.

March 1993

The Continuing Threat of Terrorism

I T TAKES AN OCCASIONAL trip abroad for an American to understand that despite the recent handshake between Yitzhak Rabin and Yassir Arafat, the threat of terrorism against Jewish civilian targets is still very much alive around much of the world.

I just returned from a brief trip to Paris during which I visited a large synagogue. It was the night of *Simchat Torah*, a joyous holiday in which Jews throughout the world celebrate the annual completion of the weekly Bible-reading cycle. It is a children's holiday, with singing, dancing, flags, and candy. I was anxious to join the celebration at Des Temple de Tournelles.

It was not difficult to locate the synagogue — or any other synagogue in Paris. Just look for a large contingent of heavily armed police. As I entered the synagogue, I was stopped by two plainclothed security officials who interrogated me as to the purpose of my visit. I was then thoroughly searched from head to toe. Every item in my pockets was removed. My body was frisked. My shoes were felt. Even my necktie was fingered to see whether I was hiding plastic explosives. (In contrast, there was no visible security when I visited Notre Dame a few days later.)

My visit to the Parisian synagogue was a scary experience, and I asked one of the guards whether there were any specific threats that night. "No," he assured me. This is the routine precaution taken every day at every synagogue. "Synagogues are their favorite target," he told me, "especially when there are many children and women attending." He reminded me of the previous terrorist attack against a large synagogue in Paris, as well as against synagogues in Rome and in Istanbul.

I asked the guard why security had not eased since the "handshake," and he replied that the threat of terrorism had not diminished. Perhaps, he suggested, it had even increased. He told me that radical Palestinian groups opposed to the peace process were planning terrorist attacks against Jewish civilian targets both inside and outside Israel. The guard added that there was no real deterrent to terrorism, and that, if anything, the handshake in Washington might well serve as a stimulus to continuing terrorism. He explained that potential terrorists may well have seen Arafat's acceptance by President Clinton as a message that past terrorism will quickly be forgiven and forgotten in the name of future peace.

The views expressed by this experienced guard — indeed, the continuing fear of terrorism by Jewish communities around the world — confirm what I have long believed: namely, that recent historical events have made it tragically clear that *terrorism works*, and that the most extreme forms of terrorism directed against innocent civilian targets work more effectively than the less extreme forms of terrorism directed against military and political targets. The assumption in the international community seems to be that any aggrieved group who would randomly kill innocent children — as the PLO did at Maalot and at numerous airports and synagogues — *must* have an extremely just cause. On the other hand, an aggrieved group that would not resort to killing children — such as the Kurds — must be less deserving of international sympathy.

Perhaps the single largest contributor to this perverse approach to reward and punishment has been the United Nations, which honored Yasir Arafat *while* he was still actively engaged in hands-on control and planning of terrorism directed against civilian targets. At least President Clinton waited until Arafat renounced terrorism and agreed to a peace process. He forgave the past in the interests of the future. The U.N., on the other hand, *legitimated ongoing terrorism* by welcoming Arafat — holster on his side — to the podium of the General Assembly just seven months after the Maalot attack and just two months before the PLO attack on an El Al plane at Orly Airport in Paris.

Why, then, should not the most radical elements within other aggrieved groups — ranging from the provisional wing of the Irish Republican Army to the Shining Path guerrillas — understand this historical event as an international green light encouraging even more violent forms of terrorism. Those aggrieved groups who have not resorted to widespread terrorism have gotten nowhere in their demands for international recognition. The perverse lesson is all too clear: Terrorism works — use it early and often!

I'm safely back home now, reading about the trial of those accused of blowing up the World Trade Center. How safe are we really? Will we all eventually pay the price for the United Nations' legitimization of terrorism? Once terrorism begins in earnest in this country, it may have a profound impact on the very character of our daily life. My visit to Paris made that all too clear.

October 1993

The German Judiciary Is Soft on Nazism

For DECADES, GERMAN apologists have defended the refusal of the German government to bring charges against Nazi criminals on the ground that too much time has passed. The genocidal injustices of the past were quickly forgotten — and too often forgiven — in the interests of building the greater German future. Those few who insisted on punishing Nazi murderers were branded as vengeful and petty.

But now the hypocrisy of that attitude has been exposed for all the world to see. On October 26, 1993, the German courts convicted a Communist of complicity in a political killing that took place in 1931 — sixty-two years ago! The defendant, Erich Mielke, is certainly not a "good guy." The eighty-five-year-old Stalinist headed the East German Secret Police between 1957 and the fall of the Berlin Wall in 1989. In the 1930s, Mielke was a Communist party operachnik and enforcer. The crimes for which he was convicted, however, pale in comparison with the crimes for which German Nazis were forgiven.

Indeed, Mielke's two victims were German policemen who

had been assigned to harass anti-Nazi political organizations, such as the Communist party. That, of course, is no justification for murder. But the killings were part of a political war that had numerous casualties on all sides. They were not randomly directed against innocent civilians on the basis of their religion or race. And the number of deaths for which Mielke was convicted is two — not the millions for which Nazi killers were responsible.

Yet Mielke's sentence of six years — he has already been confined for three — exceeds the time served by all but a few handfuls of Nazi murderers. This disparity sends a powerful message about the skewed priorities of the German government as it relates to Communists and Nazis.

Mielke is by no means the only German Communist facing criminal charges for past offenses. Several other former leaders of East Germany are now awaiting trial for actions that were legal under East German law at the time they were committed. For example, Markus Wolf, who was chief of foreign intelligence for East Germany, is currently on trial for doing to West Germany exactly the same things that West German spies were doing to East Germany in the spy-versus-spy world of the Cold War. This is an example of "victor's justice," rather than equal justice.

It is not surprising that the German judiciary is more sympathetic to Nazi criminals than to Communist criminals. Following the end of World War II, the West German judiciary was rife with former Nazis — including several notorious hands-on perpetrators of Nazi genocide. In 1959, a book was published in Germany that documented nearly one thousand Nazi judges who "today occupy positions of responsibility in the West German judicial system." These judges had been instrumental in filling the concentration camps and death camps with Jews, Gypsies, gays, political dissidents, and other enemies of the Aryan people. As a West German federal prosecutor put it in 1958: "The mass of today's judges and public prosecutors were [the] tools of illegality, the instruments of terror" between 1933 and 1945. Little was done about these disclosures, and the vast majority of Nazi legal functionaries lived honored public and private lives in both West and East Germany.

Although few of these Nazi judges continue to occupy positions of authority within the German legal system — most have died or retired — the legacy of the past is still very much alive in the German judiciary. German judges and prosecutors are still notoriously soft on Nazism.

Nor can the disparity in treatment between old Communists and old Nazis be rationalized by the argument that Communism is a more pressing current evil than Nazism. To the contrary, there is little danger of a return to Stalinism in Germany. Communism is universally despised throughout Germany, largely because its victims included virtually all Germans. Nazism, on the other hand, is experiencing something of a revival.

Indeed, Nazism was never that widely condemned within Germany, largely because its victims were mostly "outsiders" — Jews, Gypsies, gays, foreigners. This is precisely why the priorities of German law enforcement must be reversed. It is far more important to prosecute old Nazis than old Communists, and to educate about the horrors of Nazism. There is no moral equivalency between the totalitarianism of Honeker's Communist East Germany and the genocide of Hitler's Nazi Third Reich. These current prosecutions coupled with the continued softness toward Nazism send the opposite message: namely, that East German Communism was worse than Hitler's Nazism.

Old Nazis, regardless of their age, must be prosecuted if their genocidal crimes can be proved reliably. New Nazis who engage in violence must be prosecuted vigorously. Most important, all Germans must finally be made to understand that the horrors perpetrated by the German people during the Nazi regime are unparalleled in modern history.

October 1993

In May 1994, prosecutors said that Communist officials from the former East German Republic were aware of Nazi war criminals but used the information for their own purposes, usually blackmail. In fact, many of these former Nazis were employed by Stasi as informers. Recently uncovered evidence also suggests that when trials were actually held in East Germany for suspected war criminals, the proceedings were designed merely to keep up appearances with Nazi prosecutions in the West.

The German Future Is Looking Bleak

A MID THE MORE than 1,800 recent manifestations of neo-Nazi bigotry in Germany, one stands out. A poll of Germans from both sides of the formerly divided nation reveals that three-quarters of East Germans would stand idly by and do nothing if they saw Germans beating a foreigner. Among this group, 8 percent said they would "watch" and 2 percent said they would "join in" the beatings. The figures for West Germans were similar: 65 percent said they would either join in, watch, or do nothing. Only a minority would try to help the foreign victims.

The data for teenagers is even more ominous: A third agree that "foreigners have to be beaten up and kicked out" and half accept the slogan — reminiscent of Nazi propaganda — "Germany to the Germans, foreigners out." Germany's finance minister, Theo Waigel, predicts that future elections "will be won right of center." Among the emerging political parties is a racist, xenophobic "Germany-for-Germans" party headed by a former Nazi storm trooper.

The reason these recent poll results — and the attitudes they reflect — are so striking is that during the Nazi Holocaust, only a tiny percentage of Germans tried to help those who were unjustly persecuted, imprisoned, and murdered. Many joined actively in the genocide. And the vast majority simply refused to get involved as their neighbors were taken away by the Gestapo, never to return from the concentration and death camps.

Nor do I believe that there is anything unique about the German *character* that inclined — and continues to incline — so many Germans toward cowardice and passivity in the face of such evil. The fault lies largely with the failure of the United States and its World War II allies to punish those Germans who joined in, watched, and did nothing to prevent the most barbaric genocide in history. Following the Allied victory over Nazism in 1945, we decided on a disastrous double-edged policy. We would punish only several hundred of the highest-ranking Nazi leaders — and even most of those had their sentences commuted after a few short years. But at the same time, we would help West Germany become the strongest economic superpower in Europe — in effect rewarding the German people for their complicity with the Nazi horrors. And let no one deny that the vast majority of Germans were complicitous in the rise of Nazism and its predictable excesses. Hitler, after all, was *elected*, and would have received over 90 percent of the popular vote had there been a free election in the late 1930s or early 1940s. He was an extremely popular leader until the very end of the Third Reich. The vast majority of German people were thus directly complicitous in the genocidal crimes of the Nazi regime — crimes that Hitler explicitly promised he would commit, if elected.

The rationale for our decision to build up West Germany was our fear of Communism and our desire to show East

Germans — and other Europeans — the advantages of capitalism. But we picked the wrong country as a showcase for Americanism, and in doing so, we sent a dangerous message: namely, that in our ever-changing world, the international community would always quickly forget the demands of justice for past crimes in the name of expediency for future policies. That message has not been lost on other genocidal tyrants from Pot Pol to Saddam Hussein to the Serbian butchers of today.

Nor was it lost on the German people. If all these who were complicitous in Hitler's crimes had been punished and all those who resisted had been rewarded, the message would have been dramatically different, and precisely such a plan was, in fact, proposed by then Treasury Secretary Henry Morgenthau, Jr. He urged that postwar Germany should be transformed into an agrarian society, incapable of developing a new war machine for generations. Under the Morgenthau proposal, all of Germany's factories and industrial equipment would be transferred to Germany's victims as war reparations, and the German people would live at a sustenance level for a generation. At the same time, those who resisted Nazism — such as the late Willie Brandt — would have been rewarded.

Instead, we rewarded *all* Germans by bestowing on them the Marshall Plan, which artificially bolstered their economy and allowed millions of former and not-so-former Nazis to live lives of luxury and happiness.

Now the world is paying the price for our injustice in rewarding Germany for its barbarism. The German people have apparently learned an important lesson once again: that aggression is rewarded and bigotry is forgiven by an international community that cares little about justice. It should come as no surprise therefore that a majority of Germans would do today what their parents and grandparents were rewarded for doing half a century ago: standing idly by as non-Aryans are beaten — and perhaps worse — by fellow Aryans.

November 1992

In the year that this column was written, seventeen people were killed in the xenophobic and anti-Semitic violence in Germany, eight of whom were foreign nationals.

German Leaders Miss the Point

S ACTS OF BIGOTRY increase in Germany — including the murder of innocent Turkish children — the German "leadership" continues to focus on the wrong issues. Rather than addressing the underlying causes of this return to the evils of the past, German politicians insist on treating the symptoms.

Thus, a headline last week read, "Germans in Accord on a Law to Limit Seekers of Asylum." Once again, therefore, the *victims* of Nazi brutality are being scapegoated as the "cause" of the violence. The message this new law will send to the skinheads and their friends is that racist violence *works*. If neo-Nazis kill foreigners in order to protest liberal asylum laws, the response of this German government will be to toughen up the asylum laws. No wonder the great German writer Günter Grass has characterized German Chancellor Helmut Kohl — who seems to care more about retaining the support of the extreme right than preventing the violence of the neo-Nazis — as a "white-collar skinhead."

To be sure, the German leadership has directed certain

measures against the skinheads. It has banned certain *songs, salutes,* and *flags.* This resort to censorship is typical of authoritarian regimes and it is destined to failure. Already the skinheads are mocking these restrictions on free expression by simply changing the lyrics, substituting a new salute, and waving a different flag. But the message of hate has not changed one bit. It never does, when the response to bigotry is censorship. The hatred simply goes underground, or adapts to the new rules of expression.

On a more fundamental level, censorship merely addresses the overt symptoms of deeper problems. It permits the government to posture and pretend that it is doing *something* to combat the purveyors of hate. But the skinheads are laughing at the government, as they continue to recruit more members and supporters — this time under the banner of fighting censorship and championing free speech.

I am often told by my friends, including some survivors of Nazi Germany, that it was freedom of speech that brought Hitler to power. If only he and his thugs had been censored by the Weimar Republic *before* the Nazis received mass popular support, perhaps they never would have come to power. But the historical evidence is all to the contrary. There *was* censorship in Weimar Germany. Indeed, Hitler took advantage of that censorship both to delegitimate the authority of the Weimar regime and then to solidify his power by silencing his opponents. Of course, the *kind* of brutal censorship eventually used by Hitler really did work.

Short of total censorship, enforced by a Gestapo, the kind of moderate censorship now imposed by the Kohl regime can work no more effectively than the "democratic censorship" attempted by the Weimar regime.

The answer to bigotry and hate in a democratic society can never be censorship, as tempting as that futile gesture often is. Nor can it be the equally seductive response of simply giving in to the demands of the bigots, as Germany now seems to be doing. New political and moral leadership is desperately needed in Germany. The hateful arguments and ideologies of the bigots must be addressed and answered, so that they can be debated and rejected in the marketplace of ideas. No current German political leader seems both willing and able to take on the neo-Nazis and skinheads. That is the real tragedy of Germany, and it is a tragedy frighteningly reminiscent of the terrible events of sixty years ago.

Even those who condemn the bigots do so on pragmatic, rather than moral, grounds. The skinheads are hurting Germany's "image abroad." They are weakening the economy. They are endangering tourism. These arguments may work in the short run, but they will not stem what appears to be a long-term drift backward toward Aryan xenophobia. To address that problem requires a courageous, honest, and painful look at German history — a history that directly implicates the parents and grandparents of most current German citizens, including its president.

In the meantime, the German government must protect its most vulnerable minorities from the violence of the neo-Nazis. Shivers went down the spines of many Holocaust survivors when Ralph Giordano, a prominent German writer, wrote an open letter to Chancellor Kohl telling him that many German Jews now believe that they must arm themselves, because they do not trust the German police to protect them. The responsibility for protecting *all* Germans — whether of Jewish, Turkish, or Romani background — lies with the German authorities. It is imperative that this responsibility be met, *now,* while Germany tries to come to grips with its deeper, long-term problems.

December 1992

If "Ivan the Terrible" Were Tried Here

HE REVERSAL OF John Demjanjuk's conviction by the Israeli Supreme Court should make all Americans take a hard look at our own system of appellate justice. Had Demjanjuk been convicted in Texas rather than Israel, he almost certainly would have been executed, despite newly discovered evidence that cast some doubt on his guilt.

The reason for this anomaly is that Texas, as well as several other states, have unreasonably rigid rules about when newly discovered evidence can be introduced to reverse a guilty verdict, even in a death penalty case. In Texas, for example, new evidence can generally be accepted only within thirty days of the original guilty verdict. Moreover, the new evidence cannot consist of hearsay statements by dead people, who are not subject to cross-examination.

In a recent case, the United States Supreme Court declared the Texas rule constitutional, thus inviting other states to follow it. In *Herrera v. Collins*, decided on January 25, 1993, our High Court ruled that new evidence of innocence is not enough to require the reversal of a death penalty conviction, unless that evidence proves the defendant's innocence conclusively. In that case, the defendant was convicted and sentenced to death for the murder of two Texas police officers. The Supreme Court ruled that the new evidence — affidavits from two separate sources claiming that Herrera's dead brother confessed to being the actual murderer — was not sufficiently persuasive of Herrera's "actual innocence" to justify a new trial, because the government had no opportunity to cross-examine the dead brother and because the new evidence was presented several years after Herrera's trial. If the *Herrera* rule had been applied by the Israeli Supreme Court, John Demjanjuk's conviction for being "Ivan the Terrible" of Treblinka would almost certainly have been affirmed. The new evidence relied on by the Israeli Supreme Court also became available years after his trial. It consisted largely of hearsay statements of dead Nazi collaborators. The statements themselves were elicited by Stalinist interrogators, and the collaborators were either executed or died in the Gulag. None was available for cross-examination.

Moreover, Demjanjuk's conviction was obtained largely on the basis of direct eyewitness testimony of several witnesses and one Nazi collaborator, all of whom were subjected to extensive cross-examination. There was also documentary evidence that proved conclusively that Demjanjuk had repeatedly lied — committed perjury — about his whereabouts during the war years. He claimed he was a "prisoner," whereas the evidence — including evidence introduced by his *own* lawyers — proved that he was a death camp guard at Sobibór and had been prepared for that grisly role at a camp called Trawniki, where the SS trained collaborators to kill Jews in the gas chambers.

Despite this evidence, the Israeli Supreme Court reversed his conviction and ordered his acquittal on the ground of reasonable doubt — not on the ground that there was conclusive evidence of his "actual innocence," as the United States Supreme Court would require under our Constitution.

Two important lessons for all Americans must be learned from the Demjanjuk case. First, we must insist on a change in our own Supreme Court's approach to new evidence in capital cases. We claim to be the world leader in the administration of justice. Yet our Supreme Court has so weakened the constitutional rights of capital defendants that we have created a genuine risk that the innocent will be executed. Just as there is no statute of limitations on murder, there can be no statute of limitations on newly discovered evidence of innocence, especially in capital cases. To allow a defendant to be executed in the face of new evidence that casts any doubt on his guilt "comes perilously close to simple murder," as Justice Blackmun put it in his dissenting opinion in *Herrera*. We can learn something from the scrupulous manner by which the Israeli Supreme Court reassessed the evidence in the Demjanjuk case.

The second important lesson that Americans must learn is that John Demjanjuk is no hero, as Patrick Buchanan and some others have tried to portray him. He is a Nazi collaborator who had a hands-on role in the systematic murder of babies, grandmothers, men, and women at the Sobibór death camp, where tens of thousands of Jews were slaughtered for no reason except that they were Jews. Demjanjuk was ordered deported because he deliberately lied in an effort to hide his abominable past. He may not be "Ivan the Terrible" but he is certainly "Ivan the Very, Very Bad." This is not a "Dreyfus case" of an entirely innocent man who was deliberately framed, as some of his supporters have claimed. It is the case of an awful man who participated in genocide in one location rather than another.

Ivan the Very, Very Bad of Sobibór does not deserve the honor of American citizenship.

July 1993

Demjanjuk's Advocate in Robes

I N DECEMBER OF 1991, Chief Judge Gilbert Merritt of the
United States Court of Appeals for the Sixth Circuit in Cin-
cinnati picked up a newspaper and read a story about John
Demjanjuk. Thus began one of the most bizarre episodes in
American judicial history — an episode that culminated with
Judge Merritt's highly questionable order to bring Demjanjuk
back to the United States from Israel, to which he was extra-
dited in 1986.

Demjanjuk, a Cleveland autoworker, was convicted and
sentenced to death by an Israeli court in 1988 for Nazi war
crimes on the basis of eyewitness testimony that he was Ivan
the Terrible of Treblinka, who had assisted in the murder of
thousands of Jews. The newspaper story that Judge Merritt
read disclosed that new evidence had been submitted to the
Israeli Supreme Court, which was then considering his appeal,
suggesting that another man — named Ivan Marchenko —
had been identified as Ivan the Terrible of Treblinka in affidavits
obtained by Stalinist interrogators from other Treblinka guards
shortly after the end of World War II. None of those guards

was still alive, but their affidavits, which had been secreted in Soviet archives, were released several years after Demjanjuk's conviction. Judge Merritt, who had presided over the appellate tribunal that affirmed Demjanjuk's extradition, was troubled by an allegation, reportedly made by one of Demjanjuk's lawyers, that the Justice Department was aware of these affidavits even before Demjanjuk's extradition.

Instead of waiting for Demjanjuk's lawyers to file a motion before an appropriate court, Judge Merritt decided to take the law into his own hands. First, he had the clerk of the court write a letter to the Justice Department expressing Judge Merritt's interest in an investigation of the matter that, according to press reports, the Justice Department was conducting.

Judge Merritt then read another article, this one in *Vanity Fair* magazine, and on that basis filed his "own motion" to reopen the case, convened a panel of the court, over which he presided, and — not surprisingly — granted his own motion, without the help of the adversary process. He then "restored" the Demjanjuk extradition to the appellate court's docket, ordered briefs to be filed, and appointed a public defender to represent Demjanjuk, even though Demjanjuk had half a dozen lawyers representing him, a substantial defense fund, and potential book and movie deals worth millions.

As unprecedented and overreaching as these actions were, they were nothing compared to what Merritt then did. Since the original extradition case had been heard by a federal district court judge named Frank Battisti, the usual course would be for an appellate court to remand the case to that judge for further proceedings. But Judge Merritt did not trust Judge Battisti to do his bidding. There are reports that Judge Merritt spoke to Judge Battisti about how he would handle the remand. Judge Merritt denies these reports, but Judge Battisti — aware of the Merritt denial — refuses to confirm or deny them, and sources close to Battisti have characterized Merritt's decision to take the case away from Battisti as "ludicrous." In any event, Judge Merritt — without any plausible authority in the law — did take the case away from Judge Battisti and assigned another district court judge to conduct a full investigation of possible Justice Department fraud. That judge found no such fraud and recommended closing the case and leaving Demjanjuk's exclusion intact, because he had lied on his visa application.

Not satisfied with that conclusion, the Merritt panel has now scheduled its own thorough review of the case. It is in connection with this review that the panel ordered Demjanjuk to be returned to the United States, despite an unambiguous law denying him the right to return because he deliberately lied on his visa application in an effort to hide his Nazi collaboration.

The Merritt panel gave several reasons for its high-handed decision, which was issued after ten minutes of deliberation. It ruled that courts always have the power to require a "party to the litigation to appear before them." That is flat-out wrong. For example, when Kurt Waldheim was seeking to have his name removed from the "Watch List" of Nazi collaborators, he could lawfully have been required to litigate that issue from *outside* the country, with the help of American lawyers, as excluded litigants are often required to do. Nor is Demjanjuk's presence required to determine whether the Justice Department somehow defrauded the court. Demjanjuk himself has no personal knowledge bearing on that issue, and his own credibility is worthless, since he has repeatedly lied about virtually every aspect of his life in the early 1940s. If the Merritt panel's views were to become the law, then every Haitian or Chinese "boat person" could simply have an American lawyer file a lawsuit here and then seek admission in aid of that lawsuit.

The court was also dead wrong in concluding that Israel cannot properly try Demjanjuk for any crimes other than being Ivan the Terrible of Treblinka. Israel could, of course, try him for perjury committed during the trial in Israel at which he denied he was at Sobibór and Trawniki. Since Demjanjuk's perjury is a *new* crime committed *after* the extradition, Israel is free to try him for that crime without regard to the original terms of the extradition. Moreover, even on the Sobibór charges, Israel could seek a waiver from the State Department of the rather technical rules of "specialty." Such a waiver might well be granted, since the crimes committed by SS-trained watchmen at Sobibór were similar to those committed at Treblinka. In any event, the Merritt panel had itself expressed doubt in an earlier case about whether "Demjanjuk has standing to raise the principle of specialty," since that right "belongs to the . . . state, not to the individual whose extradition is requested."

Nor is there any basis for the panel's "judicial notice that a serious threat exists to the life of John Demjanjuk in Israel." Demjanjuk has been well treated and well protected by the Israeli prison authorities. Moreover, Israel had intended to send him to the Ukraine, not allow him to live among its population once it freed him.

The reality is that once Demjanjuk returns to the United States, he will almost certainly be allowed to live out his life here, in violation of our law. It took many years of litigation to remove Demjanjuk in the first place, and it would probably take just as long to remove him now, even if all the court decisions went against him.

Judge Merritt's self-generated actions are precisely the kind of judicial hyperactivism and overreaching about which so many Americans are concerned. Courts are supposed to be institutions of limited power over actual cases and controversies appropriately brought before them by the parties. Judges are not authorized to stir up litigation on their own, as Judge Merritt — who was on President Clinton's short list for the

Supreme Court — did in this case. They do not have roving commissions to inquire into allegations reported in newspaper and magazine articles.

Judge Merritt has become Demjanjuk's *advocate*, not his judge. The tone of the argument before him, as reported by several lawyers and journalists who were present, was adversarial, not judicial.

Many observers wonder why Judge Merritt has taken such a keen interest in Demjanjuk. He is not a judge who has a long record of inquiring into allegations of government misconduct in criminal cases other than those involving the Justice Department's investigations of Nazi war criminals. Nor is Demjanjuk a particularly sympathetic defendant. There is powerful evidence that Demjanjuk volunteered to become an extermination camp watchman, and was trained by the SS at Trawniki and assigned to the death camp at Sobibór. He admittedly lied about where he was and what he did during the war years in order to obtain U.S. citizenship by fraudulent means.

Traditionally, the role of a United States court in extraditing someone to a foreign country for trial is merely to determine whether there is *probable cause* to believe he may be guilty. The actual decision on guilt or innocence is left to the foreign court that will try him. In this case, Demjanjuk received a fair trial and appeal in Israel — fairer than he would have gotten in many of our own states, where newly discovered hearsay evidence of the kind considered by the Israeli court to cast doubt on his guilt could not have even been considered.

John Demjanjuk has received all the due process to which he is entitled under American law. If Judge Merritt is "not too happy with the government," as he said during the oral argument, then he has the same right as every other citizen to petition for a redress of grievances. But in his role as a federal judge, he must remain within the law and not decide to reopen cases on the basis of unhappiness generated by newspaper and magazine articles.

January 1993

According to an article that appeared in the December 31, 1993, edition of the Los Angeles Times, *Judge Gilbert Merritt has "led a campaign against the Justice Department's Office of Special Investigations. Merritt was reportedly incensed over what he saw as a deception in the Demjanjuk case. He appointed Judge Thomas A. Wiseman as a special master charged with examining whether the Justice Department office committed fraud in its handling of the Demjanjuk case. In a 210-page report, Wiseman concluded that the prosecutors acted in good faith. Undeterred, Merritt and two colleagues ruled in November that the government had indeed committed 'fraud on the court.'" The Justice Department then asked the full appeals courts to reverse that judgment, but their motion for rehearing was denied on February 24, 1994. As for Judge Merritt, after being included on President Clinton's short list of candidates to fill the Supreme Court vacancy left by retired Justice Harry Blackmun, he was passed over by the president, who instead chose to nominate Chief Justice Stephen G. Breyer of the First Circuit Court of Appeals in Boston.*

Protesting Demjanjuk's Return

JOHN DEMJANJUK IS NOW back in the United States — at least for the moment. In some quarters, he is being treated as something of a hero, despite the evidence that he volunteered to become part of Operation Reinhardt and that he actually served as a *Wachtmann* at Sobibór and other death camps.

Part of the reason why Demjanjuk has been treated as a hero is because most Americans simply do not know what Operation Reinhardt was and what the role of the *Wachtmann* was in the operation. Many believe — quite understandably but erroneously — that Demjanjuk was a mere "prison guard" who just followed orders. That is not the reality.

Operation Reinhardt was a wide-scale plan to murder every Jewish child, woman, and man in occupied Europe. In the beginning, Jews were rounded up and shot. Then mobile gas chambers were employed. Finally, death camps, such as Sobibór, were established, fully equipped with large gas chambers capable of killing thousands of Jews every day.

Five hundred volunteers, such as Demjanjuk, were trained

for this grisly task at a camp especially designed to teach *Wachtmanner* how to herd Jews from the trains straight to the gas chambers. The death camps, such as Sobibór, were not slave labor camps. They had only one purpose: to kill as many Jews as possible in as short a time as possible. There were no mere "guards" at these camps. Every *Wachtmann* was a hands-on participant in the genocide, trained to run the gas chambers and do the killing.

There can be no doubt that Ivan Demjanjuk was trained as a *Wachtmann* at Trawniki, the SS camp established to train *Wachtmanner* for Operation Reinhardt. Nor can there be any doubt that he was then posted to Sobibór. Indeed, at his trial in Israel for being Ivan the Terrible of Treblinka, Demjanjuk's own lawyers introduced the sworn testimony of a Sobibór guard named Ignatz Danilchenko as alibi evidence. Danilchenko swore that Demjanjuk was a *Wachtmann* at Sobibór, not Treblinka. He said under oath that he observed Demjanjuk "guard prisoners in all areas of the camp, from the unloading platform to the entrance into the gas chamber." Danilchenko's testimony was confirmed by a Nazi identification card from Trawniki bearing Demjanjuk's photograph and assigning him to Sobibór.

At the end of World War II, only two death camp *Wachtmanner* made it to America — both lied about their wartime experience to get in. One was Feodor Federenko, who was eventually deported to the Soviet Union, where he was tried, convicted, and executed. The other is John Demjanjuk, who was extradited to Israel where he was eventually acquitted of being Ivan the Terrible of Treblinka, because the Supreme Court had gnawing doubts based on several old affidavits from dead Treblinka guards identifying another man as Ivan the Terrible of Treblinka. But the Israel Supreme Court had no doubts, based on the evidence, that Demjanjuk was a *Wachtmann* at Sobibór.

Nevertheless, the Israeli government declined to place Demjanjuk on trial for being a *Wachtmann* — largely for procedural reasons — and a United States Court of Appeals has ordered him back to this country so that he can participate in proceedings to determine whether his deportation should be reconsidered.

It is not surprising, in light of all this, that many Holocaust survivors are protesting Demjanjuk's return to the United States. After all, federal law explicitly forbids the entry into the United States of anyone who played a hands-on role in the Holocaust. Thus, for example, the president of Austria, Kurt Waldheim, has been barred from entering this country.

But the politicians of Seven Hills, Ohio, the city where Demjanjuk lives, do not want any protests by Holocaust survivors. Accordingly, they have just enacted a special ordinance to protect John Demjanjuk from legitimate pickets and protests. The ordinance is unconstitutionally broad, prohibiting legitimate protests that are protected by the First Amendment. The cruel irony is that if this ordinance were to be enforced, it would result in a situation in which Nazis could march through Skokie, Illinois, a neighborhood in which many Holocaust survivors live; whereas Holocaust survivors could not march through Seven Hills to protest the fact that a Nazi collaborator lives there.

September 1993

On December 17, 1993, Judge Daniel Gaul struck down the Seven Hills ordinance preventing demonstrations outside John Demjanjuk's home on the grounds that the restriction was unconstitutionally broad. However, Judge Gaul did uphold some of the community's other provisions for dealing with protesters. For example, he left in place a limit on picketing hours and consented to reduce the maximum number of protesters from thirty to twenty-five. As for

John Demjanjuk, the seventy-three-year-old retired autoworker and Nazi death camp guard spends most of his days in seclusion at his suburban Seven Hills home. According to his son-in-law Ed Nishnic, Demjanjuk still maintains that he is a victim of mistaken identity.

Prosecute the Balkan Murderers

A S REPORTS OF SERBIAN death camps, massacres, and genocide proliferate, a sense of impotent rage seems to prevail throughout the civilized world.

For those who recall the Holocaust, the sense is familiar and troubling. We cannot be sure what is really happening, because the alleged perpetrators deny the allegations and attempt to deflect the blame onto their enemies.

We cannot rely on official statements by our own State Department, the Red Cross, or human rights organizations, because they all seem to have their own agendas. Our president, George Bush, reminding us of Vietnam, does not want to get us into a guerrilla ground war. Governor Bill Clinton talks about surgical air strikes, but he is not empowered to make decisions now — when there is still a chance to save lives.

But we must do something now. Not to act on the face of what we know is a crime would be a sin, especially after the Holocaust.

In that spirit, I offer a modest proposal: Let the civilized world immediately appoint a special human-rights prosecutor empowered to investigate, gather evidence, and — if warranted — prosecute all those currently perpetrating crimes against humanity in the former Yugoslavia. The special prosecutor should be an internationally recognized human-rights lawyer, perhaps a former judge or minister of justice. He or she should be authorized to gather a staff of experienced investigators, prosecutors, and other experts.

As evidence is gathered, indictments should be issued, either against named individuals, if their names can be learned, or unnamed perpetrators of designated atrocities. The special prosecutor would have no mandate — or agenda — other than enforcing the rule of law in the former Yugoslavia by prosecuting human-rights violators.

The appointment of such a prosecutorial team would give notice to the criminals that they will not be allowed to get away with what they are doing. They will be prosecuted — maybe not today, but before long. And they will be punished proportionately to their crimes.

The substantive law already exists, in customary international law and precedents such as Nuremberg. If the reports we are hearing are true, there can be little doubt that these laws are being violated.

But the mechanisms for enforcing these laws are in disarray. The United Nations has no enforceable criminal jurisdiction, nor do other international organizations. Some nations claim the power to enforce international law in their domestic courts, but they usually require some direct nexus to the events, such as the victimization of their citizens.

The United States, as the current undisputed leader of the free world, should take the lead in convening an emergency conference of all nations that have an interest in human rights. This conference should be limited to the situation in the former Yugoslavia, in order to avoid deflecting attention away from that flash point by countries with their own long-term agendas. If it were to have an impact on preventing war crimes in the Balkans, perhaps the idea could be extended to Somalia and other areas of carnage. But right now, there is a developing international consensus focusing on the former Yugoslavia, and there is no excuse for inaction even if attention is currently limited to one area of abuse.

The conference would establish a mechanism for enforcing existing laws against war crimes and appoint the prosecutorial team. The conference might, for example, establish a special court composed of judges from several countries, or it might designate one or more countries to try the cases before their existing courts. Precisely how it is done is less important than that it be done. And it should be done now, in order to add a current and future deterrent against what is going on in former Yugoslavia.

The conference would be publicized throughout the world. Copies of the rules and the punishments that it establishes would be circulated throughout the former Yugoslavia. The message would get to those who are now carrying out the barbarities that there is no defense of "just following orders." All killers of civilians will be held responsible for their individual crimes if they are eventually captured or otherwise brought into the jurisdiction of a signatory to the conference.

Deputy Secretary of State Lawrence Eagleburger's recent call for a "war crimes inquiry" is a step in the right direction, but it is vague and lacks teeth. The next step — the establishment of an effective enforcement mechanism — cannot wait the outcome of an "inquiry."

President Bush talks about a new order. This may be that new order's most critical test. If the United States can do nothing to lead the world in preventing a fifth-rate power from murdering countless civilians, it will have abdicated its claim to moral leadership. At the very least, we must try to invoke the rule of law — and the real threat of effective prosecution and punishment.

August 1992

In addition to the current arms embargo against Serbia, Bosnia, and Croatia, the United Nations recently authorized its member nations to conduct air strikes against Serbian forces in southern Bosnia. Another recent development was the appointment of Chicago law professor Sharif Bassouni to head a United Nations expert commission investigating war crimes in the Balkan region.

Part Two

The "Everyone Does It" Excuse:
Official Corruption and Misconduct

A Democrat Calls for a Clinton Special Prosecutor

T HE CLINTON WHITE HOUSE is surely correct in pointing out the hypocrisy and political opportunism of some Republicans who are now gleefully demanding the appointment of a special prosecutor to investigate the Clintons' financial dealings with a failed Arkansas savings and loan. Although the political memory of most Americans — including many media pundits — tends to be measurable in months rather than years, it is difficult to forget the shrill and ultimately successful campaign orchestrated by many Republicans to scuttle the Independent Counsel Act while their party controlled the executive branch of government. Now that the Democrats are in the White House, civic virtue has suddenly returned to those Republicans, who have conveniently changed sides and are now calling for a special prosecutor.

Nor are Democrats immune from mirror-image charges of hypocrisy and opportunism. Some Democrats who insisted on the appointments of special prosecutors to investigate allegations of Republican hanky-panky are now sanctimoniously invoking the separation of powers and the independence of career Justice Department officials, as arguments against the appointment of a special prosecutor in the Clinton matter. But it is precisely because there is so much hypocrisy and cynicism on both sides of the aisle that a special prosecutor should be appointed in this case and that the Independent Counsel Act — with some needed improvements — should be quickly revived and put in place.

It may well be true, as Attorney General Janet Reno has stated, that career prosecutors are not influenced by the political winds of the day. But it is equally true that the public will simply not trust a process in which the subjects of the investigation — in this case the Clintons — have the power to hire, fire, promote, and demote those who will be making important decisions about their political and personal futures. The appearance of fairness and equality is almost as important as its reality, especially when the integrity of the president and the first lady are at issue.

As an experienced criminal lawyer, I understand the reluctance of the White House to surrender control over the delicate fact-gathering process to an outsider who has no political accountability to the president. Were I his lawyer, I might well take the same view. It is likely — though it is too early to know for certain — that a full investigation may well show some gray areas. That is typical of these kinds of cases. It is unlikely that any clear criminal conduct will be provable by a smoking gun. Nor is it likely that a merit badge will be awarded the Clintons for their role in the financial fiasco that has come to be called Whitewater.

Accordingly, there is a palpable advantage to them in having the Justice Department, rather than a special prosecutor, conduct the investigation. When the Justice Department completes its investigation, it either secures an indictment or it announces that the investigation has been closed. It does not prepare and distribute a public report on its findings. Special prosecutors, on the other hand, generally do prepare and make public what they have found and why they believe it does not warrant criminal prosecution.

If I am correct that this may be a gray-area case, in which evidence of improprieties but not of indictable crimes may be found, then the Clintons are far better off with a Justice Department investigation, which will end with a simple statement that no indictment is being sought. Period. But as president and first lady, are they entitled to such a simple "thumbs-up, thumbs-down" decision? Is not the American public entitled to know everything investigators may learn about the financial, political, and legal dealings of our president and his wife?

In a half century that has included a flawed Warren Commission inquiry into a presidential assassination, the plea-bargained resignation of a vice-president, the firing of a special prosecutor by a president, the pardoning of a former president by his handpicked replacement, the pardoning of a former cabinet member who may have had incriminating information about the president who pardoned him, and other political actions that have made cynics of many voters, it is imperative that the current allegations be investigated without any cloud of conflict of interest. The only way to remove all such clouds is for a special prosecutor to be appointed immediately to conduct a full investigation and to report his or her findings to the American public.

As a Democrat and a Clinton supporter, my hope is that a special prosecutor will find nothing improper, unethical, or criminal in the Whitewater mess. As an American, I want the whole truth to emerge so that the voters can judge for themselves. Let there be a full and open investigation and let the chips fall where they may.

January 1994

THE ETHICS OF WHITEWATER ARE WORTH A LOOK

ROBERT B. FISKE, THE special prosecutor selected to investigate the Whitewater–Madison matter, should quickly brush up on legal ethics in general and on the Code of Professional Responsibility in particular. The investigation will probably turn up no hard evidence of criminal behavior by President Clinton. Even if Governor Clinton did use his influence to delay the closing of Madison Guaranty Savings & Loan Association, and even if he did so in exchange for campaign contributions traceable to bank funds — and there is currently no evidence of either — these elusive facts would be virtually impossible to prove.

What might be possible to prove, however, is that the Rose law firm, and some of its partners, may have played fast and loose with the Code of Professional Responsibility. That code, with some variations, governs the conduct of lawyers in virtually every state, including Arkansas. In particular, Rule 1.7 prohibits lawyers from engaging in conflicts of interest. And the Rose firm's representation of the Federal Deposit Insurance Corporation in its claims against Madison after it previously was the lawyer for Madison appears to constitute a classic conflict of interest. Exacerbating this conflict may be a letter written by Vince Foster to the FDIC soliciting the FDIC's business. In that letter, Foster apparently failed to advise the FDIC of the law firm's prior representation of the bank. If that failure to disclose a material fact was willful, it could constitute fraud. Federal bank regulators are now looking into this matter.

Then there is the potential exposure of the Rose firm to massive civil liability if it helped to cover up Madison's shaky financial condition. In recent years, both accounting and law firms have been held liable for failure to disclose adverse financial information about which it knew or should have known. The Rose firm may be particularly vulnerable on this score, because in 1985 Hillary Rodham Clinton and another partner used an audit by Frost and Co. to show that Madison was financially solvent, and then in 1989 another partner of the same firm sued Madison on behalf of the FDIC, alleging that the audit was bogus. That partner was Webster Hubbell, who is now the number two person in the Justice Department, and whose father-in-law borrowed more than $500,000 from Madison Guaranty and failed to repay it.

At a more general level is the appearance and, perhaps, reality of conflict that always exists when the spouse of a high public official practices law in front of judges, administrators, and others whose careers may be influenced by that official. There can be little doubt that clients sought out Hillary Rodham Clinton precisely because her husband was the governor. Regardless of whether the governor actually influenced — directly or indirectly — any decisions in cases in which his wife was counsel, the appearance of influence is inescapable.

Professor Paul Rothstein of Georgetown Law School, an expert on legal ethics, urges "leniency" in this area: "Unless you want to say the wife of an important man can never apply her trade, you've got to be lenient on that. You don't want to disable professional wives from practicing their trade."

But many spouses of public officials have made the decision to withdraw from practicing the kind of law that creates the appearance of improper influence. There are many ways of practicing law — both profitably and usefully — without even coming close to the line of impropriety. Hillary Rodham Clinton's practice of law was so close to her husband's base of influence that many will ask the question: Just how good a lawyer would Mrs. Clinton really have been if her husband had not been the governor?

These and other ethics issues may become the focus of the special prosecutor. I hope he or she will take these issues seriously, not so much to criticize particular individuals for past derelictions but to educate the American public about this relatively hidden but widely practiced genre of elite influence-peddling and questionable ethics. Because this form of "cheat elite" is so prevalent among big-city lawyers and law firms, I have decided to begin my legal ethics course this semester with a survey of the ethics issues surrounding Whitewater–Madison. My goal is to sensitize law students to the kinds of ethical problems they are likely to encounter when they begin to practice law.

As a Democrat who voted for President Clinton, I wish Bill and Hillary Clinton had been better sensitized to these issues when they studied legal ethics at Yale Law School in the 1970s. I hope that nothing negative turns up against the first family. But as a law professor, I understand the importance of a full and open investigation of Whitewater–Madison that will sensitize a generation of future lawyers to the ethical pitfalls of practicing law at the highest levels of government.

January 1994

Jones versus Clinton —
Hill versus Thomas Redux?

T HE LAWSUIT BEING brought by Paula Corbin Jones against
President Clinton poses problems not only for our belea-
guered chief executive, but it also raises an embarrassing
risk of inconsistency — and indeed hypocrisy — for feminist supporters of Clinton who insisted on a full airing of Anita
Hill's allegations against Clarence Thomas.

By any standard of judgment, Jones's charges against
Clinton are far more serious, have far more prima facie corroboration, and are far more consistent with other allegations
against the alleged perpetrator than were Hill's charges against
Thomas.

The Hill charges — even taken at their most extreme —
were that Thomas had used rude and suggestive language. The
Jones charges go well beyond language and include allegations
of possible criminal conduct, specifically physical assault and
lewdness.

The Hill charges lacked credible contemporaneous corroboration. Jones, on the other hand, says she told several
people about Clinton's conduct as soon as it took place, and

these people have provided contemporaneous corroboration. Moreover, several state troopers may be subpoenaed to corroborate the surrounding circumstances. Hill did not come forward with her charges until nearly a decade after she says they occurred. Jones waited less than three years.

Finally, Hill's allegations against Clarence Thomas were inconsistent with Thomas's prior conduct and reputation. That cannot be said about Jones's allegations against Clinton.

It may well be that Jones made up the entire story, or at least the most salacious parts of it. But it also may well be that Hill made up some or all of her account. The point is that many feminists took the position that women who allege sexual harassment should be believed. Indeed, Anita Hill has been speaking at conferences entitled "Women Tell the Truth." It certainly cannot be the position of the sponsors of these conferences that only liberal women who accuse conservative men tell the truth. When conservative women make allegations against liberal men, these allegations cannot be taken any more or less seriously.

No one can know for certain what took place behind the closed doors of that room in the Excelsior Hotel on May 8, 1991. There are inconsistencies in Jones's story, just as there were in Hill's. Jones and her supporters may have financial and political motivations, but so may Hill and her supporters. One fact is beyond dispute: Anita Hill has made a fortune off speaking and book fees solely on the basis of her accusation.

It is too early to make an informed judgment about the credibility of the Jones allegations. But it is not too early to insist that these allegations must be treated no differently from "politically correct" allegations of sexual harassment made against "politically incorrect" defendants. Charges of sexual harassment are too serious to be allowed to be used selectively against only certain types of people.

President Clinton's lawyer, Robert Bennett, has gotten off

to a bad start by questioning "whether a sitting president may be sued for alleged events that took place before he entered office." Of course he can. No American is above the law. Just as Vice-President Agnew could be, and indeed was, indicted for conduct that took place before he entered office, so too a sitting president is not above the law of sexual harassment and assault. By questioning whether his client can even be sued, Bennett conveys the impression that he is afraid of putting his client under oath. And perhaps he is.

But the president will almost certainly have to testify under oath — first by depositions and then in court — unless the suit is withdrawn or dismissed. Nor is it likely that a court will dismiss the complaint on legal grounds, since it appears to make out a cause of action and is being filed within the three-year statute of limitations.

It is important to remember that this is merely a lawsuit brought by a single individual. It is not an indictment or a complaint filed by an agency. Like the suit brought against Cardinal Bernadin, it may prove baseless. Certainly President Clinton is entitled to the same presumption of innocence that protects anyone charged with sexual misconduct or any other misdeed.

But as the world awaits President Clinton's response, it also awaits the response of those feminists who did not accord Clarence Thomas any presumption of innocence and who — in other cases — adopt the knee-jerk attitude that "women tell the truth." Some do and some don't — as is true of every type of allegation. Paula Corbin Jones's accusations should remind us how easy it is these days to level the thermonuclear charge of sexual harassment. Whichever way this case comes out, it should serve as an object lesson on why those accused of sexual harassment should not be presumed guilty just because some feminists believe that "women tell the truth."

May 1994

Clinton's Privacy

W HEN PRESIDENT CLINTON'S lawyer, Robert Bennett, correctly pointed out that Europeans cannot understand the obsession of the American media and public with the private lives of our public officials, he told us only half of an interesting story.

Bennett is right that most Europeans could care less about whether their presidents and prime ministers have sexual affairs outside their marriages. But the reason for this difference is not a function of American public prurience or media irresponsibility. It is a function of how our presidents — as distinguished from their political leaders — get elected. In most parts of the world, political leaders do not run for office on the basis of their personal lives. In the United States, our presidential candidates do precisely that: It is they who place their family values, their religious values, and, indeed, their sexual values at issue.

American presidential candidates rarely run on their records or platform alone. They run on their character, their charm, their charisma, their photogenic quality, their wives' popularity, and their rapport with the media. Sometimes this "beauty contest" produces surprisingly good results. President John F. Kennedy could never have been elected as a national leader of any other country at his young age and with his meager record of legislative accomplishments. But he was the right man for his time. So, too, President Bill Clinton could never have been so quickly thrust into national leadership in any other nation, based on his governorship of a small state. But these men leapfrogged over generations of more experienced politicians on the basis of their good looks, quick wit, charm, intelligence, and other personal qualities. Both placed their personal lives at issue by using their wives and children as part of their campaigns. Both won, but not because a majority of Americans agreed with their positions on substantive issues or their past records of accomplishment; they won because voters liked them better than their opponents.

It is not surprising that among the nations of Europe, the English seem to understand best our obsession with the personal foibles of our presidents. They, too, are obsessed with the personal lives of their royal family. They realize that our president — especially when he is as young and charming as a Kennedy or a Clinton — is an uncomfortable combination of their monarch and prime minister. Our First Family is more like their royal family than are the families of their European leaders. When leaders are seen as personal role models — as our president and the English queen are — it should come as no surprise that the public should be interested in their personal lives.

Another country that is quickly learning this lesson is Israel. Since its establishment forty-six years ago, the Jewish state has had a parliamentary system of selecting its prime minister. Under that system, experienced parliamentary politicians generally worked their way up the hierarchy. No one cared much about their private lives. Now Israel is moving toward popular election for prime minister, and young, charismatic, and photogenic candidates — such as Benjamin Netanyahu — are emerging. Not surprisingly, Netanyahu's private life — an acknowledged extramarital affair — became big news. Welcome to the world of personality politics.

President Clinton insists on confiding to the American public the most personal details of his religious beliefs and practices. Such revelations by a European politician would be as unthinkable as the disclosure of what kind of underwear he or she wears. The queen does, of course, speak about religion, because an important part of her role is "defender of the faith" in a nation with an established church. But the American president is supposed to be the defender of the Constitution rather than the defender of the faith, as Walter Mondale had to remind President Reagan during the 1984 election campaign, after Reagan constantly invoked his religious beliefs. American presidents should not wear their religion on their sleeves.

American politicians cannot have it both ways. If they seek election on the basis of their religious and family values, they should not be heard to complain when the public and the media hold them to their campaign rhetoric. Only if they eschew reliance on such personal revelations should they be heard to invoke a right to privacy.

The cycle can be broken only if presidential candidates were to resist the easy temptation offered by the TV camera to run on personal qualities, rather than issues. The truth is that most of our politicians don't want to keep their personal lives private — so long as making them public helps them win elections. They only want to keep their personal lives private if making them public may cause them to lose. The American voter cannot be expected to accept such selective invocation of the right to "privacy" by their elected officials.

May 1994

The Political Right Learns from the Left

I WAS RECENTLY SENT a letter inviting the recipient to a fund-raising event honoring a well-known criminal defendant facing indictment for what his supporters believe is a "political" crime. It reminded me of similar letters I had received back in the 1960s and 1970s for the "Chicago 7," the "Spock 5," the "Berrigan 3," the "Wilmington 10," the "Elsberg 2," and other such leftist political conspiracies. ("Numbered defendants" were so common in those days that some young people thought the Indianapolis 500 was a massive conspiracy.)

Liberals who attended such events and contributed to "defense funds" were considered — by people like Richard Nixon, Edwin Meese, Lyn Nofziger, Ronald Reagan, and Richard Viguerie — as disloyal Americans, who sided with the forces of crime rather than the forces of law enforcement. It was Meese who characterized the American Civil Liberties Union as the "criminal's lobby."

It came as something of a shock when I read the list of names supporting this particular criminal defendant and urging contributions to his "defense fund." It read like a Who's

Who of the "law-and-order" right. Its co-chairmen are the three living former Republican presidents — Reagan, Ford, and Nixon. Its members include Meese, Nofziger, and Viguerie as well as Elliott Abrams and Maurice Stans. Others who have publicly supported this defendant include former secretaries of state James Baker and Henry Kissinger and Senate Minority Leader Robert Dole.

The honoree is, of course, Caspar Weinberger, who is facing a prison term for allegedly perjuring himself before Congress and lying to investigators. The issue in his case will be quite simple: Did he deliberately lie when he made certain statements regarding arms sales to Iran, which appear to be contradicted by his own handwritten notes?

The only way that perjury can be considered a "political" crime is by believing that lying under oath to further the administration's political agenda is permissible. This is a cynical variation on the-ends-justify-the-means theme for which Weinberger demanded that Jonathan Pollard — the American who spied for our ally, Israel — must be sentenced to life imprisonment. No American can take the law into his own hands, railed Weinberger, even when he believes the administration is acting improperly. Yet Weinberger's supporters now seem to be arguing that lying should be excused if it was done to protect the administration. Some of his supporters are claiming, of course, that he did not lie, and that factual issue should be placed before a jury or judge.

At least one invitation was sent to a sitting federal judge, urging him to make "a contribution" to the "Weinberger Defense Fund." The mailing list must be very broad indeed, considering some of the people whom the invitation reached.

When I called the RSVP number to ask who would be at the event, I was told that "just about everybody" would be there — "senators, congressmen, cabinet people, the military." Edwin Meese was going to be addressing the expected eight hundred guests, who were shelling out nearly $30,000 to hear how the former law-and-order attorney general beat his own rap and what advice he may have for Weinberger. I would love to be a fly on the wall listening to these recent converts to the gospel of civil liberties condemning selective and arbitrary prosecution, lauding the Bill of Rights, and singing the praises of confrontational defense lawyers. There is nothing like the occasional indictment of one of their own to make law-and-order right-wingers understand the virtues of our adversary system. Converts are always the most zealous believers, and I fully expect to see the Meese crowd enroll en mass in the ACLU, now that his friends need the help of the "criminal's lobby."

The point, of course, is that civil liberties are for everybody, from the most lowly homeless person accused of sleeping on a park bench to former members of the cabinet. Just as the criminal law — including the law of perjury — must be applied equally to all, so too the Bill of Rights must be applied equally to everybody.

Caspar Weinberger deserves a zealous defense. He has the right to collect contributions to his defense fund. He has the right to take advantage of the privilege against self-incrimination and other protections that Meese used to say only the guilty need. Meese himself took full advantage of several of the "pro-defendant" safeguards of the Bill of Rights, including wisely hiring one of the toughest criminal-defense lawyers in Washington when he was under investigation by a special prosecutor.

I don't think I'm going to send Weinberger my own contribution, since he is a wealthy man. But I do send him my sincere hope that justice prevails in his case. And I want to remind him of the old joke about the lawyer who cabled his client, "Justice has prevailed" — to which his client cabled back, "Appeal immediately."

September 1992

Bush Pardon Should Be Probed

PRESIDENT BUSH'S DECISION to pardon Caspar Weinberger, though constitutionally authorized, may well have constituted an obstruction of justice. It certainly reflected a classic conflict of interest.

If it is true, as it has been widely reported, that President George Bush might have been personally disadvantaged by the scheduled criminal trial of Weinberger, then President Bush's decision to cancel the trial by a preemptive pardon raises serious ethical and legal issues, notwithstanding the president's constitutional power to pardon.

President Bush might have been personally disadvantaged by the full-blown criminal trial of Weinberger in several different ways. First, he could have been subpoenaed as a material witness by the prosecution and examined under oath as to his own role in the Iran/Contra conspiracy or in the cover-up. Second, other witnesses could have put the lie to his self-serving claims that he was not in the loop and that he was unaware of the extent of Weinberger's opposition to the arms-for-hostages deal — including Weinberger's expressed view that it was illegal. Third, President Bush could have been subject to sanctions for nondisclosure of his own relevant notes. And fourth — and perhaps most important — had Weinberger been convicted and sentenced to prison, the former secretary of defense may well have been willing to bargain for his own freedom by incriminating higher-ups, including Mr. Bush. Indeed, Weinberger himself has alleged that he was offered freedom in exchange for incriminating former President Reagan. President Bush had every reason to fear that if convicted, an unpardoned Weinberger might be willing to sing the prosecution's tune to save himself from jail. Many "loyal" subordinates find their prior loyalty challenged by imminent imprisonment.

If any of these considerations could even arguably have played a role in President Bush's decision to pardon Weinberger, then President Bush had a clear conflict of interest, which should have precluded him from participating in the pardon decision. A conflict of interest exists whenever a decision-maker — a judge, a senator, a lawyer, a cabinet member — has a personal stake, or even the appearance of a personal stake, in the outcome of a decision that is supposed to be made in the public interest. The policy that forbids conflicts of interest applies to presidents as well. For example, when President Nixon fired special prosecutor Archibald Cox, there was a conflict of interest, since the reason for the firing was to protect Richard Nixon from prosecution or public disgrace. The American public recognized that President Nixon had acted improperly and he paid a heavy price. So did Nixon's designated hitter, Robert Bork, who obeyed President Nixon's unethical order to fire Mr. Cox, after both the attorney general and the deputy attorney general refused to do so. Mr. Bork's participation in the unethical decision to fire Mr. Cox played a role in his not being confirmed to the High Court.

Just because a president has the constitutional power to pardon does not mean that he may exercise that power in cases in which he has a personal stake. For example, no one would deny that if a president pardoned a convicted drug dealer after secretly accepting a million-dollar payment from him, that president would be guilty of accepting a bribe. Indeed, several governors have gone to prison for exercising their constitutional power to pardon, in exchange for personal consideration. Nor could it be disputed that if a criminal threatened to inculpate a president in criminal activity unless he were pardoned, a presidential decision to pardon would be a criminal obstruction of justice.

It is particularly ironic that it is President Bush who has issued a pardon under circumstances suggesting a conflict of interest. It has been the Bush administration's Justice Department that has, for the first time, tried to criminalize conflicts of interest by lawyers. Thus, the Bush administration's Justice Department has indicted several criminal lawyers on the ground that their conflicts of interest — for example, representing one member of a drug or organized-crime conspiracy while taking orders from the "boss" of the conspiracy — constituted a criminal obstruction of justice. By the standards currently being enforced by the Justice Department, an investigation should be opened concerning the Weinberger pardon. If the special counsel does not open such an investigation, then the new Justice Department should. Now that Weinberger has been pardoned, he no longer has a Fifth Amendment privilege to refuse to testify — unless, of course, he is at risk of self-incrimination for his role in securing the pardon. Reports are now circulating that Weinberger may be subpoenaed by the special counsel. But if neither the special counsel nor the new Justice Department opens an investigation of the circumstances surrounding the pardon, then Congress should. The

American public has the right to know whether President Bush's decision to pardon Caspar Weinberger was in any way influenced by self-serving considerations.

January 1993

Should the CEO of a Criminal Corporation Govern Yale?

ERNON R. LOUCKS, JR., is the senior trustee of the Yale University Corporation. In that capacity, Loucks is supposed to help raise funds from other alumni and help direct university policy. He is also supposed to be a role model of success for Yale alumni in the world of business. The problem is that Loucks's company, Baxter International, just pleaded guilty to committing a serious felony over a four-year period. Under Loucks's direction — he is chairman of the board and chief operating officer at Baxter, which is the world's largest hospital supplier — the company violated American law by cooperating with the Arab boycott of Israel.

Following extensive negotiations, the corporation copped a plea, thus avoiding the possibility of criminal charges being brought against individuals who made the actual decisions to break the law.

When the investigation was first made public, Loucks made a solemn promise to Yale University. He promised that if the investigation showed that his company had violated the antiboycott statute, he would step down from his position on the Yale Corporation. Now the company itself has admitted that it "is in fact guilty of the charges," to which it has pleaded guilty. As the *Yale Daily News* put it in a recent editorial:

> In January 1992, Vernon Loucks said he would re-sign from the Yale Corporation if federal investiga-tors found that the company he runs had broken the law. They did, and now he must. Loucks' company, Baxter International Inc., pleaded guilty last Thurs-day to undertaking a four-year, orchestrated effort to have itself removed from the Arab League's boycott list. The company agreed to pay a $6.5 million fine, the largest in history for such a violation, avoiding a messy trial in which more details would have sur-faced. The settlement between Baxter and the Justice Department makes clear that as Baxter's chairman and chief executive officer, Loucks had knowledge of — and may have even directly overseen — the scheme.

The scheme itself was nefarious indeed, involving the payment of "penalty" money — a euphemism for bribes — to Arab officials. One Syrian official with whom the company worked closely was a general who has written anti-Semitic tracts denouncing the Jews for murdering Christians in order to use their blood to bake "the matsoh of Zion." Loucks's company will apparently get into bed with anybody for the almighty dollar.

But the issue goes beyond complicity with anti-Semitism or sympathy with the Arab boycott against Israel. It is a serious crime — a felony — under the law of the United States to do what Loucks's company has admitted it did over a considerable period of time. Nor was this the company's only brush with the law under Loucks's stewardship. It was also investigated for what *Business Week* described as a "payola" scheme to pay "kickbacks" to doctors. Some role model for Yale students and alumni!

Vernon R. Loucks, Jr., is trying his best to distance himself from his company's problems and his own broken promises. He has fired several of the designated flack-catchers, as CEOs often do when problems have arisen on their watch. Now he is using all of his charm and grace to try to put the problems behind him without accepting any of the responsibility for the criminal actions from which his company tried to profit. But it is doubtful that his John Wayne bearing and background — he stands six feet five inches and still looks like the Yale football player and marine he once was — will be enough to get him out of the mess he has created for himself, his company, and his university.

Within the past few days, one of his company's largest customers said that it might curtail tens of millions of dollars of business because of the company's criminality and its "concern over Baxter's business methods, ethics and behavior over the past four years." Other customers, particularly hospitals, have expressed similar concerns.

The newly designated president of Yale, Dr. Richard Levin, has stated that he has not yet formed an opinion on whether Loucks should remain on the Yale Corporation, but several student groups and influential alumni are pressing for his removal, and it seems unlikely that Yale's new president will want to start his term with an ethics stain that was not of his making.

The issue in the Loucks case goes beyond Baxter and Yale. The relationship between university governance and business ethics is being more thoroughly scrutinized throughout the country. In the old days, any rich and generous alumni could serve on a university's corporation. Today, students, faculty, and concerned alumni are asking tough questions about the ethics of those who govern institutions of learning. Alumni can no longer buy their way onto governing boards. They must earn that honor by their life's work. Under that test, Vernon Loucks, Jr., gets a failing grade, and so will Yale if it allows him to remain on its corporation.

May 1993

On September 10, 1993, Vernon Loucks resigned his post as a senior trustee and campaign chairman of Yale University. Loucks denied that his resignation was motivated by student pressure and said that he intended to continue working as an alumnus on behalf of Yale's major fund-raising campaign.

An Anti-Jewish Judge Is Allowed to Sit on the Bench

IN HITLER'S GERMANY, one could imagine a Nazi judge referring to Jews as "kikes," or declaring, "It's time to warm up the ovens," when a Jew walked into his courtroom. But it is difficult to conceive that an American judge would be allowed to continue to sit on the bench if he were found to have made such anti-Semitic utterances in 1993. Yet, Judge B. Joseph Fitzsimmons, Jr., associate justice of the Probate and Family Court of Massachusetts, will be eligible to continue his service as an associate justice on July 1, 1993, after he admitted using "anti-Semitic terms describing or referring to certain attorneys of the Jewish faith."

The bigoted judge had no choice but to admit these allegations since — according to the findings of the Commission on Judicial Conduct — "various court personnel" heard him say, "It's time to warm up the ovens," when he was advised "that an attorney of the Jewish faith was waiting in his courtroom to argue" a case. Nor were these quoted remarks isolated instances of insensitivity in an otherwise distinguished judicial career.

So pervasive were Judge Fitzsimmons's anti-Jewish feelings that he and his brother — a crony who hung around the courthouse with the judge, selling his influence — actually devised "a form of double-talk or verbal code" to disguise their references to Jewish lawyers in front of witnesses. The judge admitted that he used the code so "that they won't know that we are talking about them."

Nor was Judge Fitzsimmons's bigotry limited to Jews. He made numerous sexist remarks as well, insulting women, especially women who were unemployed. He told them to "get a job," without inquiring as to whether they were able to obtain employment.

In addition to these crass manifestations of bigotry, Judge Fitzsimmons repeatedly engaged in the serious crime of theft of payment for services not rendered. Although he was obliged to work from 9 A.M. to 4 P.M., with an hour off for lunch, he repeatedly arrived at work late and then spent the entire afternoon playing golf. During the few hours he spent in the courtroom each day, "Judge Fitzsimmons spent substantial periods of time in his lobby occupied with paying personal bills, attending to personal correspondence, and making personal phone calls." He simply refused to conduct trials, because they would take too much time out of his golfing afternoons. As the commission put it: "During his first ten years on the bench, from 1980 until [the investigation began], Judge Fitzsimmons sought to avoid the trial of contested matters that came before him, particularly those that were lengthy or complicated." Put simply, the lazy bum in robes simply refused to work. Yet he received full pay. That constitutes theft of payment for services not rendered. Public employees are prosecuted for such theft, when it is as overt and sustained as it was in Judge Fitzsimmons's case. Recently, an exposé on *60 Minutes* of New York School employees who worked on their boats and played golf instead of working at their school maintenance jobs resulted in indictments.

Despite these and other violations of the judicial office — there were eight serious charges in all, each of which had numerous examples — Judge Fitzsimmons was not removed from the bench. He was merely fined and suspended for six months. Thus, in July of this year, an anti-Semitic and sexist bigot will again put on his robe and administer "justice" in Massachusetts. Perhaps his language will change, at least in front of witnesses, since he knows that the commission will be observing him — at least for a while. But his attitudes will not change, especially since he received only a slap on the wrist for his outrageous misbehavior. B. Joseph Fitzsimmons, Jr., simply does not belong on the bench. He belongs in prison, for stealing money from the taxpayers, for not giving a full day's work for a full day's pay. He belongs in the Ku Klux Klan or the Nazi party, where the views he expressed are commonplace. He should be wearing a robe, but it should be a white one with a hood, rather than a black one with the power to enforce his bigoted conception of the law.

As a Massachusetts attorney, I will refuse to appear in his courtroom, even if I am assigned a case there. I will not appear before a bigot in robes who regards me as a "kike." I will take the consequences of this act of civil disobedience, rather than recognize the authority of this bigot as a judge. And I urge all other Massachusetts lawyers of good will, regardless of religion or ethnicity, to boycott Judge Fitzsimmons when he returns to the bench in July. If the Massachusetts judiciary cannot or will not clean its own house, then the lawyers, who are also sworn to administer justice, must do something to assure that bigoted bums like B. Joseph Fitzsimmons do not pervert our system of justice.

January 1993

On September 13, 1993, Eileen M. Shaevel was unanimously confirmed as the replacement for former Norfolk County Probate Court Judge B. Joseph Fitzsimmons, Jr., who left the bench under fire in May. Fitzsimmons chose formally to resign his judgeship, after having been suspended for his anti-Semitic remarks, just days before a legislative hearing was to be conducted on his suitability for the bench. Interestingly, Judge Fitzsimmons had spent part of his time during the suspension in an extensive training and education course, sponsored by the New England Regional Office of the Anti-Defamation League, entitled "The Roots and Prevention of Anti-Semitism."

An Anti-Arab Bigot Is No Better Than an Anti-Jewish Bigot

A N ACTING JUSTICE of the New York Supreme Court was recently censured for directing anti-Arab remarks at an attorney of Syrian ancestry.

According to the findings of the Commission on Judicial Conduct, Justice Stewart L. Ain — who is Jewish — asked the attorney to spell his name. When Paul Saqqal did, Justice Ain asked, "You're not an Arab, are you?" When Saqqal said that he was of Arab ancestry, Justice Ain shot back, "You're our sworn enemies." Mr. Saqqal, who was representing a client and did not want to endanger his case, attempted to mollify the judge by assuring him that he was of "Christian Arab ancestry," rather than of Islamic Arab ancestry. But Justice Ain was not mollified. Demonstrating that he is an equal-opportunity bigot who does not discriminate between Christians and Muslims — so long as they are Arabs — Justice Ain replied: "You're still our enemies." Then, as if in a schoolyard or a barnyard, Justice Ain turned to the lawyer, and, saying "Here's what I have to say to you," extended his middle finger at Mr. Saqqal.

Just to make sure the lawyer got his point, Justice Ain shouted "What the f—k do you people want anyway?" He then gave the lawyer the finger again, saying "You know what this is, don't you?"

The justice then turned to the opposing lawyer and asked whether he was Jewish. When that lawyer replied in the affirmative, Justice Ain inquired whether he had ever met General Ariel Sharon. Justice Ain then spoke of his admiration for General Sharon's "hawkish views toward Arabs."

Justice Ain's defense to this outrageous misconduct is that he was trying to be funny. Saqqal did not appreciate his humor: "I didn't take it for a joke, not for a second." The commission rejected Justice Ain's explanation, finding that it "lacks credibility" — legalese for "Justice Ain is not only a bigot, he's a liar as well." Stewart L. Ain also sounds like he may need emotional help.

The question is why the commission let Justice Ain off with a slap-on-the-wrist "censure" for misconduct that it characterized as "a series of biased and abusive actions." It could have ordered the harsher sanction of removal, but instead it imposed no punishment other than "the strong public criticism of the censure itself." It concluded that Justice Ain had not actually been biased in his decision, but had "conveyed the impression that he was biased against Mr. Saqqal because of his ethnic background." It is impossible, however, to determine whether an *apparently* biased judge *acted* on his bias in a complex case involving the exercise of judicial discretion. That is why the appearance of justice is so important.

Bigots like Stewart L. Ain do not belong on the benches of our state and federal courts. Nor is Ain alone in his bigotry. What is unique about him is that he was prepared to express his bigoted views so crudely, rather than more subtly, as some other judges do.

I recently experienced the appearance of religious favoritism by a judge in a federal defamation suit brought by a rabbi (Avraham Weiss) against a cardinal (Joseph Glemp of Poland). Cardinal Glemp had falsely accused Rabbi Weiss of going to Poland to kill nuns and destroy a convent, when he knew that the rabbi had conducted a peaceful pray-in at the Auschwitz convent. The judge, Robert Patterson, shocked courtroom observers when in the course of this religiously divisive case, he expressed the view that the pope was the individual singularly responsible for the fall of the Berlin Wall. He then went on to credit the testimony of the Catholic witnesses, while accusing the Jewish witnesses (and a black witness) of lying. He also went out of his way to take a cheap shot at me, my book *Chutzpah*, and an affidavit I had filed. He dismissed the rabbi's case on the extraordinary ground that an experienced process server had failed to serve the cardinal properly, when she tried to hand him a summons on an Albany street.

Judge Patterson's questionable behavior went beyond the appearance of religious favoritism; he also made bizarre statements about how he "got in a little trouble" in the supermarket "dancing" and "pretending the music was better than it was." He told startled courtroom observers that "the checkout girl thought I was a real oddball." So did many in the courtroom, especially when he continued to ramble on about his friend who brought refrigeration to Eastern Europe, his father, who worked to bring Jews and Christians together, and the "Jewish church in Russia."

I would hope that organizations committed to equal justice — including Jewish organizations — would urge the removal of judges who express anti-Arab bias or any kind of bigotry or religious favoritism. There is no room for any kind of bigotry, favoritism, or emotional instability in our legal system.

October 1992

Although Judge Stewart L. Ain was censured in October 1992 by the New York State Commission on Judicial Conduct, he is still sitting on the bench in Nassau County. Judge Patterson also continues to sit on the federal bench in New York.

Too Eager to Classify in the Pollard Case?

J ONATHAN POLLARD, THE American who pleaded guilty to spying for Israel, has now served longer in prison than any American in history convicted of spying for an ally. Indeed, he has served longer than most Americans convicted of spying for enemies. This is especially surprising in light of the plea bargain that the government struck with Pollard. In exchange for pleading guilty and cooperating with the government, Pollard was promised that the government would not seek life imprisonment. But the judge nonetheless imposed a life sentence and the very prosecutors who made the promise are now breaking it by insisting that the president not reduce the life sentence. Under current guidelines, Pollard may not be eligible for parole until 2015.

In light of all this, it is not surprising that President Clinton is reported to be considering some form of reduction that would bring Pollard's sentence more in line with those who have pleaded guilty to spying for allies and more in line with the government's promise. But now, in a calculated effort to keep Pollard in prison, Pentagon officials have made public a letter from outgoing Secretary of Defense Les Aspin to President Clinton alleging that Jonathan Pollard had slipped classified information into fourteen letters he sent from prison. The implication is that this information might endanger United States security. If there were any truth to this tall tale, it would show unparalleled stupidity on the part of the American intelligence officials, who monitor all of Pollard's letters. If they had spotted any dangerous classified material in the first letter, they clearly would have stopped it — as they had the right to do — from being sent. To wait until all fourteen letters had been sent would — if true — have constituted government complicity in the publication of dangerous classified information. Indeed, Pollard had the right to rely on the fact that he was advised that his letters were being passed through the national security censorship.

As one of Pollard's legal advisers, I have read many of his letters in which he defends himself against charges that he seriously endangered our national security. If any of his letters inadvertently included information that was technically classified, then it was information that had either already been made public or was of no real importance. The best proof of this is that Joseph deGenova, the prosecutor in the Pollard case, has publicly called for all the classified information in that case to be made public. Indeed, some of the classified information was already leaked to *Time* magazine by government sources in an effort to deny Pollard's request for commutation. I have written to Attorney General Reno asking her to open an investigation of this recent leak.

Several years ago the government claimed that thirteen of Pollard's letters contained classified information. On November 23, 1992, the director of naval intelligence confirmed that the material in those letters had been declassified "because they no longer possess the potential to damage national security." Les Aspin must be aware of this statement, yet in his letter to the president, he conveyed the false impression that the contents of Pollard's letters currently have the potential to damage our national security.

What we are seeing here is yet another abuse of the classification system by the Pentagon to serve political rather than national security interests. The entire classification system reeks of arbitrariness. Insiders leak classified information with impunity. I was recently told by a former intelligence official that he had been shown classified information in the Pollard case in order to give him ammunition to oppose Pollard's release.

The government continues to play fast and loose with the facts regarding Pollard's case. In another recent leak, intelligence officials assert that information provided by Pollard to Israel may have inadvertently found its way to the Soviet Union. Yet prosecutor deGenova asserted during a public debate that he had no information to confirm that speculation.

In a democracy, it is unfair for the government to argue against the rights of a citizen by relying on classified information without giving that citizen the right to defend against its charges. Accordingly, the only appropriate course for the government to follow now is that suggested by prosecutor de-Genova: All the material on which the government is relying in its efforts to keep Pollard in jail should now be declassified so that the public can determine for itself the actual extent of damage done by Mr. Pollard. I am convinced that a full, fair, and open review of the facts will lead to the conclusion that the information provided by Pollard to Israel was largely tactical and regional rather than global and strategic. It related primarily to Iraq's plans for chemical and gas warfare and to Syrian-inspired terrorism directed against civilians. Jonathan Pollard has more than paid his debt to society for engaging in an act of civil disobedience calculated to save innocent lives.

January 1994

On March 23, 1994, relying upon the recommendations of Defense Secretary Aspin, Attorney General Reno, as well as the opinions of unnamed officials in the Central Intelligence Agency, President Clinton held a press conference to announce his decision not to commute Jonathan Pollard's life sentence. President Clinton cited "the enormity of Mr. Pollard's crime, the harm his actions have done to our country and the need to deter every person who might even consider such actions." Unfortunately for Jonathan Pollard and his many supporters, this decision reflects little more than the currently harsh political climate in Washington, D.C., toward individuals who have been caught spying in the United States; it certainly does not represent an honest assessment of Jonathan Pollard's crimes or the proper punishment for those offenses.

Bombing Story Has Two Sides

NOW THAT VIRTUALLY every American — including potential jurors — has been told the essence of the government's case against the alleged bombers of the World Trade Center, the judge has imposed a gag order on *all* parties. This is the same kind of "equality" mocked by Anatole France when he quipped: "The law, in its majestic equality, forbids the rich as well as the poor to sleep under bridges, to beg in the streets, and to steal bread." Similarly, the law equally forbids prosecutors and defense attorneys to leak information — *after* the prosecution has presented its side of the case to the public. Now that the prosecution's horse — or is it bull? — is out of the barn, the judge is unfairly closing the door to deny the defense equal access to the media.

This unlevel playing field is all too typical of the unfair way in which courts treat proactive disclosures from the prosecution and reactive disclosures from the defense in highly publicized criminal cases. The prosecution always gets an unfair advantage over the defense in the court of public opinion, because it gets its case out to the media and then sanctimoniously demands a gag order on both sides so that the defense cannot try to level the playing field and neutralize the damage that has been done. This often translates into an unfair advantage as well in the court of law, since jurors are influenced by what they read and hear — especially when it comes from "reliable government sources." The prosecution's case thus starts with a heavy factual presumption of guilt, rather than the constitutionally required presumption of innocence.

From the moment of the first arrests in the World Trade Center bombing case, government agents have been busy disclosing and leaking selected details of their version of the case. We "know" what was found during the various searches, who the "ringleader" allegedly is, what the motives were. An incriminating letter, supposedly written by one of the defendants, has been publicized in the press. How much of this "evidence" will actually be admissible at trial is unclear, but it certainly sounds convincing to readers of the one-sided press accounts orchestrated by the government.

Nor will government leaks suddenly end now that a gag order is in place. Prosecutors and their agents are masters of the discreet leak. They have long-term institutional relationships with favored reporters, who would never blow a good government source. The prosecuting attorneys themselves rarely have to dirty their own hands by actually dropping the dime. FBI agents and other law-enforcement officials — who are less concerned about the judicial reaction — are perfectly willing to do the dirty work for the government lawyers. Government lawyers are almost never caught — indeed, there is rarely even an investigation — and they know that if they were to be caught, nothing would happen. Defense attorneys, on the other hand, are terrified of leaking information in violation of a gag order. They know that they and their clients would pay a heavy price indeed for trying to play catch-up with the prosecution. Nor can defense attorneys have anyone else do their leaking for them, since they do not have FBI agents or police working for them.

I certainly have no personal sympathy for the defendants charged in the World Trade Center bombing. But the issue of press bias in high-visibility cases transcends any particular case. Practices that have become acceptable in cases of unpopular defendants become precedent for all cases.

Nor do I have any sympathy for gag orders. I believe they violate the First Amendment's guarantee of freedom of speech, and when applied to defense attorneys in criminal cases, they may also violate the defendant's Sixth Amendment right to an effective defense. The best answer to prosecutorial leaks is the open marketplace of ideas, in which *both sides* can tell their stories to the press. Juries would then have to be picked more carefully and sequestered more often. That may take more time and create some inconvenience. But it is a reasonable price to pay for balancing the right of free speech against the right of fair trial. It is surely better — from any point of view — to have both sides talk to the press than to continue the present one-sided approach, which implicitly encourages prosecutorial leaks to the media, while denying defense efforts at responding to the prosecutor's trial by media.

The public has a right to know about ongoing investigations of terrorism, especially terrorism that hits home, as the World Trade Center bombing did. But the public has a right to know *both* sides of the story — in the media and in the courtroom — so that it can make its own judgment, rather than simply being spoon-fed the government's self-serving account.

April 1993

Louis J. Freeh, who replaced William Sessions as director of the Federal Bureau of Investigation, recently suspended James Fox, head of the FBI's New York office, on grounds that he had violated the federal judge's gag order by commenting on television about the World Trade Center bombing case.

Keeping Hoover's Name on the FBI Building Sends the Wrong Message

A S I READ Anthony Summers's book on the life of J. Edgar Hoover, I couldn't help thinking how close we allowed ourselves to come to a dictatorship. Although many of the revelations in *Official and Confidential* were known previously, this compilation of abuses into one volume should send shudders down the spine of every American who cares about democracy and due process of law.

Summers's portrait — even discounting the loosely documented but titillating gossip of transvestism and homosexuality — is of a cynical tyrant who blackmailed presidents, drove innocent people to suicide, and used the most despicable means to try to destroy his enemies.

But the most interesting and disturbing disclosures are not about the blackmailer, but about those who submitted to his blackmail — namely several presidents of the United States, ranging from Roosevelt to Kennedy to Johnson and Nixon.

If information is power, then negative information capable of destroying the most powerful people in the world is a veritable nuclear weapon. J. Edgar Hoover had that weapon, and he knew exactly how to use it to achieve his personal ambitions and to settle personal scores against his perceived enemies.

Hoover specialized in collecting — and selectively disseminating — sexual information about the private lives of public people. Under the pretext of gathering this information to *prevent* the blackmail of high officials with national security secrets, the director of the FBI used it as a sword for his own blackmail rather than as a shield against the blackmail of our enemies.

Hoover was indeed a master. But his mastery was of public relations and propaganda. He fooled a gullible nation into believing that he and his agents were all that stood between Americanism and totalitarianism.

He sure fooled me. As a twelve-year-old, I took my first trip to Washington, as part of a class outing. I have only vague recollections of my visit to Congress, the White House, the Supreme Court, and the Smithsonian. But I will never forget my morning at FBI headquarters, where I learned about the dangers of "Godless Communism," where I saw the "death mask" of John Dillinger, and where I watched agents taking target practice — I saved my souvenir target and cartridge shell for a decade. In the years that followed, I became an FBI groupie, reading Hoover's *Masters of Deceit* and watching as his G-men systematically captured the "most wanted criminals" in America.

It was only while in college that I began to learn about the darker side of Hoover's FBI, but even then I could not believe that a high official of our government could be guilty of what radicals were claiming Hoover had done. Then in 1971, I was told — by a former government official whose word I trusted — about Hoover's taping of Martin Luther King. Hoover hated King and set out to destroy him. He put in motion a secret plan calculated to get King to commit suicide.

The plan required the Kennedy administration to approve the wiretapping of King, so that Hoover could secure hard evidence of King's sexual involvement with white women. Initially, the Kennedy administration resisted Hoover's demands, but eventually — after Hoover employed his usual blackmail — they acquiesced. They had to know that the wiretaps were not being installed "for the protection of Dr. King," as former Attorney General Nicholas Katzenbach once tried to rationalize it, or to protect the "national security" of our country, as others tried to explain. But they did not suspect the use to which the tapes would be put by Hoover. He had the King sex tapes sent to Dr. King's wife, with an anonymous note suggesting that suicide was "the only thing left for [Dr. King] to do."

The King plan did not work, as many of Hoover's harebrained schemes did not work. But Hoover did apparently succeed in driving actress Jean Seberg to suicide, after leaking a story that she was carrying the child of a "prominent Black Panther." Whether they were effective or not, Hoover's dangerous plots created an atmosphere of fear and intimidation throughout the nation. I wrote about the King episode while Hoover was still alive and subsequently discovered that Hoover began a file on me as a result of my critical article. That was his way of trying to control his critics.

Despite this legacy of tyranny and blackmail, J. Edgar Hoover's name is still honored in Washington. The FBI building is called the J. Edgar Hoover Building. This sends precisely the wrong message to young FBI agents and to the public in general: namely, that extortion, blackmail, and outright criminality in law enforcement will be honored and rewarded. It is time to remove Hoover's name from all places of honor and to recognize him for the dangerous criminal he was.

April 1993

The Prosecution Buys a Witness

IMAGINE THE FOLLOWING scenario: A highly publicized and controversial white-collar criminal trial is under way. There is one crucial witness who used to work for the major defendant. Both the defense and the prosecution want him to testify for its side. What the witness observed falls into the gray area: the witness could — without lying — slant his testimony either *for* or *against* his former boss, since it is largely a question of perspective and emphasis.

As the witness contemplates his options, he receives a phone call from the defense attorney imploring him to testify in favor of his former boss. The lawyer invokes old friendships and loyalty. The witness is still vacillating. Suddenly the defense lawyer raises the ante: "If you testify for my client, I will try to get you a high-paying job with another of my clients. I will also give you $12,500 in cash, and if my client wins, I will see to it that you get a $100,000 bonus." The witness accepts this hard-to-refuse offer and testifies for his former boss. He doesn't lie, but he clearly slants his testimony in favor of the defendant.

Had a defense attorney been caught making such an offer, he would almost certainly be prosecuted for bribery, obstruction of justice, and subordination of perjury. Yet that is not nearly as much as what the *prosecutor* in the notorious BCCI case did for one of his witnesses in that case. Manhattan District Attorney Robert Morgenthau wrote a letter to Merrill Lynch urging it to hire a key prosecution witness. And a letter to Merrill Lynch from Morgenthau is not just another letter of recommendation, since — as one legal expert pointed out — "the District Attorney of Manhattan is in effect one of the regulators to whom Merrill Lynch reports." He characterized the letter as "very ill advised." Morgenthau also wrote to his own cousin recommending the witness for a job.

What makes these recommendations all the more extraordinary is that the highly recommended witness was himself facing charges of bank fraud by British authorities, even after Morgenthau had given him total immunity from prosecution in New York. As a lawyer involved in the BCCI case put it: "It's amazing to me that a prosecutor would recommend a person he knows had [allegedly] committed numerous acts of criminal fraud. . . . It's irresponsible."

In addition to the powerful job offers, Morgenthau also paid the witness $12,500, reminded him just before he testified that he was eligible for an additional $100,000 reward, and paid to have his furnace repaired. Little wonder the witness sang the song the prosecutor wanted him to sing. As one lawyer put it: "He who pays the piper calls the tune, and in this case the one who paid also wrote the lyrics."

There is something very wrong with what Morgenthau did, but it is only the tip of the iceberg. Prosecutors do this — and more — all the time in order to obtain favorable testimony from witnesses. Indeed, Morgenthau's defense of his highly questionable conduct is that what he did is "perfectly routine" for prosecutors. And it is! Prosecutors all over the country buy and rent witnesses every day. They claim that they have to — otherwise the guilty will go free, because witnesses are often reluctant to "fink" on their friends, colleagues, and employers. That is certainly true in some cases, but the dangers of paid-for testimony place our entire system of criminal justice at risk. Witnesses should not be auctioned to the highest bidder. Imagine if the defense were permitted to try to outbid the prosecution, with even better job offers and cash rewards. The system would break down.

What may be even more dangerous is the current one-sidedness of the bidding war. Prosecutors are free to offer almost anything. Some courts have actually permitted *contingency* rewards: The prosecution witness gets *more* money if the prosecution *wins*. Consider the incentive that gives the witness to tailor his testimony to what the prosecution wants. Defense attorneys, on the other hand, may not even suggest to witnesses that they may benefit financially from testifying for the defense.

Nor is the solution to give *both* sides the equal right to buy witnesses. The only acceptable rule is for neither side to be able to offer anything of value to a witness in order to obtain favorable testimony for its side. But what about immunity from prosecution? Prosecutors must remain free to immunize witnesses who would otherwise invoke their privilege against self-incrimination. And immunity from prosecution may be even more valuable than money or jobs. The answer to this inequality is to reassign the immunity decision to the *judge*, who would have the power to grant immunity *both* to necessary *prosecution* witnesses and to necessary *defense* witnesses. In that way, both sides would be placed in an equitable position in the quest for truth.

July 1993

Despite New York District Attorney Robert Morgenthau's successful efforts to secure his star witness's testimony against Robert Altman in a highly publicized trial stemming from the BCCI scandal, a New York jury wasted little time in exonerating Altman of criminal wrongdoing in August of 1993.

Police Perjury? "I'm Shocked!"

F OR ANYONE WHO HAS practiced criminal law in either the state or federal courts, the recent disclosures about rampant police perjury cannot possibly come as any surprise. "Testilying" — as it has come to be called by the police themselves — is an open secret among prosecutors, defense attorneys, and judges. When I read about the disbelief expressed by some prosecutors at the conclusion of the draft report of the Mollen Commission that police perjury is "widespread," it reminded me of Claude Rains's classic response in *Casablanca* upon being told that there was gambling in Rick's bar. "I'm shocked! Shocked!"

More than a quarter of a century ago, legendary district attorney, Frank Hogan, anticipated the problem. One of the arguments he made against rules that exclude evidence obtained by police in violation of the Constitution was that such exclusionary rules encourage police perjury. He understood that policemen would be unsympathetic to rules that freed guilty defendants, and that they would fudge the facts to circumvent these barriers to efficient justice.

A few years after the Supreme Court applied the exclusionary rules to the states, a New York City criminal court judge described police testimony in search-and-seizure cases: "When one . . . looks at a series of cases, [it] then becomes apparent that policemen are committing perjury, at least in some of them, and perhaps in nearly all of them." Judge Irving Younger — who had practiced and taught law with distinction before ascending the bench — was focusing on one particular genre of police perjury, namely "dropsy" testimony:

> Were this the first time a policeman had testified that a defendant dropped a packet of drugs to the ground, the matter would be unremarkable. The extraordinary thing is that each year in our criminal courts policemen give such testimony in hundreds, perhaps thousands, of cases — and that, in a nutshell, is the problem of "dropsy" testimony.

Judge Younger concluded that the solution to this pervasive problem "is prosecutors' work," since the "courts can only deplore," while the prosecutors can refuse to put perjuring policemen on the witness stand and can prosecute them if they lie.

Judge Younger was correct in identifying the problem, and he was certainly right in arguing that prosecutors bore considerable responsibility for the persistence of this problem. But he was tragically wrong in letting the courts off the hook so easily. The central villains in the scandal of police perjury are precisely the *judges* who, for decades, have pretended to believe the tallest of tales told by perjuring cops in the face of overwhelming evidence of the pervasiveness of police perjury. The main reason why the sickness of police perjury persists decades after it was diagnosed is that we refuse to hold judges accountable for their role in legitimating it.

Without the knowing complicity of judges, police perjury would be reduced considerably. Policemen know that in the courtrooms of many judges, they can get away with the most blatant perjury without fear of judicial rebuke or prosecution. I have seen trial judges *pretend* to believe perjuring policemen whose testimony is contradicted by common sense, documentary evidence, and even unambiguous tape recordings. And I have seen appellate court judges close their eyes to such patently false findings of fact. Judicial acceptance of obviously false testimony sends a subtle, yet powerful, message of approval, if not encouragement, to perjuring police.

- A judge in Detroit, after listening to more than a dozen "dropsy" cases on a single day, chastised the police for not being more "creative," but nonetheless accepted their testimony.

- In Washington, D.C., the Court of Appeals held that "spontaneous apologies" by the accused to the victim would be admissible even in the absence of a Miranda warning. Following this decision, there was an epidemic of "spontaneous apologies" that were believed by trial judges.

- In Boston, Massachusetts, police routinely made up imaginary informants to justify searches and seizures, and the judges believed them.

- In a federal case in New York, a judge credited the testimony of a policeman even though he was caught on tape telling an informant that if he testified truthfully, he would run him "over with a truck" and if the informant ever said "that I said it, I'm gonna deny it." The cop then denied saying it, and despite the tape, the judge pretended to believe him.

• In Nassau County, a policeman showed a key witness photographs of a suspect before the witness was asked to pick the suspect out of a lineup, and then denied under oath that he had done so.

Most trial judges are experienced in the ways of police perjury, many having been prosecutors themselves. They know police perjury when they hear it, and they hear it often enough to be able to do something about it. Yet many continue to tolerate it, because they know that most victims of police perjury are factually guilty of the crimes for which they stand charged. Many prosecutors and judges themselves oppose exclusionary rules that sometimes free the guilty. They are prepared to wink at the *means* of police perjury if it produces the *end* of convicting the guilty.

Some judges have, to their credit, refused to close their eyes to police perjury, but it is fair to say that they are the rare exception to a rule of blindness, deafness, and muteness that has characterized the vast majority of judges and prosecutors.

Unless the Mollen Commission — which includes a former judge and prosecutor — broadens its focus to include judges and prosecutors who subtly encourage police perjury, nothing will change. A few policemen will be prosecuted, and a quarter century from now yet another blue ribbon commission will express shock at the pervasiveness of police perjury in the criminal justice system.

April 1994

WHO SHOULD PROBE WACO?

I N THE AFTERMATH of the tragic deaths in Waco, everyone seems to be calling for investigations. President Clinton has ordered the Justice and Treasury departments to investigate their own actions. Senators have called for a Senate investigation, Congressmen for a congressional probe.

Although the reactions have not been precisely along party lines, there can be little doubt that partisan politics are at work. In an uncharacteristically tough "law and order" posture, Congresswoman Patricia Schroeder — who has long been a critic of Justice Department machismo — was praising Attorney General Janet Reno for not wasting taxpayers' money on further negotiations. On the other side of the aisle, congressmen who nearly always side with law enforcement were second-guessing the FBI and Justice Department.

It is imperative that politics be removed from any investigation of the events in Waco, if the findings are to have any credibility and impact on future situations like Waco. We should have learned from the fiasco of the Warren Commission that politics and objective inquiry are incompatible. What is needed now is a professional and objective investigation outside the influence of politics and without any predetermined agenda or point of view.

In other Western democracies, there are preexisting institutions capable of conducting such inquiries. In Great Britain there is a long tradition of Royal Commissions to investigate and recommend. In Israel, judicial commissions of inquiry have been helpful in assessing the responsibility for disasters such as the Falangist massacres at Shatila and Sabra. But in our country there is no existing nonpartisan institution geared up to conduct a credible investigation and to make professional recommendations.

Perhaps such an ongoing institution should be created under the auspices of independent professional, scientific, and academic institutions, such as the National Academy of Sciences. In the absence of such a continuing investigative body, an ad hoc professional commission of inquiry should be convened immediately. But it should *not* be like the Warren Commission, which was composed of politicians, patriots, and apologists, with almost no professional expertise.

What is needed here are objective, outside experts in terrorism, hostage situations, cults, law enforcement, civil liberties, technology, and psychology. The object of the inquiry should not be to lay blame for the past, since it seems clear that whatever mistakes were made were honest miscalculations, not acts of venality or corruption. It must be to learn from these mistakes in order to assure that they are not repeated.

Such an inquiry cannot credibly be conducted by anyone with a political or personal stake in the outcome. Those involved in the decision-making process — the Bureau of Alcohol, Tobacco and Firearms, the FBI, the Justice Department, and the White House — should have no influence on the scope, nature, methodology, or conclusions of the inquiry. Indeed, the FBI and ATF should not even be involved in the gathering of evidence from the crime scene, since they have a stake in proving certain conclusions, for example that the fire was deliberately set by the Branch Davidians rather than started accidentally by the FBI tanks. There should be no conflicts of interest or even appearances of conflict.

Maybe then the world can really learn what went wrong and what can be done to maximize the chances that the next standoff will end less tragically. But this learning can occur only if hard questions are fairly asked and honestly answered. Among these questions are the following:

- Should the ATF have initiated the confrontation by entering the armed compound to effect its arrest warrants, or should it have waited for Koresh to leave on one of his routine trips to the outside world and arrest him *outside* the compound?

- Once the ATF learned that the cultists were lying in wait for them, should they have backed off, rather than walking into an ambush?

- Once the siege began, did the ATF and FBI employ the best psychology by isolating the cultists and blasting them with loud sounds, rather than by using family members to demonstrate that they had alternatives to remaining with Koresh?

- Should the FBI have continued the siege indefinitely, rather than moving in as they did?

- If moving in was the correct tactic, should it have been done as a lightning strike in the

middle of the night with overwhelming numbers
in an effort to rescue as many children as
possible?

• Were there better technological means for
disabling the cultists quickly, or is old-fashioned
tear gas the best we could do?

These and other questions must be addressed scientifically
and objectively — not by internal or political investigators —
if we are to get answers that can prevent the fire next time.

April 1993

*On April 19, 1994, lawyers for the Branch Davidians along with
a small band of demonstrators marked the one-year anniversary of
the destruction of the cult's complex by calling on President Clinton
to authorize an independent investigation of the Waco tragedy. Thus
far, only the Treasury and Justice departments have been asked by
the White House to investigate the events leading up to the final
siege of the Branch Davidian compound. To her credit, Attorney
General Janet Reno made no excuses for her role in approving the
ill-fated raid.*

PART THREE

The Political Correctness Excuse:
Sexual Harassment, Censorship,
Feminism, and Equality

Politics As Sexual Harassment

MASSACHUSETTS JUDGE recently rendered a troubling free-speech decision, which endangers the very core of the First Amendment. He ruled that a constitutionally protected election satire could be prohibited because it constituted "sexual harassment."

The case involved a union election in which the supporters of a male candidate distributed photocopies of the female opponent's face pasted on top of photographs of nude and seminude women in lewd positions. Objectionable as such campaigning may be, it is within the zone of constitutionally protected political speech. From the earliest days of our republic, politicians have juxtaposed the faces of their opponents on jackasses, snakes, members of the opposite sex, and assorted other objects for the purpose of ridicule and derision. As the defendant in this case put it, his rude collage was intended as political satire designed to make the candidate he opposed "look ridiculous." He wanted to degrade her, as politicians from time immemorial have tried to degrade opponents.

The answer to such crass and low campaigning is for the

opponent to make a campaign issue of his or her opponent's dirty tricks. Under the First Amendment, the answer to bad speech is good speech, not censorship or damage suits. We must leave it to the marketplace of ideas — not the judgment of the censor — to regulate campaign literature. There can be no speech codes for political campaigns.

The implications of this wrongheaded decision are frightening. Certainly women — who constitute a majority of Americans, with enormous voting power — cannot be given greater protection from degrading or offensive speech than minorities, such as blacks, Jews, Hispanics, or gays. Thus, if this "politically correct" but constitutionally infirm decision were to be taken to its logical conclusion, then judges would have the power to punish all campaign rhetoric or literature that denigrated any minority candidate.

Perhaps such a rule would produce cleaner elections, but it would cut the heart out of the First Amendment by giving judges the power to regulate campaign rhetoric and literature. Freedom of speech includes the right to denigrate, ridicule, insult, offend, burlesque, and stereotype. And it does not make an exception for racism, sexism, anti-Semitism, or homophobia. The lawyer for the woman candidate believes that there should be an exception to the First Amendment for "sexual degradation." But the First Amendment does not and should not make any such exception. Nor does it permit "affirmative action" in the area of speech under which women candidates are given more protection than their male counterparts.

A female candidate for office has the right to urge the voters to vote against men because "they just don't get it," because we "need" more women in the Senate, or because women are more sensitive than men. To make her point, she could juxtapose a picture of her opponent on a male sexual organ or a nude male. A male candidate could respond by arguing that women belong at home, that they aren't tough enough for politics, or that they are too influenced by their menstrual cycles. To make his point, the candidate could juxtapose his opponent's picture on a female sexual organ or on a nude woman. Under the First Amendment, any idea that can be expressed verbally may also be expressed visually or symbolically.

The judge in this case tried to circumvent the strictures of the First Amendment by pretending that this was a "workplace" case rather than an election case. He ruled that "First Amendment concerns are subject to various restrictions in the workplace where employees may be a captive audience." But this case arose in the context of a political campaign for president of the union. Employees are not children. They have the right to refuse election handouts, or to tell the candidate what they think of his mudslinging.

It is simply not sexual harassment when a political candidate — who has chosen to run for election — is degraded as part of an election campaign. Nobody was seeking sexual favors from the candidate. Nobody was threatening her job if she refused to submit. She decided to get into the rough and tumble of union politics, and then when she lost, she ran to the court for protection.

Sexual harassment should be limited to cases in which power is used to extort sex. It should not extend to the creation of a so-called hostile environment. This case shows the illogical extremes to which the hostile environment approach can be taken. All political campaigns are by their nature hostile environments. And women candidates are entitled to no special protection from the slinging of mud. Harry Truman would have put the crybaby candidate in this case straight by telling her, "If you can't take the heat, get out of the kitchen."

July 1993

Following the publication of this column, the defendant asked me to represent him on appeal on a pro bono basis. Because of the troubling nature of the judge's decision in this case and the serious First Amendment issues involved, I agreed. That case is currently pending before the Massachusetts Court of Appeals in Boston. See Sylvia Smith Bowman v. Commonwealth of Massachusetts Department of Public Welfare.

Advertising As Sexual Harassment

C AN WOMEN EMPLOYEES claim sexual harassment on the basis of sexist ads used by their employer to sell its product? That perplexing issue is now being raised by several women who work for Stroh's Beer, whose television ads show a Swedish "bikini team" descending on a group of beer-drinking male campers. The employers allege that the ad — which portrays women as sex objects — contributes to "a hostile work environment" at the brewery.

Their lawsuit has dangerous implications for the First Amendment that go well beyond beer advertisements. Sex has been a powerful advertising symbol for many products, ranging from automobiles to clothing to cigarettes. Even under the less protective rules for "commercial speech," there can be no doubt that sexually oriented ads — even blatantly sexist ones — are fully protected by the First Amendment.

The Stroh's lawsuit is a clever attempt to circumvent the protections of the First Amendment by arguing that the ads are part of a pattern of harassing behavior. Professor Maria

Angel of Temple Law School argues that "the ads and behavior are connected; you can't separate them."

But speech is always connected to behavior. As Oliver Wendell Holmes once put it, "Every idea is an incitement" to action. Under our First Amendment, we must separate the speech component from the act component of any mixed communication. For example, burning an American flag is both speech and action. The speech component is fully protected — if you burn your own flag. But the vandalism component is not protected — if you burn someone else's flag.

Similarly, direct sexual harassment of female employees — such as touching, conditioning promotions on sex, or creating a "hostile work environment" — may be lawfully prohibited. But speech — even commercial speech — is constitutionally protected unless it comes within specific exceptions to the First Amendment.

It is the last genre of sexual harassment — the creation of a "hostile work environment" — that raises potential clashes between the rights of female employees to be free from prohibited harassment, and the rights of male employees to freedom of expression. For example, does a male employee have the right to pin up a *Penthouse* centerfold in "his" work area, in a common work area, or in the men's room? Does a female employee who is offended by nudity have the right to have the pinup removed? What if it stimulates male employees to whistle at or even touch female employees? What if it stimulates no improper behavior, but simply annoys or distracts the woman? Who has the burden of proving a claimed relationship between the picture and the behavior?

These are the kinds of questions being raised in sexual harassment cases around the country. In one case, off-color jokes are on trial. In another, the issue is pinups and lewd comments. And now television ads are being included in the mix, despite the lack of any direct relationship between how

Stroh's advertises its product and the behavior of its employees at the brewery. The female employees are arguing that the ad, by portraying women as sex objects, "condones" similar treatment in the workplace. It is an obvious stretch, and one that seems to lack empirical support.

I am aware of no data even suggesting a link between the nature of a company's advertising on television and the way in which its female employees are, in fact, treated in the workplace, either by management or by fellow employees. Some religious institutions, for example, have terrible records of discrimination against female employees — and sexual harassment is a form of gender discrimination; while some adult magazines — which use women and nudity in their advertising — have exemplary records in their treatment of female employees.

The inclusion of the "bikini team" ad in the Stroh's suit is part of a continuing effort by some radical feminists to outlaw sexism in the marketplace of ideas and commerce. Despite its lack of connection to behavior in the workplace, the ad is simply (and understandably) offensive to some women. And they are using the pretext of sexual harassment in an attempted end-run around the First Amendment. It shouldn't work. But if it does, the entire theory of the First Amendment is in danger. Female employees would be given an "offensiveness veto" over freedom of speech — a veto that would know no bounds. As the executive director of the National Organization for Women's Legal Defense Fund recently put it: "The issue is what women perceive." If women's perceptions can serve as a basis for censorship, why not also the perceptions of blacks, gays, Jews, Hispanics, Evangelical Christians, and David Duke supporters. If that subjective test ever becomes the law, we can wave goodbye to the First Amendment.

February 1992

Although the women who filed a sexual harassment lawsuit against Stroh's Beer lost that case, based upon a Minnesota County Court judge's ruling that the plaintiffs were not permitted to introduce any commercials or posters that were not actually distributed at the plant as evidence in support of their "hostile work environment" claim, the Supreme Court recently reaffirmed the standard for determining when a workplace constitutes an "abusive or hostile" environment. See Harris v. Forklift Systems, *114 S. Ct. 367 (1993).*

THE TALMUD AS SEXUAL HARASSMENT

THE RULES GOVERNING "hostile environment sexual harassment," especially on university campuses, are quickly becoming an excuse for old-fashioned censorship. There are generally two types of sexual harassment prohibited by current law. The first — quid pro quo harassment — involves threats or promises by superiors directed to subordinates in order to obtain sexual favors. This form of sexual harassment lies at the core of the prohibition.

The second — hostile environment sexual harassment — actually has little to do either with sex or harassment. It is directed at the general environment in which people work, attend school, or live. In the context of academic institutions, it has often come to mean a classroom environment free of any perceived hint of sexism, or at its extreme, a classroom that affirmatively reflects the tenets of radical feminism.

A recent case in point demonstrates the dangers to academic freedom implicit in giving one group the power to dictate the proper environment for learning.

For more than three decades, Professor Graydon Snyder,

a venerable scholar at the Chicago Theological Seminary, has been using a story from the Talmud to illustrate the difference between Jewish and Christian concepts of responsibility. In the Talmudic tale, a workman accidentally falls off the roof and into the arms of a woman below in a manner that constitutes a sexual coupling. Under Jewish law, the accidental coupling does not amount to a punishable sexual contact, since — according to Professor Snyder — "the Talmud says if you do the act, but didn't think about it, you didn't do it." But the "New Testament says that if you think about doing the act, you've done it." This ecumenical variation on "how many angels can dance on the head of a pin" seems harmless enough for discussion at a school of theology. But predictably, in this age of politically correct hypersensitivity, a women student filed a charge of sexual harassment against Professor Snyder, claiming that his quotation of the Talmudic account constituted insensitivity toward rape. "She said in the complaint that men are always saying that they don't intend to do any harm and in fact they do." After learning of the complaint, Snyder apologized to the student. But she persisted with her formal charges.

Instead of advising the foolish student to shape up, the school agreed with her and placed Professor Snyder on probation, ordering him to undergo therapy! Since virtually every old religious book — ranging from Genesis to Luke to the Koran — is loaded with sexism, I guess this means that the Chicago Theological Seminary is going to have to ban the Bible, lest it be charged with creating a hostile environment for hypersensitive feminists. And what would other universities have to censor: Shakespeare, Renoir, Mailer, Tolstoy?

In another recent case, an English professor was charged with hostile environment sexual harassment for using the following tasteless example to illustrate a simile: "Belly dancing is like Jell-O on a plate with a vibrator under the plate." He, too, was convicted of sexual harassment and sentenced to undergo therapy and suspension. Thankfully, both professors are suing their schools. But most teachers who have been found guilty of hostile environment sexual harassment simply take their lumps and try to rebuild their damaged academic careers.

Several years ago, a group of women students threatened to charge me with sexual harassment because I spent too much time — in their view — discussing false charges of rape during my classes on the crime of rape. I welcomed such a charge, hoping for a needed test case, but the students backed down.

These cases and others are intimidating professors into teaching only what their most radical feminist students want to hear. A single hypersensitive student can bring a charge of sexual harassment, and such a charge, regardless of how unfounded, can be a career-ender, especially for an untenured teacher. But even many tenured professors do not want to incur the wrath of organized feminists on campus. Journalist Cathy Young recently characterized this phenomenon as part of a power play by radical feminists, "to dictate the curriculum and write campus codes that would turn 90 percent of the men into rapists."

The time has come to end this new tyranny of censorship. Sexual harassment should be limited to quid pro quo efforts to obtain sexual favors from subordinates. It should not apply to the marketplace of ideas, which should be somewhat hostile, especially when highly volatile issues are being discussed. If a student disagrees with a professor's statements, she has ample opportunity to respond, rebut, picket, even heckle. But there is no place in a university setting — or anywhere else — for censorship of hostile ideas regarded by some to be sexist. Sexual harassment laws must not be allowed to become speech codes designed by radical feminists to circumvent the First Amendment.

May 1994

Graydon Snyder's suit against the Chicago Theological Seminary for defamation of character was recently filed in Cook County Court. His claim is based not only upon the seminary's decision to place him on probation in response to the woman's complaint, but also upon a memorandum that the school circulated to every teacher and student at the seminary telling them that Snyder had "engaged in verbal conduct of a sexual nature" that had the effect of "creating an intimidating, hostile, or offensive" environment. Although Snyder's case is yet to be decided in court, legal experts say that this case could force the Supreme Court to decide whether some sexual harassment codes violate the First Amendment right to freedom of speech.

CENSORSHIP FROM THE LEFT

OME OF OUR most basic constitutional liberties are in danger of being crushed between the pincers of a two-flanked assault from elements of the right and the left. Civil libertarians always have their guard up to protect against anticipated attacks from the right flank. But when their friends of the left surprise them by joining assault on our liberties, civil libertarians are often caught with their defenses down.

Much has already been written about the Machiavellian pact between some feminists and fundamentalists in the war against sexist pornography. And there are other, equally dangerous efforts at censorship emanating from groups not normally allied with the repressive right. Some cases in point:

- Environmentalists and antinuke activists in some cities are pushing legislation that would ban research — even pure thinking and writing — on nuclear issues.

- Several years ago, a coalition of blacks and civil rights activists banded together to get the liberal attorney general of Massachusetts to enjoin a restaurant chain from using the offensive name "Sambo's."

- The United Nations — with the blessing and encouragement of some American foes of apartheid — has published a formal "blacklist" of entertainers who have performed in South Africa. No one on the list is permitted to perform at any UN-sponsored event, and city councils and universities throughout the country are urged not to hire blacklisted artists.

- Some Jewish activists are seeking legislation — modeled on a Canadian statute — that could make it a crime for anyone to deny that the Nazi Holocaust occurred, or to advocate genocide or race hatred.

- Some children's rights advocates have proposed censorship of TV programs aired on Saturday morning and other times when children are likely to be watching.

Nor is the attack limited to the First Amendment.

Several feminist groups recently persuaded the New York Court of Appeals to create a new crime — marital rape. Now, there is nothing wrong with making it a crime for a husband to rape his wife. The legislatures should enact new laws recognizing that a married woman has as much right to control her body as a single woman does. But there is something very wrong with an appellate court creating a new crime. It has long been an important part of the American constitutional tradition that the decision to use the powerful weapon of the criminal law should never be made unless the legislature — representing the popular will — votes for it. As the Supreme Court put it more than 150 years ago: "The legislative authority of the Union must first make an act a crime. . . ."

Many feminists — joined by some civil libertarians — have been demanding that occasional consumers of sex for hire (the johns) must be prosecuted along with full-time purveyors (the prostitutes). The implications of this "if-the-purveyor-goes-to-jail-so-must-the-consumer" approach are frightening. It will mean the mass arrest of occasional pot-smokers, two-dollar bettors, porn readers, and women who seek abortions from illegal clinics.

Many "do-good" causes — whether of the left or right — tend to be impatient of constitutional barriers to their goals. They want action on their agenda now, even if it means circumventing or ignoring the Bill of Rights. When the goals are obnoxious to civil libertarians — as most right-wing goals are — it is easy to mount a united front against the unconstitutional means employed by the right. But when the goals are agreeable to civil libertarians — as many left-wing goals are — it is far more difficult to maintain a united front against left-wing means that raise serious questions of constitutionality.

An important reason for this phenomenon is that the existing civil liberties movement in this country — whose most important spokesperson is the ACLU — is really a convenient coalition of true civil libertarians and political liberals. That coalition thrives when the Constitution is violated by a common enemy: groups seeking to impose a right-wing political agenda by unconstitutional means. But that coalition experiences real tension — sometimes to the point of rupture — when the Constitution is violated by a friend. In that situation the true civil libertarians — those who put the Bill of Rights before their own political agendas — remain willing to join battle against their erring friends. But some of the liberal pretenders abandon the civil liberties ship and join their political friends, or remain silent, in the face of left-wing assaults on the Constitution.

It is not surprising — though it is extremely disturbing — that the American Civil Liberties Union (and its local affiliates) have remained silent in the face of some of the dangers outlined above. They will probably seek to justify their silence by claiming that they didn't know about them. But that is a symptom of the problem, rather than a justification. The ACLU tends to "know" more about civil liberties violations from the right than from the left.

An even-handed approach to civil liberties is essential if we are to preserve the Bill of Rights. Especially now, when the U.S. Supreme Court is joining in on the assault, it is more important than ever for all civil libertarians to stand as firm against attacks on the Constitution from our political friends as from our political foes.

July 1985

FEMINIST CENSORSHIP IN CANADA

F EMINIST CENSORSHIP is alive and well in Canada. A recent decision by the Supreme Court of Canada approved a law that would permit the banning of sexually oriented material deemed "degrading" to women. In becoming the first Western nation to justify censorship on this broad ground, Canada has bought into the repressive philosophy of radical feminists Catharine MacKinnon and Andrea Dworkin. That philosophy — which would establish rules of censorship singling out women for special protection from "dangerous" speech — has been repeatedly rejected in this country.

But repression is contagious, and already efforts are under way to adopt the Canadian approach in several of our states and at the national level. Immediately following the Canadian decision, MacKinnon announced that "there are going to be several pieces of legislation in Congress soon, predicated on the harm approach and recognizing that both the making of pornography and its use do harm to women." A bill has already been introduced in the Massachusetts legislature mimicking the Canadian law.

But the Canadian approach does not fit as comfortably into our First Amendment as it does into the very different Canadian Charter of Rights and Freedoms. Our First Amendment is written in absolute terms: "Congress shall make no law . . . abridging the freedom of speech, or of the press." The Canadian charter, on the other hand, expressly authorizes the courts to strike a balance between freedom of expression and other values. The charter "guarantees the rights and freedoms set out in it subject only to such reasonable limits prescribed by law as can be demonstrably justified in a free and democratic society."

Canada has a long tradition of censorship to protect minorities. It has "hate crimes" legislation on its books, which permits the banning of public speech that "willfully promotes hatred against any identifiable group." Pursuant to such legislation, Holocaust-deniers and other bigots have been convicted of hate crimes.

In the United States, it is unconstitutional to censor hate speech, whether it is directed against blacks, Jews, gays, or women. Holocaust-denial, racist diatribes, and sexist rantings are all protected by our First Amendment. Unless the speech constitutes an actual incitement to immediate violence against a specific target, it cannot be banned in this country. And even MacKinnon acknowledges that what she calls "pornography" does not meet that stringent test. We do allow the censorship of "obscenity," but that is permitted under a very different theory, which MacKinnon rejects — namely, that obscene material is offensive to community standards and lacks literary, scientific, or political value. MacKinnon and her censorial minions analogize pornography to hate crimes — an argument that works in Canada, but not in the United States.

Nor should we be looking to our northern neighbors for guidance in this complex area. The concepts of "hate crimes" and of promoting "hatred against any identifiable group" are simply too broad and open-ended to be borrowed by a nation like ours, with so many divisive issues about which people feel so strongly. A few examples:

- Fundamentalist Christians (and Supreme Court justices) who express the belief that homosexuality is an abomination are certainly guilty of promoting hatred against gays.
- Both pro- and anti-abortion groups often express hatred against each other.
- Radical feminists, such as MacKinnon and Dworkin, constantly express hatred against men in general and against men and women who defend "pornographers" in particular.
- Atheists who mock religion, and religious people who regard atheists as immoral, both engage in hate-mongering.
- Many pro-Palestinian activists express hatred against Jews, and many pro-Israel activists express hatred against Palestinians, especially after episodes of violence and retaliation.
- Some African Americans express hatred against whites and vice versa.

It would, of course, be more civilized if all legitimate disagreements could be resolved without any expressions of hatred. But from the earliest days of our history, it has been clear that for freedom of speech to work, it must include the hateful as well as the civil. We are not a people who always speak in muted tones or with the politeness of charm school graduates. We are a vibrant people who do not hold back our true feelings.

And there is no room under our First Amendment for a special exception for women. If speech degrading to women is subject to censorship, then so must speech that is degrading to Asians, to Fundamentalists, to puritans, to Communists, to environmentalists, to veterans, and to all other identifiable groups. If our country ever came to that, we could say goodbye to talk radio, to Pat Buchanan — no great loss, perhaps — and eventually to the First Amendment. The answer to degrading speech must be in the marketplace of ideas, not in the scissor of the censor.

July 1992

Soon after the Canadian Supreme Court adopted the ban on sexually oriented material deemed "degrading" to women, the first two cases that were prosecuted by the Canadian authorities under this new standard were a lesbian magazine and a gay and lesbian bookstore in Toronto.

HATE SPEECH

T HE TREND SEEMS finally to be turning against laws and rules that would ban so-called hate speech. For nearly a decade, the radical left — along with some well-meaning but misguided civil rights groups — have been pressuring universities, cities, and towns to enact regulations that would outlaw all speeches, writings, symbols, and other expression that might offend racial minorities, women, gays, and other sensitive groups.

Several major universities around the country raced to outdo each other about how much they could censor. Stanford and Wisconsin were among the worst offenders. Wisconsin's rule, for example, prohibited speech intended to "create a hostile learning environment" by demeaning a person's race, sex, religion, color, creed, disability, sexual orientation, or ancestry. Suddenly, students and faculty had to guard against the inadvertent comment, the off-color joke, or even the deeply felt political argument that might offend — or be alleged to offend. Under some such rules it became a possible "speech crime" to argue insensitively against affirmative action, rape-shield laws, gay rights legislation, or abortion on demand.

Nor was the circle of censorship ever symmetrical. African-American groups could sponsor speeches by race-baiters such as Louis Farrakhan, Leonard Jeffries, and Steve Cokely. Feminists could invite sexists such as Andrea Dworkin and Catharine MacKinnon to rail against men. Third World bigots could attack Western culture and Zionist colonialism. Speech codes on many campuses were little more than muscle flexing by newly empowered minorities against the expression of the old guard. It was affirmative action for some speech coupled with negative reaction against other speech.

Some cities and towns, looking for a quick fix to deeply divisive racial conflict, also enacted hate speech criminal laws. In St. Paul, Minnesota, for example, the law criminalized the display — on public or private property — of all symbols, objects, or writings intended to arouse "anger, alarm or resentment in others on the basis of race, color, creed, religion or gender."

Imagine the implications of such a law, if enforced across the board. When I was growing up in a Brooklyn ghetto, my immigrant grandparents surely resented displays of the cross — a symbol that had been used to encourage pogroms against them in Poland. I am certain that some Palestinians are angered by the Israeli flag or the Star of David. My socialist friends resent ostentatious displays of wealth, which are offensive to their Marxist "creed." Patrick Buchanan's bigotry alarms me, as does David Duke's. Surely Martin Luther King intended to create "anger, alarm [and] resentment in others on the basis of race" when he marched through the city of Cicero, Illinois, in the 1960s. Almost no form of controversial expression would be safe under the St. Paul ordinance.

The Supreme Court understood that and unanimously

struck down the St. Paul law during its past term, in a case involving a cross-burning on a black family's lawn. The city remains free to punish those who set fire to other people's property, of course, but it may not criminalize the content of expression by a prohibition as broad as the one covered by the St. Paul law.

Now, the University of Wisconsin — by a 10 to 6 vote of its Board of Regents — has rescinded that school's "hate speech" rule. It had earlier tried to narrow it, but that proved unworkable, especially in light of the Supreme Court's decision in the St. Paul case.

Private colleges and universities remain free — subject only to state restrictions — to bar hate speech, since the First Amendment does not apply to purely private actions. But they would be well advised to forgo this doomed experiment in censorship. There is no place for content censorship on university campuses. Peer pressure against "politically incorrect" speech already imposes informal barriers to full, candid, and open discussion of many sensitive issues. But courageous individuals can fight against the informal constraints of the political correctness cops. When the official imprimatur of the university is placed on such censorship, it is far more difficult to fight back without endangering careers.

There is far less racism, sexism, homophobia, and anti-Semitism on campuses today than there was in the past, when these pernicious bigotries were often given the imprimatur of university administrations and admission committees. There is still too much bigotry, because any bigotry is too much. But censorship has never been an effective remedy against bigotry. Victor De Jesus, co-president of the Wisconsin Student Association, originally favored the "hate speech" code. But he changed his mind when he came to believe that it was being used as an excuse to avoid the real problems facing minority students.

What he has said about Wisconsin is surely applicable to other universities as well: "Now they can finally start putting their efforts into some of our major concerns like financial aid, student awareness and recruitment retention."

Censorship may drive some of the problems underground, but it will never make them go away.

January 1993

FEMINISTS FIGHT AGAINST CENSORSHIP

AS A RESULT OF SUCH censorial radicals as Andrea Dworkin and Catharine MacKinnon, feminists often become stereotyped as prudish advocates of banning all pornography. These two contribute to this stereotype by branding all women who oppose their brave new world of censorship as pseudofeminists, pornocrats, or hate-mongers. Such stereotyping is sexism, pure and simple.

Now some feminists are fighting back with a vengeance. A working group on women, censorship, and pornography, sponsored by the National Coalition Against Censorship, boasts some of the most prominent names in the feminist movement, including Betty Friedan (who is among the founders of modern-day feminism), Karen DeCrow (a former president of the National Organization for Women), Nadine Strossen (the president of the American Civil Liberties Union), Faye Wattleton (a former president of Planned Parenthood), and numerous prominent writers, artists, and political figures. Their goal is "education and advocacy against censorship," and their specific target seems to be the Dworkin-MacKinnon effort to equate true feminism with censorship.

Not surprisingly, Professor MacKinnon has dubbed these efforts by women as a "hate campaign." That choice of words is significant, since MacKinnon believes that "hate" speech is not constitutionally protected. The implication, then, is that if she could, she would censor her political opponents as hate-mongers.

What, then, is the hate campaign that some feminists are conducting against Dworkin and MacKinnon? It is an effort to explain the implications of the Dworkin-MacKinnon theory. Though rejected by courts in the United States, the theory has been accepted by the Canadian Supreme Court. In a recent newsletter, the National Coalition Against Censorship showed that "an explosion of censorship against women has come in the wake of the 1992 Supreme Court decision." According to *Feminist Bookstore News*, the new Canadian standard has been applied "only to seize lesbian, gay, and feminist material." The coalition reports that there is "widespread anger at MacKinnon, Dworkin, and their followers among women artists, writers, readers, activists, and scholars." As one woman writer recently put it, "Why do we have to keep our legs crossed for [MacKinnon]?"

In what has to be deemed the ultimate act of poetic justice, among the books recently seized by Canadian Customs were two by Andrea Dworkin. Although the Dworkin books were eventually released, as sexologist Lenore Tiefer recently put it, "There is nothing like a little taste of state repression to put one back in touch with reality."

But neither the Canadian experience nor the counterattack by feminist opponents of censorship has put Dworkin or MacKinnon in touch with reality. They continue to deny that they have handed the religious right a powerful weapon in its campaign against sexual freedom. Yet it is clear that without right-wing support, MacKinnon's "model" censorship statute would not have been enacted anywhere. Even Jerry Falwell now mouths the rhetoric of Dworkin and MacKinnon while continuing to oppose a woman's right to choose. Dworkin and MacKinnon support the right of women to choose only what *they* favor. Their theory is the best thing that has happened to the right-wing campaign to censor pornography — and they know it.

Fortunately, wise women are taking back the Bill of Rights from those who would create a false dichotomy between freedom and feminism.

May 1994

Censoring Sex

R EADERS BEWARE. PROFESSOR Catharine MacKinnon — the Lorena Bobbitt of academia — is after our erections and our orgasms. And this time she means business. In her latest screed — published by the respectable Harvard University Press — the radical feminist makes an "argument" that goes well beyond mere book burning. MacKinnon's illogic goes something like this: Pornography causes erections and orgasms; "an erection is neither a thought nor a feeling"; an orgasm is not an "idea" or "an argument"; therefore, the entire pornographic "experience" — from consumption to erection to orgasm — is unprotected by the Constitution and subject to governmental regulation.

The analysis applies, of course, only to the male masturbatory experience. The comparable female experience is constitutionally protected, because only male erections and orgasms are based on male domination and "support aggression against women."

MacKinnon seems to believe that every male reader of sexually oriented magazines will eventually become a rapist or sexual harasser. "Sooner or later, in one way or another, the consumers want to live out the pornography further in three dimensions. Sooner or later, in one way or another, they do. It makes them want to; when they believe they can, when they feel they can get away with it, they do." To make matters worse, the consumers of pornography do not even realize they are raping, "as pornography makes rapists unaware that their victims are not consenting." What a great defense for rapists: "The pornography made me do it, and I wasn't even aware I was doing anything wrong." But don't expect to see MacKinnon in court defending any accused rapists on this theory, since she argues that rapists and pornographers should be held "jointly responsible for rapes they can be proven to have caused." On this theory, should radical feminists also be held "jointly responsible" if it can be shown that their rhetoric may have contributed to the act of Lorena Bobbitt or other women who attack men?

Moreover, MacKinnon seems to believe that all pornography is the product of sexual coercion and rape, and that no adult woman — like no ten-year-old child — is capable of consenting to appear in a nude photo spread: "Empirically, all pornography is made under conditions of inequality," since most models come from humble economic backgrounds. Of course the same observation could be made about hamburgers. Few short-order cooks — male or female — would choose to sweat over a hot stove if they could do investment banking instead. But MacKinnon goes even further, suggesting that most of what she regards as pornography could not be made without women actually being "gang raped" and "killed." MacKinnon seems obsessed with so-called snuff films, which have little to do with traditional pornography and, if they exist at all in the real world, are extremely rare.

Pornography also "silences" all women, according to the

never-silent MacKinnon: "Pornography and its protection have deprived women of speech. . . ." As with her other questionable assertions of "fact," MacKinnon offers no credible support for this demonstrably false proposition. If anything, the debate over pornography has empowered many women and given a loud — if not always persuasive — voice to radical feminists like MacKinnon and her equally censorial colleague Andrea Dworkin.

In light of MacKinnon's shoddy research, illogical reasoning, and polemical writing, it is remarkable that she is taken seriously by anyone. But she is, for several reasons. First, many of her critics are afraid to speak out against her, because she immediately accuses them of being under the influence of pornography. Professors who teach about rape "from the viewpoint of the accused," judges who write "judicial opinions" in favor of free speech, and doctors who "use pornography to teach sex education in medical school" are all trying "to keep the world a pornographic place so they can continue to get hard from everyday life." Second, she and her radical colleagues have formed an unholy alliance with the reactionary right, especially the religious right. Though they have little in common, both regard pornography as an evil that should be subject to censorship.

No one should really be surprised by this alliance between the extreme right and left. Much of MacKinnon's book could have been written by Joseph McCarthy. Like McCarthy, she would ban "dangerous" speech without waiting to see if it really causes harm. Like McCarthy, she cannot understand how a nation can have a commitment to a principle — in this case equality, in McCarthy's case anticommunism — while still allowing dissenters their right to disagree with that principle. Like McCarthy, she claims to be protecting the rights of the majority of Americans. Like McCarthy, all of her critics are under the influence of the "evil" — pornography in her case, communism in his. And like Joseph McCarthy, Catharine MacKinnon can be ignored only at great risk to the liberty of all Americans. She is after our privacy, our sexuality, and our freedom of speech. We must not let her succeed.

April 1994

FALSE REPORTS OF RAPE

APE IS BOTH THE most underreported and overreported serious crime in America. It also presents our criminal justice system with some of the most controversial civil liberties issues of the day. Some feminists claim that for every reported rape, there may be as many as ten that remain unreported. Although there is no hard evidence to back up these numbers, there can be little doubt that many women who are raped do not go to the authorities.

The other tragic side of this coin is less well known. According to FBI crime statistics, 8.4 percent of all reported rapes turn out to be "unfounded." That percentage translates into more than eight thousand false rape reports each year. This number is dramatically higher than the number of false reports of other serious crimes. The comparable figures for assault, for instance, are 1.6 percent; burglary, 3.8 percent; larceny, 1.2 percent; motor-vehicle theft, 4.2 percent; murder, 2.3 percent; and robbery, 3.5 percent.

Falsely reporting a rape should be a serious crime since it

can destroy a life, even in cases where the complainant publicly recants.

Remember the case of Gary Dotson? He was falsely accused of raping Cathleen Crowell Webb and spent six years in prison before Webb recanted, prompting DNA tests that corroborated her retraction. Recently, the Massachusetts State Supreme Court unanimously reversed the date-rape conviction of a Brandeis student, finding the alleged victim's account was "inconsistent" with the allegation of rape.

In the days following the Palm Beach prosecutor's decision to charge William Kennedy Smith with rape, various women's rights leaders took up their position. The president of the Massachusetts chapter of the National Organization for Women declared that "feminists" are "obviously pleased" with the prosecutor's decision to charge Smith with rape. The national vice-president of NOW echoed this view and their statements were replete with references to what the "victim" had been through. They were also very concerned about "how long it took for the investigation to get off the ground" and whether "she can get a fair trial."

Perhaps these feminists have access to a videotape of what happened that night, but the rest of us have no idea who is telling the truth. The complainant has provided an account that the defendant has called an "outrageous lie." The reason we have jury trials is to determine whether the defendant — who is presumed innocent until a verdict is reached — is guilty or not guilty.

Some feminists seem to believe that the women's movement has a stake in Smith's being found guilty. That view is a perversion of both feminism and civil liberties. All fair-minded people have a stake in Smith's being found guilty only if he *is* guilty. They also have a stake in Smith's being found innocent if he is innocent — or if there is a reasonable doubt as to whether he raped the complainant or not.

A former president of the Massachusetts Civil Liberties Union once complained that "some radical feminists regard rape as so heinous a crime that even innocence should not be a defense." That may be a burlesque of their views, but statements made by some feminist leaders make it sound as if they are more interested in how a guilty verdict in the Smith case might advance their cause than in the discovery of truth, which will arise only through a fair trial and the rendering of justice.

May 1992

On December 12, 1991, after deliberating for only seventy-seven minutes, a jury in Florida acquitted William Kennedy Smith of charges that he raped a woman at the Kennedy family's Palm Beach estate.

THE OTHER RAPE EPIDEMIC

T HERE ARE TWO EPIDEMICS of rape in this country, but only one of them is receiving public attention. According to the FBI statistics, approximately 110,000 rapes are committed each year in the United States. This is surely an underassessment, since we know that many rapes — both by stranger and by acquaintance — go unreported. It is also an underassessment because it does not include the estimated 200,000 to 300,000 rapes committed by male prisoners against other male prisoners, and the undetermined number of rapes committed by female prisoners against other female prisoners.

We hear little about intragender rape because highlighting this serious problem does not serve the political agendas of those who use the terrible problem of male-against-female rape as a metaphor for all male exploitation of women. We also hear so little about prison rape because we don't seem to care very much about what happens to prisoners.

But what does, in fact, happen to thousands of young male first offenders in prison is a national scandal. They are raped — often repeatedly and by gangs of older inmates — as a rite of passage into prison life. Their bodies are traded like cigarettes. And worst of all, they contract AIDS in significant numbers. Thus a short sentence imposed for "rehabilitation" may become a death sentence. Yet many prison authorities turn a blind eye to this crisis, regarding it as simply another consequence of the punitive regime of incarceration.

As many Americans rail against the recent caning of an American teenager in Singapore, few pause to ask themselves what they themselves would opt for, if given the choice of four lashes with a Singaporean cane or four months in an American prison where rape and the risk of AIDS was rampant. I, for one, would not hesitate a moment before selecting the cane. A bruised backside heals with time, whereas HIV only gets worse.

Even those who support the caning of Michael Fay should be appalled at the reality of American imprisonment in many of our states. No civilized person supports the death penalty for first-offender, nonviolent criminals. Yet that is precisely what some get when they are sent to prisons where rape is a way of life. In New York State, the rate of HIV infection among prisoners may be as high as 15 percent — and rising. In Massachusetts, where rape is common and HIV is at about 7 percent, condoms are contraband in state prisons. In some states condoms are permitted in prison, but they are rarely used by the rapists.

Nor are prisoners the only victims. The vast majority of prisoners who are raped and contract the human immunodeficiency virus will be let out of prison within a few years. Many will not even know they have been infected, since testing is rare in prison. They will infect others outside prison, thus contributing to the spread of this deadly virus throughout the general population.

Yet despite the seriousness of this rape epidemic, prison rapists are rarely prosecuted or even disciplined. To be sure, prison rape is not easy to prevent. It is part of a general lawlessness that prevails in many prisons.

Almost all prisons are overpopulated and understaffed. But some effective measures can be taken. In most federal prisons, there is far less rape and violence than in most state prisons. That is partly because federal prisons have a better (and older) class of inmates than state prisons. It is also because many federal prisons are smaller, better staffed, and better equipped. Indeed, the federal system is so much safer that defendants often plea-bargain just to get into a federal rather than a state prison.

If this problem continues to get worse, we can expect lawsuits by inmates alleging cruel and unusual punishment. Already, some prison escapees have tried to defend their actions on the ground of "necessity" — a legal doctrine that justifies committing a lesser evil when necessary to prevent a greater evil. This defense is a combination of the "abuse excuse" and self-defense, but it is far more compelling here since some prisoners really do have no other recourse. They cannot simply leave; nor can they call the cops, since prison guards routinely shut their eyes to inmate rape. The necessity defense is similar to the abuse excuse in another respect as well: It asks the courts to acknowledge that law enforcement does not work and that the law of the jungle governs. The sad reality is that the law of the jungle does, in fact, govern in many of our state prisons. The time has come for all concerned citizens to take "the other rape epidemic" as seriously as we rightly take the rape epidemic we all know about.

May 1994

POTTY PARITY VERSUS SYMMETRICAL INEQUALITY

SOMETIMES REAL EQUALITY requires a recognition of differences and an increase in numerical access for some. No, I'm not talking about affirmative action. I'm referring to "potty parity." This attempt to achieve equality of access to public restrooms for women is on the rise around the country.

Massachusetts is now likely to join several other jurisdictions in mandating twice as many toilets for women as for men in all newly constructed public buildings. This number is based on a 1987 study that found women, on average, taking about twice as much time in the john as men. When this apparently immutable law of nature is combined with anachronistic allocations of restrooms, which have traditionally favored men — because far more men than women *used to* work and attend public events — the predictable effect has been long lines at the women's room and no lines at the men's room.

Any woman who has tried to use the toilet during halftime at a basketball game or intermission at a Broadway show can attest to the palpable inequality in facilities. For men, too, this inequality can be galling, as they wait for their wives, daughters, or women friends to reach the front of the line. But it is the women themselves who have the most to complain about.

Some literal-minded egalitarians — mostly men, I suspect — will shout "discrimination" at the new "two-for-one-potty" rules. If "one-person-one vote" is good enough for elections — they will argue — why isn't "one-person-one-potty" good enough for bathrooms? But this kind of symmetry elevates formalism over realism.

Potty parity requires an asymmetry in the absolute number and proportion of bathrooms to users. This numerical advantage is designed not to remedy a difference that is capable of being eliminated by greater individual efforts. To paraphrase an old song, "I'm going as fast as I can." The double-time difference is purely a matter of physiology. Even the most zealous advocates of the "just-work-harder" opposition to all numerical disparities will have to acknowledge that it is not the fault of women that they take longer.

Some Jurassic sexists will surely argue — or at least think — that there is nothing wrong with women having to wait a little longer since men's time, on average, is so much more "valuable" than women's. That kind of attitude is simply another manifestation of the thinking that produced buildings with fewer women's than men's rooms.

A case in point is Harvard Law School, where I have been teaching for thirty years. A decade and a half before I arrived in Cambridge, there were no women students at the law school, and some faculty opposed their admission on the ground, among others, that there were not enough ladies' rooms. It was easier to keep women out — went this argument — than to convert a few urinals into women's toilets. Finally, in 1950, reason and fairness prevailed, and women were finally admitted. But even by the mid-1960s, when women were being appointed to the faculty, there was only one "faculty" rest room. It didn't even have to be identified by gender. Everyone knew what gender the word "faculty" referred to.

To some, potty parity may seem a trivial issue. It is not. It symbolizes a pervasive lack of sensitivity to women's concerns. It also reflects a more general response to what I call "symmetrical inequality" — real inequality that is based on formal symmetry. Symmetry does not constitute equality in an asymmetrical world — especially where the asymmetry is a function of intractable differences that are not within the control of the person.

There are other areas of life in which symmetry also produces inequality. Some examples are: "equal" access to stairways for those unable to walk; "equal" visual access to floor numbers on elevators for those unable to see; "equal" audibility of television for those unable to hear. We are responding to these real inequalities by requiring special accommodations to these and other differences. Although the female physiology is not a "handicap," it is a relevant consideration in the allocation of resources. The time has come to recognize the reality of differences in our quest for equality.

Three cheers for potty parity.

April 1994

On May 5, 1994, the Massachusetts Board of State Examiners of Plumbers and Gasfitters voted to approve the new regulations that require all public buildings, such as schools, theaters, stadiums, and restaurants, constructed after this month to provide roughly twice as many toilets for women as for men. Unfortunately, since these new regulations are not retroactive, planned projects for which plumbing permits have already been obtained, such as the new Boston Garden, will not be affected.

Needed: Honesty in Affirmative Action

AST WEEK, THE Berkeley Law School (which is part of the University of California) agreed to comply with a demand by the U.S. Department of Education that it end its practice of setting aside a certain number of student slots for minority applicants. This widely publicized "victory" by the Department of Education's Civil Rights Office — following a two-year-long investigation — will do little more than to force Berkeley into doing what most other law schools are already doing: namely, hiding the ball more effectively from the probing eyes of government enforcers.

Since the Supreme Court's landmark decision in the 1977 *Bakke* case, universities have been playing a dangerous game with government enforcers. The *Bakke* decision — one of the most ambiguous and confusing in Supreme Court history — sent out a mixed message. The majority approved of the educational goal of a diverse student body, including but not limited to a racially diverse student body. But it disapproved of the means then being used by many universities to achieve that end — namely, racial quotas, set-asides, and other mechanisms that made admissions decisions turn essentially on the race of the applicant. Thus, no university that received government funds could adopt any two-track system under which white applicants competed for admission against other white applicants, while minority applicants competed only against other minority applicants for a designated number of spots.

Most universities — and especially law schools — figured out ways to circumvent the strictures of the *Bakke* case. They allocated admissions decisions to committees with broad discretion, few criteria, and almost no accountability to the faculty, the alumni, or the public. While eschewing overt quotas or set-asides, admissions officers saw to it that virtually every new class contained almost the same percentage of minority applicants as other classes since the beginning of affirmative action. If the number of minority admissions were to go down, the school could expect protests, sit-ins, and even lawsuits. A new word — "targets" — was substituted for "quotas" and "set-asides," but the concept was essentially the same: A certain percentage of places was reserved for qualified minorities. And most of the minority applicants — certainly at places like Harvard and Berkeley — were highly qualified. Those who were admitted did well, some very well indeed. That was not the issue.

The issue was, and continues to be, whether it is fair and legal to reject a *more* qualified white applicant — more qualified by grades, test scores, extracurricular activities, and other criteria relevant to success in school and in the outside world — and to accept a *qualified, but less qualified* minority candidate in order to achieve a targeted racial mix.

It has been difficult to debate that controversial issue, since law schools rarely admit that they are giving preference on racial grounds. Instead, they argue that various diversifying elements — including but not limited to race — are *part* of the applicants' qualifications. Berkeley acknowledged what it was doing and thus ran afoul of the government's rules. As Richard Stamp, chief counsel of the Washington Legal Foundation — a conservative antiquota group — put it:

> Colleges around the country know that "quota" is a dirty word so they lie and cover up to make it look as though they are using race as just one factor. The only difference between Berkeley and hundreds of other schools is that Berkeley simply didn't cover up what it was doing.

It is possible, though not likely, that some universities will take the Berkeley decision seriously and actually change their admissions criteria to comply with the central thesis of the *Bakke* decision. That thesis is that *real* diversity within the student body is a desirable and constitutional educational goal, but that *superficial* diversity — based on race alone — may not be achieved by admissions criteria that make decisions turn on race. Some universities have made efforts to broaden their definition of diversity beyond race, to include the physically challenged, the economically disadvantaged, and other individuals who have overcome hardships and barriers.

The challenge posed by the Berkeley decision is for universities to stop being *lazy* about their admissions decisions, and to begin looking beyond *group* criteria such as race. It is more difficult to base affirmative action decisions on *individual* criteria and accomplishments. But it is well worth the effort.

It is particularly unseemly for law schools — which are supposed to be teaching their students fidelity to the law — to be contriving to circumvent a Supreme Court decision with which most of the faculty disagrees. It would be far better to make serious efforts to comply both with the letter and spirit of the *Bakke* decision. In the alternative, law schools could seek to challenge *Bakke* and have it overruled, but with the current Supreme Court, that seems highly unlikely. For the present, at least, law schools will have to live with the restrictions of *Bakke*, but they must live with those restrictions in the spirit of compliance and not circumvention.

October 1992

Iran's Unrebutted Threat to Rushdie

THE IRANIAN MAFIA — otherwise known as the Islamic Republic of Iran — has renewed its three-million-dollar contract on author Salman Rushdie. On the fourth anniversary of the original contract, it is urging its fundamentalist hit men all over the world to "execute" — a euphemism for murder in cold blood — the author, because his book, *The Satanic Verses*, is deemed blasphemous. Rushdie must take this threat seriously and remain in virtual hiding to avoid what Iran's Islamic republic leaders assure him is "the arrow" that is "moving toward its target" and that will "sooner or later hit it."

Despite this outrageous threat, made by the official representatives of a member nation of the United Nations, the world community is doing virtually nothing to protect a respected author. The United States, as the leader of the free world, has a special obligation to protect international freedom of expression from what George Bernard Shaw once called the "ultimate form of censorship" — namely "assassination."

Yet we have been among the least aggressive in defending

Rushdie. A year ago, several congressional leaders were considering extending an invitation to Rushdie to address Congress. Former Secretary of State Baker prevailed on them not to extend the invitation. He also persuaded President Bush to refuse to meet with Rushdie, and the White House justified this refusal by describing Rushdie as "just an author on a book tour."

Of course, it is Rushdie's fondest dream to be just another author on a book tour. Other authors don't have to have bodyguards and remain in hiding. Other authors look forward to publishing contracts, not murder contracts. The Bush administration's hands-off attitude toward this manifestation of international Iranian terrorism simply emboldens its practitioners.

Nor is the problem limited to Rushdie or Iran. Islamic fundamentalism is being exported all over the globe. Recent disclosures of Hamas influence in Great Britain, the United States, and elsewhere have caused the FBI and other agencies to increase their surveillance. The murder of Rabbi Meir Kahane several years ago is widely believed to have been inspired by Hamas hatred of his rhetoric. Unless the civilized world begins to do something concrete to stop this fundamentalist censorship by violence, we can expect it to increase.

Some governments have, at least, taken symbolic steps to demonstrate their commitment to international free speech and against censorship by death threat. The German government has issued a warning that those who have issued the death threats will be held legally responsible for any harm that might befall Rushdie. It is a warning without teeth, since Germany does not have extraterritorial jurisdiction to punish crimes committed outside its borders, but it is better than nothing. Britain has vowed to continue its breach in relationship with Iran until it calls off its contract on Rushdie.

The Clinton administration should move quickly to change the tolerant tone our government has expressed toward the

Iranian murderers. It should send an unmistakable message that it will not tolerate death threats against authors. Such threats are clearly our concern for several reasons. We have the largest and most important publishing industry in the world. The Iranian "contract" is a direct threat to American publishing. It is also a direct threat to American readers, who must be free to read anything they choose, without regard to the sensibilities of foreign fundamentalists.

Unless the international community, led by the United States, succeeds in getting the Iranian mullahs to withdraw their contract, we will never know how many potential authors and speakers throughout the world are refraining from writing and speaking freely, out of fear that they will be next on the Iranian hit list. If we allow our freedoms to be held hostage to fundamentalist threats, we can only be certain of one conclusion: These threats will increase and expand to other areas.

The Bush administration rationalized its permissive attitude toward the Iranian mullahs by pointing to our need to renew relationships with that oil-rich and strategically located nation. But it sent precisely the wrong message to suggest that we place politicoeconomic concerns over human rights concerns. We no longer have the excuse of the Cold War. The days of tolerance of tyranny in the name of realpolitik must end. We have a real opportunity to make clear that human rights are very high on the foreign policy agenda of the new administration. We can have our cake and eat it too in this instance. Iran needs us much more than we need Iran. We should extend an olive branch to all of our enemies, but we must ask in return not only for an olive branch, but also for an assurance that inhuman practices of the sort conducted by Iran will not be tolerated.

February 1993

Salman Rushdie remains under a death sentence with a bounty on his head. Rushdie, who has lived in hiding under police protection since the Iranian edict was issued in February of 1989, recently met with President Clinton at the White House in a high-profile visit designed to call the public's attention to his continuing plight.

Defense Lawyers As Censors

DEFENDERS OF THE First Amendment must always be prepared for new and unexpected attacks from new and unexpected enemies of free speech. We have fought back against censors from the right and left.

Now, what may be the most dangerous attack on freedom of the press in this century is coming from some liberal criminal-defense lawyers who are calling for censorship in the name of protecting a defendant's right to a fair trial.

This issue suddenly came to an ugly head in the Manuel Noriega case. As all criminal-defense lawyers well know, prison authorities monitor inmates' phone conversations, ostensibly for the purpose of preventing jailbreaks and other threats to prison security. If a lawyer wants to have a confidential conversation with a confined client, that lawyer generally either comes to the prison and meets with the client in a special lawyer's room or makes arrangements for an unmonitored lawyer-client telephone call at a special time.

In the Noriega case, the prison authorities — either deliberately or inadvertently — monitored some conversations between Noriega and members of his defense team. Tapes of these conversations found their way to Cable News Network (CNN), which announced that it intended to broadcast them.

Noriega's lawyers obtained an injunction from the trial judge against broadcasting the tapes, arguing that any airing would endanger their client's right to a fair trial. Since that injunction constituted an unprecedented form of prior restraint, CNN decided to violate it and broadcast one of the tapes. (The ban has since been lifted because the tapes were found to contain little significant information.)

CNN thus set in motion a constitutional crisis: an alleged conflict between two equally important provisions of our Bill of Rights — the First Amendment's freedom of the press and the Sixth Amendment's guarantee of a fair trial.

It is a phony conflict, in my view, for several reasons. First of all, the Bill of Rights imposes restrictions only on the government, and not on private parties. The First Amendment does not assure freedom of publication for all. It only precludes the government from interfering with it. Second, the Sixth Amendment does not assure that all trials will be fair; it only requires that the government do nothing to deny defendants a fair trial.

Moreover, if the exercise of First Amendment freedoms by the private press has made it difficult for a defendant to obtain a fair trial, the courts can move the trial, delay it, or in the very rare case, even reverse a conviction or dismiss an indictment.

Finally, the courts do have the power to prevent government officials from leaking prejudicial information to the press and to punish those officials who do. Most information that endangers fair trials emanates from government officials — as did the Noriega tapes. Yet courts are often reluctant to exercise their authority over those officials and more willing to muzzle the press.

I see no real conflict between the First and Sixth amendments. A free press, in my view, is the ultimate guarantee of a fair trial.

March 1991

CENSORING LAWYERS

SHAKESPEARE'S REVOLUTIONARY character Dick the Butcher announces in *Henry VI*, Part II, "The first thing we do, let's kill all the lawyers." In real life, revolutionary tyrants — from Robespierre to Stalin to Mao — did, in fact, go after the lawyers first. Attorneys are, after all, easy targets. A current joke asks, "What's a load of lawyers sinking at sea?" The answer: "A good beginning." Lawyers are important targets for tyrants because lawyers help citizens secure their rights against government tyranny.

It is not surprising, therefore, that the American judicial and prosecutorial establishments are now going after lawyers, especially criminal-defense lawyers, with a vengeance. They are currently trying to put outspoken criminal lawyers in jail for responding to prosecutorial press leaks.

The leading case involves Bruce Cutler, the New York criminal lawyer who infuriated the legal establishment by securing several acquittals for his client John Gotti. When Gotti was brought to trial again, prosecutors employed two weapons against his successful defender. First, they got Cutler disqualified from representing Gotti. Now they are prosecuting Cutler for criminal contempt on the basis of remarks he made before he was disqualified.

The remarks at issue seem entirely within the orbit of protected speech under the First Amendment. They include such rhetorical flourishes as accusing the government of "throwing the Constitution out the window" in its "continuing vendetta" against Gotti. As if to prove Cutler was right, the trial judge charged Cutler with criminal contempt, and now he faces imprisonment.

As usual, the real villain is Rehnquist's Supreme Court, which, in 1991, gave prosecutors and judges the green light to go after noisy defense lawyers. The decision did not, of course, distinguish between prosecuting attorneys and defense lawyers; it gave the courts the power to punish both equally. But such false equality is reminiscent of Anatole France's ironic quip about the law's majestic equality. The courts rarely go after prosecutors who leak information to the press.

What makes this asymmetry worse is that prosecutors are the primary cause of the problem. Defense lawyers speak to the media almost always in an attempt to level a playing field that has been unleveled against their clients by deliberate prosecutorial leaks. The Gotti case is an example in point. For years the government's lawyers have been prosecuting John Gotti in the press. Bruce Cutler had an obligation to defend his client in whatever forum the prosecutors selected for their trial. If Gotti was prosecuted only in a court of law, then that is where he should be defended. But if he is being prosecuted in the court of public opinion, then he should be defended there as well.

In picking Bruce Cutler for its test case, the government has chosen wisely, if not fairly. Cutler is crude, boisterous, and a bit too close to his clients for the taste of many in the legal establishment. His detractors outnumber his defenders, though some establishment groups are worried about the free-speech implications of an adverse judgment against Cutler. They are right to be worried. Any ruling against Cutler — no matter how narrow — would stifle the free speech of all defense attorneys.

Bruce Cutler will weather this storm because he is a survivor. The real question is whether or not the First Amendment will.

August 1993

Bruce Cutler was tried for contempt before Judge Thomas C. Platt, chief judge of the United States District Court for the Eastern District of New York. Chief Judge Platt found Cutler guilty of criminal contempt for violating the gag order imposed by Judge I. Leo Glasser in the John Gotti case. See United States v. Cutler, *840 F. Supp. 959 (E.D.N.Y., 1994). Cutler's appeal of that conviction is pending.*

Censorship by a Newspaper

I F THERE WERE AN award given for displaying a lack of
courage in journalism, it would surely go to the *Boston Globe*
for its recent decision to assist a Massachusetts district attorney in a censorship crusade.

The *Globe*'s capitulation grew out of a Massachusetts
statute that set forth a procedure to censor allegedly obscene
material. Under that procedure, a district attorney who deems
it necessary and wise to ban books or magazines must first
publish their titles in at least two newspapers of general circu-
lation. The D.A. of Hampden County found a Springfield, Massachusetts, paper willing to accept a notice listing the targeted
titles, but both the *Globe* and the *Boston Herald* refused to print
it. Their rationale was that the titles themselves — which included *Hand 2 Mouth, Backside to the Future II, Good-Cum-Pany,*
and *Hot Pizza Ass* — were obscene and violated the standards
of their family newspapers.

The D.A. then threatened to sue them. The *Herald* stuck
to its guns, but the *Globe* wimped out and ran the notice. The
publisher of the *Globe*, William O. Taylor, explained, "We're

performing a public service here to remove these magazines. [The district attorney] can't prosecute unless they had this notice placed, and so, yes, we're helping the situation."

Since when is censorship a public service, especially when it's facilitated by a newspaper? And since when is a newspaper supposed to be "helping" a district attorney do the dirty job of prosecuting dirty books?

Is the *Globe* now going to continue "helping" prosecutors and performing "public service" by disclosing confidential communications between journalists and their sources? This kind of cooperation would have been a boon for Senator Joseph McCarthy's blacklisting. Imagine the purge he could have unleashed if newspapers had printed the names of Communist and fellow travelers back in the 1950s.

The *Globe* also explained its capitulation by saying that it wanted to avoid litigation. But this is the same newspaper that litigates virtually every subpoena and every libel suit. The *Globe* is quick to wrap itself in the First Amendment when it chooses to fight, but the paper conveniently forgets it when throwing in the towel. The paper's publisher also forgets that the towel it is throwing in does not belong to the *Globe* alone. Every newspaper is a trustee of the First Amendment — as the *Globe* is quick to remind us when it seeks support in its libel battles.

The courts clearly would have supported the *Globe*'s right to refuse to publish the D.A.'s notice. More than fifteen years ago, the Supreme Court ruled that no government agency could compel a private newspaper to print an item that it chose not to publish.

The *Globe* knew the paper would win if it fought. Its publishers just did not want to spend the money required to do battle nor did they want to alienate a local prosecutor. No self-respecting newspaper should take orders from government officials about what to publish. Once one newspaper buckles, it will be more difficult for other papers to fend off such pressures. Once a newspaper agrees to publish items at the command of government officials, it will be easier for these officials to demand that newspapers refrain from publishing certain items. The *Boston Globe* has brought us one small step closer to totalitarianism by its unprincipled capitulation to the Hampden County district attorney.

Shame should be placed on publisher William Taylor, who regards his newspaper as one of the nation's most liberal big-city daily newspapers. He should contemplate what those words mean and then go back to school to do some reading on the history of the First Amendment.

August 1991

People Says: We're Wrong. So?

NOW THAT AUTOMATED informational retrieval systems
have all but replaced manual library research, it is more
important than ever for newspapers and magazines to
correct their errors. If they do not, these errors — which
can damage reputations and subvert truth — will quickly become part of the conventional "wisdom" and be repeated over
and over by other newspapers and magazines.

Recently, I encountered a remarkable instance of journalistic arrogance and irresponsibility that warrants recounting.
The August 10, 1992, issue of *People* magazine featured a
story on "celebrities" who are serving time in prison. After
each celebrity's name, the magazine listed the "offense" for
which he or she had been imprisoned. One of the celebrity
inmates was my client Michael Milken. The offense listed for
him was "insider trading."

As soon as I saw the article, I called *People* and advised
them of their mistake. I told them that Michael Milken had *not*
been convicted of insider trading. He had pleaded guilty to
other, less serious, violations. The government had initially

alleged that he had also committed insider trading, but the charge was unfounded and Milken vigorously denied it. The trial judge gave the government ample opportunity to prove its allegation of insider trading at Milken's presentence hearing, but the government came up short. The judge concluded that she was "unable to find" that Milken had traded on inside information, and she refused to consider that allegation in sentencing him.

The bottom line is that Michael Milken is innocent of insider trading. He is now finishing up his two-year prison sentence (reduced recently from ten years) for a handful of technical violations, which the judge found caused a total loss of $318,086. *People* was simply in error when it listed his "offense" as "insider trading," and it was a serious error, since insider trading is a far more culpable crime than are the offenses for which Milken is serving his sentence.

Several days after I advised *People* of its mistake, *People*'s lawyer called me and acknowledged the error. He told me, however, that after an extensive "staff" discussion, the decision had been made not to correct or retract the error. Nor would they even print a letter from me or anyone else setting the record straight. The reason the lawyer gave me was even more appalling than the decision itself. He told me that since *People* is not the *New York Times* or *Wall Street Journal*, its readers do not expect the kind of precision or accuracy expected of "financial or legal journals." In other words, *People*'s own lawyer was defending his publication's error by arguing that *People*'s readers expect imprecise, inaccurate, and flat-out false information — like the readers of the *National Enquirer* and other "Elvis Weds Alien" tabloids. I wonder if *People*'s readers will agree to this insulting assessment of their expectations.

The lawyer's second reason for refusing to correct the record was even more dangerous. He told me that since Milken had "originally been charged" with insider trading, it was no big deal for *People* to list that as his offense. In other words, at *People* magazine, being "charged" with a crime is the journalistic equivalent of being *convicted* of that crime, even if the judge — after hearing days of testimony — has declared the person not guilty. "Why do we need judges or juries when we have *People* editors to determine guilt or innocence?" is the question that I'm sure the *People* lawyer must be asking.

Nor is *People* the only arrogant and irresponsible media giant that refuses to correct its errors. *People* made its mistake because it *copied* other media accounts, which had similarly confused what Michael Milken had been charged with and what he is serving his sentence for. And therein lies the danger of perpetrating falsehoods in our age of automated information-retrieval systems. For once a mistake is made, it remains in a widely accessed computerized database, waiting to be spit out to those unwary researchers who believe they are receiving facts, not fiction. Thus, any mistake takes on a life of its own, being repeated endlessly with little hope of the truth ever catching up to the lie.

There is a relatively simple and inexpensive solution to this recurring problem, but it requires the cooperation of both the responsible media and those who run the retrieval systems. When errors are documented — as they were in the Milken case — the mistakes should immediately be corrected by the newspaper or magazine that published them, and the corrections and documentations must be made part of the database in the retrieval system. Every time the false information in the original story is retrieved, the correction and the true information would be retrieved along with the original story. This is not being done today. If it were, the marketplace of ideas would indeed produce truth, not the kind of imprecise, inaccurate misinformation that *People* magazine believes its readers expect.

September 1992

WIVES ALSO KILL HUSBANDS — QUITE OFTEN

Though O. J. Simpson vehemently denies that he murdered his former wife, his case has provoked a flurry of media attention toward other husbands who kill their wives. Coincidentally with the Simpson case, the Department of Justice has just released the first detailed empirical study of "murder in families." It contains some surprising information, which contrasts sharply with the media headlines.

The most shocking finding of this study — which analyzed nearly ten thousand cases — is that wives murder their husbands far more frequently than press reports would suggest. To put the issue in context, women in general account for only about 10 percent of defendants charged with all murders. But for all spousal murders, women accounted for more than 40 percent of defendants. And "among black marital partners, wives were just about as likely to kill their husbands as husbands were to kill their wives." Not surprisingly, when it comes to parents who kill their children, mothers kill more often than fathers.

The real headline of this report, therefore, is that women kill almost as often as men do in the context of *all* family murders, though men much more often kill strangers — nearly always other men.

The other shocker in this report is that husbands who kill their wives are not treated more leniently than men who kill strangers, despite the media myth to the contrary. Indeed, they were as likely to be charged with first-degree murder, were no more likely to have their cases dismissed or diverted, and were as likely to be convicted. Nor were their sentences significantly different, when relevant "case characteristics" — such as prior criminal record — were taken into account. Indeed, the only real difference is that spousal murderers "required less time to disposition than other types of murder cases."

Despite this hard data, the myths persist that spousal murders consist almost exclusively of husbands who kill their wives and are then treated leniently by the criminal-justice system. Indeed, there is one figure that is strikingly missing from this otherwise thorough report: namely, whether women who murder their husbands are treated more leniently than husbands who murder their wives. I phoned the author of the report and asked if that data was available. He told me that it was but that it had not been compiled. I asked him if he would compile it and he did, faxing me new tables that compared the outcome of prosecution based on the gender of the victim and the accused. This previously unpublished data dramatically undercuts the myth that husbands who kill their wives are treated more leniently than wives who kill their husbands. The available evidence points overwhelmingly in the opposite direction.

Wives who kill their husbands were acquitted in 12.9 percent of the cases studied, while husbands who kill their wives were acquitted in only 1.4 percent of the cases. Women who were convicted of killing their husbands were sentenced to an average of six years in prison, while men received an average of seventeen years for killing their wives. Sixteen percent of female spousal killers get probation, compared to 1.6

percent for males. By almost every other measure as well, female spousal killers are treated more leniently than male spousal killers. To be sure, some of the differences may be attributable to gender-neutral factors such as prior record, provocation, or mental illness. But there is absolutely no support in this data for the claim that husbands who kill their wives are systematically treated with kid gloves by the justice system.

Despite the unexpected data produced by this Justice Department study — that wives kill husbands much more frequently than media accounts suggest and that they are treated more leniently than husbands who kill — the press release issued by the Justice Department to accompany the report buried this politically incorrect data under the following politically correct headline: "Wives are the most frequent victims in family murders." But even that conclusion obscures the real picture: that for all family murders — which includes killing of parents and children as well as spouses — 55.5 percent of the victims were males and 44.5 percent females, and "female defendants were more likely than male defendants to have murdered a person of the opposite sex."

The Justice Department report on "murder in families" sheds important light on a subject that is being obscured by the heat of political rhetoric. The new data strongly suggests that spousal murder is not primarily a male-versus-female political issue, as some radical feminists and media commentators insist. Instead, it is primarily a psychological issue of pervasive familial violence on all sides, generated by the passions of family interaction. Misdiagnosing this important psychological problem to fit into a political agenda will delay its proper treatment and cure. The problems of spousal abuse and violence are far too serious to be turned into divisive "we versus them" political or gender issues.

July 1994

CONCLUSION

A S THIS BOOK GOES to press, national — indeed, international — attention is being focused on the sensational double murder case against O. J. Simpson. Having been asked to consult on the constitutional issues in the Simpson defense, I can no longer remain neutral about that specific case, nor do I know, at this point, how the case will unfold. It is noteworthy, however, that in his letter to the police, which was read while Simpson was apparently contemplating suicide, the former football star said that he had "nothing to do with Nicole's murder." Simpson also wrote the following: "At times I have felt like a battered husband or boyfriend. . . ." It is too early for anyone to know whether this variation on the abuse excuse will play a role in the Simpson case, since the prosecution has the burden of proving beyond a reasonable doubt that the defendant has committed the criminal act with the necessary mental state. In this case, Simpson denies any connection with the act. But the prosecutor has publicly predicted that Simpson will eventually admit that he committed the act and will raise "a Menendez-type defense" — namely, an abuse excuse.

Simpson's chief counsel has disputed this prediction and has criticized the prosecution for making it. Indeed, on the basis of the massive pretrial publicity generated by the prosecution and police, a California judge ordered the grand jury dismissed. Yet there are many who believe that if the DNA tests were to prove positive, Simpson would have little choice but to make a "mental state" defense, such as insanity, self-defense, provocation, or some variation on the abuse excuse. The case is a long way from any such point, since the law is in a state of flux as to DNA testing. It is clear that DNA testing, if properly done on appropriate samples, can *exculpate* a suspect, since all that is needed to exculpate is a reasonable doubt about guilt. But it is far less clear whether DNA testing, especially on crime-scene samples, which are often tainted, can ever *inculpate*, since the prosecution must eliminate all reasonable doubt. Put another way, the DNA testing in a given case may well be scientific enough to *raise* reasonable doubt, but not scientific enough to *erase* reasonable doubt. Unless and until the prosecution were to prove its case beyond a reasonable doubt, the defense would have no obligation to put on any defense.

For purposes of concluding this book, however, it is interesting to explore — in an entirely hypothetical fashion — the implications of the prosecutor's prediction that O. J. Simpson may raise a "Menendez-type defense." This prediction — even if it proves to be erroneous — demonstrates the pervasiveness of the abuse excuse in the contemporary American mind. If O. J. Simpson — the most famous American ever to be charged with murder — were to invoke an abuse excuse, his case would focus world attention on this troubling phenomenon.

Even if Simpson's case does not involve any excuse, we are likely to see little abatement in the national — indeed international — blame-a-thon that has come to characterize the current age. Any retrial of the Menendez brothers is certain to thrust the abuse excuse into sharp focus once again.

Indeed, their lawyer and chief spokesperson, Leslie Abramson, has already gone on the counteroffensive against "critics" who label the defense she offered in the Menendez case as "the 'abuse excuse.'" She suggests that "denizens of the law schools' ivory towers" who disagree with her about the Menendez brothers are racists and sexists. She argues that "the recent cases of O. J. Simpson, Lyle and Erik Menendez, and Lorena Bobbitt have opened a public debate on . . . gender bias. . . ." Her inclusion of the Menendez brothers in this list is a bit difficult to follow, since these young men killed their mother as well as their father. Abramson characterizes the Menendez brothers — who are twenty-six and twenty-three — as "children" and then argues, quite fallaciously, that "women and children . . . rarely kill, but when they do they don't do it out of wounded pride or from affronts to their sexuality or in the anger of the rejected" — as she says men do. In fact, young men the age of Lyle and Erik Menendez commit among the highest rates of murder. Moreover, women kill family members and loved ones at about the same rate that men do, and for the same basic reasons. Abramson is trying to bootstrap her clients' unsympathetic case — rich, young, mobile men murdering their parents for money — into the more sympathetic category of the battered woman syndrome. By doing so, she delegitimates geniune cases in which battered women strike out in self-defense. In any event, I welcome the continuation of the debate over the Menendez brothers and hope that the next jury will be able to place their abuse excuse in its proper legal and moral perspective.

If William Kunstler does indeed raise the "black rage" defense in the Colin Ferguson case, a racial dimension will be added to the debate over whether abuse should excuse. Daimian Osby, whose "urban survival syndrome" defense resulted in a hung jury, will probably also be retried, and Joel Rifkin, who claims "adoptive child syndrome," is scheduled to be retried for more murders of prostitutes who reminded him of his mother. In addition, we are likely to see new and even more imaginative variations on the abuse excuse, especially if jurors continue to accept these defenses.

Nothing in this book is intended to deny that the issue of criminal responsibility is complex and not subject to simple "either-or" solutions. Responsibility is a matter of degree, and a history of abuse may well be one relevant factor in the calibration of responsibility and the calculation of punishment. Surely a Mafia hit man who cold-bloodedly murders a stranger for profit is more culpable than an abusive wife who strikes back in frustration or fear. For a criminal-justice system to earn the characterization of "civilized," it must reflect differences in degrees of guilt. Judges should take such differences into account in imposing sentences, and jurors should be presented with an array of staircased verdicts representing different degrees of culpability. This is supposed to be done under the existing law of homicide, by its breakdown into degrees of murder and manslaughter. But these distinctions often make little sense, as for example the difference between first-degree murder, which generally requires "premeditation," second-degree murder, which generally requires "malice aforethought," and voluntary manslaughter, which often requires that the act be "intentional" but "provoked." Jurors have understandable difficulties comprehending such terms and differentiating among them, thus encouraging lawyers to make emotional appeals such as those in the Menendez and Bobbitt cases.

The time has come for our legal system to confront the issues of responsibility in a rationally calibrated manner that is comprehensible to jurors and citizens. A people who does not take responsibility seriously places liberty at risk. As George Bernard Shaw once put it: "Liberty means responsibility. That's why most men dread it." Today, many men and women seem unwilling to take responsibility for their actions. Excuses abound in every sphere of life from the most public to the most private. Evasions of responsibility breach the social contract and rend the very fabric of democracy. We must stop making excuses and start taking responsibility. What is at stake is far more than the punishment of criminals and the deterrence of crime. It is the very nature of our experiment with democracy.

August 1994

Glossary of Abuse Excuses

ACCOMMODATION SYNDROME In this pattern of behavior, a child may keep abuse secret, accommodate it out of helplessness, delay its disclosure, present an unconvincing account of the incidents, or even recant the testimony later in court. Although this syndrome is considered by many psychologists to be a valid theory, it has nonetheless been rejected by the courts in a number of recent criminal cases. See *State v. J. Q.*, 599 A.2d 172 (N.J. Sup. Ct., 1991) (rejecting the testimony of experts concerning the accommodation syndrome primarily because "the scientific community does not yet exhibit a consensus that the requisite degree of scientific reliability [of the accommodation syndrome] has been shown").

ANTISOCIAL PERSONALITY DISORDER This condition is a psychological syndrome whose victims are possessed with little conscience or empathy for others. According to medical experts, it is precisely this "missing" aspect of the personalities of individuals who suffer from antisocial personality disorder that causes them to experience chronic fits of anger and violence in which the subjects often take pleasure in violating social norms and harming others. Although this disorder is well recognized by the medical and psychological communities and evidence about this condition has been admitted in court for several years, the fact that an individual suffers from antisocial personality disorder does not generally satisfy the legal requirement for a defendant to be declared either incompetent to stand trial or legally insane. See the *New York Times*, February 7, 1993, p. 1.

ATTENTION DEFICIT DISORDER The essential features of this disorder are developmentally inappropriate degrees of inattention, impulsiveness, and hyperactivity. Symptoms typically worsen in situations requiring sustained attention, such as listening to a teacher in a classroom, attending meetings, or doing class assignments or chores at home. Attention deficit disorder is typically treated by medication and professional counseling. See *Diagnostic and Statistical Manual*, Version III (revised), p. 50. A recent example in which attention deficit disorder was invoked as a legal defense to criminal conduct or as a mitigating factor during sentencing was the Michael Fay case in Singapore. Fay's family sought clemency for their son on the grounds that he suffers from attention deficit disorder, which they also claimed could lead to severe problems, possibly even suicide, if the caning were carried out. See the *Los Angeles Times*, May 4, 1994, p. 1.

BATTERED PERSONS SYNDROME This condition is a modified version of the battered woman syndrome, expanded to include male victims of long-term physical or sexual abuse, that was first articulated by psychologist Lenore Walker in her book *The Battered Woman*. Battered persons syndrome arises from the cycle of abuse that individuals are forced to endure in abusive situations at the hands of their spouses. The constant and unpredictable nature of this abuse gradually leads the individual to develop a companion condition known as "learned helplessness." Learned helplessness makes the abused person feel that he or she has no control over the situation and that he or she is powerless to stop the abuse. Since this condition was first diagnosed in the early

1980s, thousands of defendants have invoked battered persons syndrome as an excuse for murdering their abusive spouses, boyfriends, girlfriends, and even parents. Recent examples include the case of seventeen-year-old Andrew Janes, who ambushed and shotgunned his abusive stepfather, and the killing of a forty-one-year-old woman by her thirty-seven-year-old husband, a city fire department captain in Hickory, North Carolina, allegedly out of fear for his safety. See the *Seattle Times*, March 31, 1994, p. B4; *North Carolina News & Observer*, May 11, 1994, p. 1.

BLACK RAGE DEFENSE This defense, which was created by Manhattan attorney William Kunstler after reading a 1969 book, *Black Rage*, written by black psychiatrists William H. Grier and Price M. Cobbs, asserts that black people who are constantly subjected to actions that are perceived by them to be unfair and oppressive become angry, despite an appearance of external calm. According to William Kunstler, this anger over racial injustice can cause an individual to commit acts of violence by becoming the "catalyst" for an individual who already suffers from severe mental problems. Kunstler's theory will soon be tested in court when his client Colin Ferguson, the man accused of murdering six passengers on the Long Island Railroad, goes to trial later this year. See the *New York Times*, April 7, 1994, pg. B6.

CHERAMBAULT-KANDINSKY SYNDROME According to John Money, a prominent sexologist and medical psychologist at Johns Hopkins University, this psychological syndrome is an "erotomanic type delusional disorder" which causes its victims to suffer helplessly under "the spell" of lovesickness. This defense was recently suggested in the case of Sol Wachtler, the chief judge of New York State's highest court, after he was arrested for extortion and threatening to kidnap the fourteen-year-old daughter of his ex-lover. In that case, Professor Money railed against the FBI's treatment of Sol Wachtler, who he believed should not be held responsible for his actions because he was manifesting advanced symptoms of Cherambault-Kandinsky syndrome (CKS) at the time of his crimes, calling their "law-and-order treatment of people with CKS . . . the equivalent of making it a crime to have epileptic spells." See *U.S. News & World Report*, December 7, 1992, p. 22.

CHRONIC LATENESS SYNDROME This condition, which was recently used by a former school district employee as grounds for suing his former boss after he was fired for consistently showing up late for work, seeks to explain the tendency to arrive late for appointments as some sort of psychological disorder, rather than the product of an individual's carelessness or conscious efforts. See the *Chicago Tribune*, September 20, 1992, p. 16.

CULTURAL NORMS DEFENSE This defense involves using one's cultural background and practices as a defense for having committed acts that may be typical in one's homeland but illegal in the United States. An interesting case where cultural norms were raised as a defense occurred in Los Angeles when a Japanese immigrant named Fumiko Kimura was charged with first-degree murder in the drowning deaths of her two young children. Ms. Kimura's defense alleged that she was attempting to commit suicide, in a traditional Japanese method called *oyako-shinju*, or parent-child suicide, by walking out into the ocean holding her two children's heads under water. While this form of ritualistic suicide is not considered murder in Japan, Ms. Kimura was charged with first-degree murder in the United States. Ms. Kimura was eventually allowed to plead guilty to voluntary manslaughter, a crime for which she received a one-year jail sentence. See *People v. Kimura* (L.A. Superior Ct., No. A-091133).

DISTANT FATHER SYNDROME This condition purports to explain why some adults, who were raised by a father who failed to play a significant role in their emotional development, experience feelings of anger, betrayal, and vindictiveness toward their fathers. One self-styled expert on the distant father syndrome, Robert Bly, whose book *Iron John* focuses on the changing relationship between young boys and their fathers from the nineteenth century to the present, commented that "[w]hen the son does not see his father's workplace, or what he produces . . . demons move into that empty place — demons of destruction." See *Men's Health,* July 1993, p. 26.

DRUG ABUSE DEFENSE This excuse contends that an individual is not criminally responsible for offenses that were committed while he or she was under the influence of drugs or alcohol. A recent example of the drug abuse defense was the case of a California man who claimed that he should not be held responsible for the sexual molestation and murder of a nine-year-old girl because he was high on drugs at the time of the offenses. See *People v. Richard Lucio Dehoyos* (Santa Ana County Superior Ct., 1989).

ELDERLY ABUSE SYNDROME This condition affects elderly Americans who come to believe, as a result of being subjected to constant abuse often taking the form of emotional, physical, and even sexual maltreatment, that they are unable to escape their situation. In many of these cases, the victim feels reluctant to report the abuse to the authorities because his or her abuser is a family member, usually a son or daughter, but in some cases a spouse. One such case involved a seventy-eight-year-old woman in Cobb County, Georgia, who killed her fifty-eight-year-old abusive husband after years of physical and emotional abuse. See the *Atlanta Journal and Constitution,* June 23, 1991, p. 1.

"EVERYBODY DOES IT" DEFENSE This claim focuses on the actions of other, similarly situated individuals in an effort to excuse the defendant's conduct. The "everybody does it" defense is most often invoked by politicians who have been accused of improperly exercising the authority of their office for personal gain. One such case involved Texas's newly elected senator, Kay Bailey Hutchison. Senator Hutchison was accused of using public employees to perform personal and political chores for her while serving as that state's treasurer. In her defense, Senator Hutchison's lawyer released research that demonstrated that Texas Governor Ann Richards, Mrs. Hutchison's predecessor as Treasurer, also used that office's resources for political purposes. See the *New York Times*, September 10, 1993, p. A16.

FAILURE-TO-FILE SYNDROME This condition seeks to explain why individuals fail to file their IRS income tax returns before the April 15 deadline. New York University psychiatry professor Stephen J. Coleman has described this "syndrome" as the result of an "overall inability to act in one's own interest, all while one is actively anxious about a clear and present danger." Failure-to-file syndrome has emerged as a legal defense in some cases in New York State, although it has yet to be raised as a defense in a criminal tax case. See the *Atlanta Journal and Constitution*, April 18, 1994, p. A5; the *Wall Street Journal*, April 18, 1994, p. B1.

FAN-OBSESSION SYNDROME This syndrome was first invoked by psychiatrist Park Elliot Dietz who testified in the murder trial of Robert Bardo, the Newport Beach, California, man who was accused of killing actress Rebecca Schaeffer. Dr. Dietz claimed that "fan obsession syndrome," which he believes is a psychological condition created over time by repeated exposure to, and identification with, a particular celebrity. Despite Dr. Dietz's testimony, the jury in the Bardo case convicted the defendant of first-degree murder. See the *Washington Times*, March 4, 1992, p. E1.

FETAL ALCOHOL SYNDROME This syndrome seeks to explain why many children and adolescents exhibit severe behavioral problems, poor judgment, and are easily deceived by others by pointing to the fact that their mothers consumed large quantities of alcohol during pregnancy. See *Calgary Herald*, May 15, 1994, p. B2. This condition has also been purported to cause psychological problems similar to those produced by a mother's use of other drugs during pregnancy. See fetal trimethadione syndrome, discussed below.

FETAL TRIMETHADIONE SYNDROME This condition asserts that a mother's use of epilepsy medication during pregnancy can cause her children to behave aggressively after they are born. The first defendant to invoke fetal trimethadione syndrome as a defense was Eric Smith, a fourteen-year-old boy whose lawyer says that he was driven to beat a four-year-old boy to death because of his uncontrollable "sadistic side" produced by his mother's epilepsy medication taken while she was pregnant with Eric. See the *New York Times*, May 20, 1994, p. B20.

FOOTBALL WIDOW SYNDROME This defense, which was first employed by a Florida woman who shot her husband after he changed the channel to watch a Sunday afternoon football game, is presumed to reflect the frustration that some wives feel when they never get to watch what they want on television. See the *Orlando Sentinel Tribune*, January 2, 1994, p. 9. There is, of course, an analogue to this condition called Super Bowl Sunday syndrome (see below), which gives a husband an excuse for beating his wife.

GENETICS DEFENSE This defense asserts that an individual's genetic makeup is at least partially responsible for his or her criminal behavior. The most common form of this excuse is the XYY genetic phenomenon, a chromosomal abnormality purported to cause individuals afflicted with this condition to have a severely disordered personality characterized by violent, aggressive behavior. Although several studies have shown that the XYY phenomenon is particularly prevalent among prison inmates, most courts have been unwilling to allow cytogenetic evidence of chromosomal abnormality to be considered at a defendant's trial. See *People v. Yukl*, 83 Misc. 2d 364 (N.Y. Sup. Ct., 1975).

GONE WITH THE WIND SYNDROME This condition, named after the movie, has been identified by rape experts as a belief on the part of some men that sex "has to be spontaneous — you have to push through the resistance and, finally, the woman will give in if you push hard enough." One of the dangers of Gone With

The Wind syndrome, according to rape educators, is that these sorts of images, which appear so often in the media, depicting men who pressure women into having sex have contributed substantially to the current rape epidemic in America. See the *Los Angeles Times*, October 17, 1993, p. 1.

GULF WAR SYNDROME Although the causes and symptoms of this disorder are still not very well understood by the medical community, hundreds of Persian Gulf War veterans have reported experiencing some of the following symptoms since their return from Saudi Arabia: rashes or sores on their bodies, muscle or joint aches, and disabling fatigue. There is speculation that this disorder, which has yet to be recognized as an official medical diagnosis separate from other similar conditions such as chronic fatigue syndrome, may have been caused by the exposure of Gulf War veterans to chemical agents used by the Iraqi government during the conflict. See *MacNeil/Lehrer NewsHour,* January 20, 1994.

HOLOCAUST SURVIVAL SYNDROME This disorder, also referred to as concentration camp syndrome, was first described in 1952 by Per Helweg-Larsen and other Danish colleagues among Danish non-Jewish survivors, primarily from the resistance, who had been imprisoned in German concentration camps. Victims of this syndrome suffer symptoms such as difficulty in concentration, irritability, emotional instability, impaired memory, and sleep disturbances, including nightmares of captivity. This syndrome is another manifestation of posttraumatic stress disorder. In fact, torture inflicted in death camps is listed in the *Diagnostic and Statistical Manual*, Version III (revised), as one of the most common stressors producing posttraumatic stress disorder. See the *New York Times*, February 5, 1994, letter to the editor from Robert Krell, professor of psychiatry, University of British Columbia.

LEGAL ABUSE SYNDROME According to Karin Huffer, a social worker who coined the term, victims of this disorder are "first, assaulted by crime, and secondly, by abuses of power and authority administered by the systems their tax dollars support to provide due process of law. . . . In short, they get a 'double whammy.'" In her book *Legal Abuse Syndrome,* Huffer describes how many victims of white-collar crime, court abuse, and bureaucratic "bungling" have come to suffer from posttraumatic stress disorder as a result of having brushed up against various phases of our legal system. Although legal abuse syndrome seems similar to many of the other abuse excuses, including black rage, urban survival, and failure-to-file syndromes, it has yet to be offered as a legal defense against charges of criminal conduct.

MEEK-MATE SYNDROME This syndrome was first invoked by a Los Angeles man named Moosa Hanoukai, who claimed that he was driven to beat his wife to death with a wrench as a result of the psychological emasculation that she had caused him. His lawyer argued successfully (Mr. Hanoukai was convicted of manslaughter instead of murder) that it was his client's wife's constant ridiculing of him and decision to make him sleep on the floor that forced him to kill her. See the *New York Times,* May 20, 1994, p. B20.

"THE MINISTER MADE ME DO IT" DEFENSE This defense was first used by Michael Griffin, the man convicted of killing Florida abortion clinic physician Dr. David Gunn, whose attorneys argued unsuccessfully for an acquittal based upon Griffin's testimony that he had been driven to a nervous breakdown by anti-abortion arguments and he was being made to take the blame for others involved in the killing. See the *Dallas Morning News,* March 12, 1994, p. A30.

MOB MENTALITY DEFENSE According to Dr. Philip McGarry, a consultant psychiatrist in Belfast, Northern Ireland, the central features that compose mob mentality are a core group identity and the presence of a victim who is considered by the mob to be a member of the "out-group" and thus vulnerable to attack. See the *Irish Times*, April 16, 1994, p. 7. The fact that mob mentality involves a number of people acting in concert to perform some violent act has made this condition a popular defense of individuals who have been accused of criminal acts committed as a part of the larger group. For example, in a recent case in Bothell, Washington, two young men who helped put a seven-foot burning cross in the front yard of an African-American family's home attempted to excuse their conduct by claiming that their actions were not "a gesture of racial hatred, but a stupid prank fueled by a mob mentality." See the *Seattle Times*, February 23, 1994, p. B3.

MOTHER LION DEFENSE This excuse, which is in many ways similar to the battered woman syndrome defense, seeks to absolve a mother of criminal responsibility for violent actions taken to protect herself or her children against an attacker. According to a recent poll conducted by the *National Law Journal*, 89 percent of Americans said that they would find it a "compelling" defense if a mother said she'd committed a serious crime to protect her children from a physically abusive father. See the *National Law Journal*, April 18, 1994, p. A1.

MULTIPLE-PERSONALITY DISORDER This condition is most often seen as a response to childhood abuse, which causes the victim's memory, identity, and consciousness to become fragmented. This state of mental disorder also leads to the creation of a separate personality in an effort to distance the individual from the painful memories of abuse. A recent case where multiple-personality disorder was claimed as a legal defense involved an Arizona man named James Carlson who claimed to have eleven personalities, only one of which was aware of the sexual assaults that Mr. Carlson's body was alleged to have committed. After his insanity defense was rejected by a jury, Carlson admitted that he had lied about having multiple-personality disorder because he "was so scared of going to prison." See the *Arizona Republic*, April 20, 1994, p. A1; the *New York Times*, May 9, 1994, p. 1.

MUNCHAUSEN-BY-PROXY SYNDROME This syndrome, which causes parents to falsify or cause their children's illnesses, is thought to involve a pathological need for attention, possibly to strike back at the medical system for some perceived wrong, or to bask in the nurturing concerns of doctors, nurses, and friends. See the *New York Times*, March 29, 1994, p. B1. In Texas, a thirty-five-year-old woman named Tanya Reid was accused of murdering her eight-month-old daughter, Morgan, who died on February 7, 1984, in an Amarillo hospital. During her trial, evidence was presented that Ms. Reid's other child, Robert, had been rushed to the emergency room by his mother on twenty separate occasions, each time under very peculiar circumstances. See the *Dallas Morning News*, December 5, 1993, p. A45.

NICE-LADY SYNDROME This condition emphasizes how, as a result of the lessons learned during childhood, many women tend to play only a supporting role in relationships. The reason is that these women have become "obsessed with reading other people" to the point of becoming "less and less expert about their own thoughts and feelings." This syndrome therefore seeks to explain why many women who are unhappy with their current relationship do not leave their spouses or boyfriends — namely, because they care more about their mate's feeling than they do about their own. See *Cosmopolitan*, February 1993, p. 180.

NICOTINE WITHDRAWAL SYNDROME According to the *Diagnostic and Statistical Manual of Mental Disorders*, Version III (revised), nicotine dependence is categorized by psychologists as a psychoactive substance abuse disorder that causes people afflicted with this disorder to become "distressed because of their inability to stop nicotine use, particularly when they have serious physical symptoms. . . . In many cases, they may experience a period of nicotine withdrawal lasting from days to weeks." The American Psychiatric Association has also concluded that nicotine withdrawal is "an organic mental syndrome and disorder . . . [which] includes craving for nicotine, irritability, frustration or anger, difficulty concentrating, restlessness, increased heart rate, and increased appetite or weight gain." Despite the fact that millions of Americans probably suffer from at least some of the symptoms of nicotine withdrawal syndrome, this disorder has apparently yet to be offered in court as a legal defense against charges of criminal conduct.

NIMBY (NOT IN MY BACKYARD) SYNDROME This condition reflects the hypocrisy of those who claim to want to help solve some of society's problems but are then unwilling to sacrifice their own time, money, or community resources in order to further these goals. A recent example of NIMBY syndrome was a case in Miami in which city officials sued the federal government, who had donated an unused five-acre Naval Reserve site in the upper-middle-class Coconut Grove neighborhood for construction of a shelter for the homeless, arguing that the land grant was improper because it bypassed various local ordinances. The jury who heard the case found otherwise and chastised the plaintiffs for showing "little if any concern for the humanity and dignity of those who were less fortunate and homeless. Residents worried for their property values; business owners feared loss of their patrons; and governments claimed a lack of funds." See the *San Francisco Chronicle*, July 5, 1992, p. 10.

PARENTAL ABUSE SYNDROME This syndrome claims that years of emotional, physical, or sexual abuse inflicted upon a child at the hands of his or her parent can cause that person to lose control of his or her behavior, usually manifested in an act of revenge against the abusive parent. This theory has most recently been invoked as a defense against first-degree murder in the case of Lyle and Erik Menendez, who claimed that parental abuse drove them to kill their parents. The Menendez brothers won a mistrial in that case, largely on the basis of expert testimony about the affects of parental abuse on Lyle and Erik's mental state. See *Time*, October 4, 1993, p. 68; the *Chicago Tribune*, January 2, 1994, p. 3; the *New York Times*, February 13, 1994, p. 14.

PARENTAL ALIENATION SYNDROME This term was coined by psychologist Richard Gardner, who claims that by alienating children and turning them against one parent, usually the noncustodial parent, the other parent is inflicting a form of emotional abuse on the child, which some people believe is as psychologically damaging as sexual abuse. See *The Guardian,* September 20, 1993, p. 10. In a recent case, the Supreme Court of Israel awarded custody of three children to Steven Foxman, a resident of Montreal, Canada, after the children's mother kidnapped them in March 1992 and took them to Israel, where experts say they had been taught to hate their father. See *The Gazette* (Montreal), November 27, 1992, p. A3.

PORNOGRAPHY DEFENSE This defense asserts that pornography is responsible for causing men to commit criminal acts of violence against women, including spousal abuse, rape, and even murder. Two of the most vocal advocates of the link between pornography and sexual violence are Andrea Dworkin and Catharine MacKinnon, both of whom have been involved in drafting legislation in the United States that would make sellers of pornography liable to the victims of sexual violence that can be linked to an individual who has been exposed to these same materials. See *The Atlantic,* November 1992, p. 110. However, as recently as 1992, the Seventh Circuit Court of Appeals rejected a defendant's claim that his death sentence for rape and murder should be mitigated because he was acting under the influence of pornography at the time of the crimes. See *Schiro v. Clark,* 963 F.2d 962 (1992).

POSTTRAUMATIC STRESS DISORDER According to the *Diagnostic and Statistical Manual of Mental Disorders,* Version III (revised), this disorder is triggered by a psychologically distressing event "that is outside the range of usual human experience (i.e., outside the range of such common experiences as simple bereavement, chronic illness, business losses, and marital conflict)." Characteristic symptoms of the disorder include recurrent and intrusive recollections of the event or recurrent distressing dreams during which the event is reexperienced, deliberate efforts to avoid stimuli associated with the traumatic event, a numbing of general responsiveness (referred to as "psychic numbing" or "emotional anesthesia"), feelings of detachment or estrangement, hypervigilance, and difficulties falling or staying asleep. Posttraumatic stress disorder is most commonly known as a combat-related illness affecting male veterans. However, in recent years, the disorder has been discovered frequently among women who were sexually assaulted or the victims of sexual harassment during their military service. (See the *Orlando Sentinel Tribune*, November 8, 1993.) A recent example in which posttraumatic stress disorder was invoked as a mitigating factor during sentencing was the June Marie Burkett case in Bellevue, Washington. Burkett was arrested in 1990 after robbing a Bellevue bookstore. Prosecutors said that the defendant fired a shot, which narrowly missed the store clerk's head. A charge of attempted first-degree murder was dropped in exchange for Burkett's plea to first-degree robbery. At the time of her sentencing, Burkett's defense attorney argued that his client suffered from posttraumatic stress disorder stemming from abuse. See the *Seattle Times*, February 19, 1992.

PREMENSTRUAL STRESS SYNDROME DEFENSE This claim asserts that a woman can be so profoundly affected by the hormonal changes that she undergoes each month that she could be driven to commit acts of violence that would be unthinkable to her at other times. A well-known case in which premenstrual stress syndrome was raised as a defense against criminal charges involved a Virginia surgeon named Geraldine Richter. Ms. Richter was acquitted of drunken driving charges on the basis of the testimony of a gynecologist who told the judge that her conduct was consistent with many of the symptoms of PMS. See the *Toronto Star,* June 24, 1991, p. B1.

PROZAC DEFENSE This claim focuses on the controversial drug Prozac, which is ordinarily prescribed for depression, but has recently been linked in a number of cases to violent behavior on the part of its users. In one particularly grisly case, a modern languages instructor at the University of San Francisco, who had been taking Prozac, pleaded innocent to charges that she bit her eighty-seven-year-old mother so badly that police discovered pieces of flesh on the floor of the family home. See the *St. Petersburg Times*, November 8, 1991, p. 6A.

RAPE TRAUMA SYNDROME The term "rape trauma syndrome" (RTS) was coined by Ann Wolbert Burgess and Lynda Lytle Holmstrom as a result of a research project that studied women who entered the emergency room of Boston City Hospital alleging they had been raped. Since its discovery in 1974, RTS has since been recognized as one of the most common traumata producing posttraumatic stress disorder. See *Diagnostic and Statistical Manual*, Version III (revised), p. 248. RTS is marked by an identifiable cluster of psychological symptoms, often with physical manifestations, that most victims experience in varying degrees and intensity following a sexual assault. RTS consists of two phases: The acute phase is marked by intense fear, shame, anger, self-blame, irritability, changes in eating patterns, and somatic symptoms such as headaches, nausea, and exhaustion. Within two weeks to six months after the assault, the victim enters the second phase, a long-term process of reorganization, characterized by a change in lifestyle (e.g., change in residence), nightmares, insomnia, depression, sexual dysfunction, and the development of fears and phobias specific to the circumstances of the attack. Despite what is know about RTS in the medical and psychological communities, RTS has received a mixed reception in the legal context. See *State v. Marks*, 647 P.2d 1292 (Kan. Supreme Ct., 1982) (allowing the testimony of RTS expert to refute the defense of consent); *State v. McGee*, 324 N.W.2d 227 (Minn. Supreme Ct., 1982) (RTS expert testimony inadmissible to counter the defense of consent).

REPRESSED MEMORY SYNDROME Proponents of this syndrome contend that memories of traumatic events, formed while a person is in an altered state of mind induced by terror, are frequently inaccessible to ordinary consciousness. These memories are thought to be indelible and can be triggered years — even decades — later by a related sensation or event. In recent years, the legal system has been forced to adjudicate lawsuits brought by plaintiffs on the basis of their repressed memories of traumatic events. In one of these cases, a jury in Napa County, California, recently awarded $500,000 in damages to former winery executive Gary Ramona who had accused his daughter's therapists of implanting "memories" of childhood incest into her mind. See the *New York Times,* May 14, 1994, p. 1. In another case in California, a Redwood City jury convicted George Franklin, Sr., of rape and murder of his eight-year-old daughter's friend, based largely on his daughter's sudden memory of the murder twenty years after the fact. See the *Washington Post,* April 12, 1994, p. Z12.

RITUAL ABUSE SYNDROME Coercive persuasion, or thought reform, has been extensively studied and documented by researchers and psychologists in the context of prisoner of war camps, religious cults, and captives of outlaw or extremist groups. Factors such as isolation, physiological depletion, assertions of authority, guilt manipulation, and peer pressure, when applied together to an individual, can have the effect of bringing about behavioral compliance and attitudinal change. See Paul H. Robinson. *Fundamentals of Criminal Law* (Little, Brown, 1988), pp. 883–884. Perhaps the most famous case in which ritual abuse syndrome was invoked as defense against criminal charges is the Patty Hearst bank robbery trial in which Ms. Hearst's lawyer, F. Lee Bailey, called a battery of psychiatrists to testify that Hearst was not responsible for her conduct during the Hibernia Bank robbery because she had been brainwashed by her kidnappers. See *United States v. Hearst,* discussed in Robinson's *Fundamentals of Criminal Law* (cited above), pp. 897–899.

ROCK AND ROLL DEFENSE This defense alleges that subliminal messages contained in rock and roll, or in some cases rap music, were the cause of the defendant's conduct. An early case where this theory was offered was the case of two teenagers in Nevada whose families sued the rock band Judas Priest after their sons committed suicide while listening to the Judas Priest album *Stained Class*. See *Entertainment Law Reporter,* December 1990, p. 1.

SELF-VICTIMIZATION SYNDROME This condition is a sociological phenomenon that describes how the constant anger that an individual feels about his or her position in society can have inhibiting effects on his or her creativity, happiness, and ability to take social and intellectual risks. Self-victimization syndrome, which is also referred to as the internalization of oppression, is not limited to particular social, economic, or racial groups, although many proponents of this syndrome cite the cycle of poverty that many African Americans experience in the inner cities as a prominent example of the evils of this condition. See the *Washington Post,* March 26, 1994, p. B1; the *San Diego Union-Tribune,* September 12, 1993, p. G4.

SITTING DUCK SYNDROME This condition usually arises in an individual who has been abused, either physically, emotionally, or sexually, early in life. Sitting duck syndrome postulates that an individual who has a history of abuse is more likely to passively accept new relationships, even those which are abusive or exploitative, because he or she has become accustomed to this type of maltreatment. An important implication of this type of reasoning is that, similar to what the proponents of battered woman syndrome have argued, our legal system should not hold those people who choose to remain in abusive relationships responsible for the consequences of that decision because they had no control over their situation. See *Psychology Today,* May 1993, p. 64.

STEROID DEFENSE According to Dr. David L. Katz, a lawyer and psychiatrist at Harvard Medical School, research has demonstrated that anabolic steroids, growth-promoting compounds typically ingested by athletes and professional bodybuilders to increase muscle mass, may be responsible for causing increased levels of aggression in their users, a phenomenon that is commonly referred to by steroid users as "roid rages." This defense was recently raised in a San Francisco, California, courtroom by Gordon Kimbrough, a thirty-one-year-old bodybuilder and avid steroid user, who claimed that his long-term use of anabolic steroids caused him to fly into an uncontrollable rage during which he stabbed and strangled his girlfriend to death. See the *New York Times,* July 3, 1993, sec. 1, p. 45.

STOCKHOLM SYNDROME This syndrome, which was first identified after a hostage incident in Sweden where hostage-takers and their victims drew closer together the longer the siege continued, seeks to explain why hostage-takers, as well as their captives, tend to bond closely together during a crisis situation, even to the point where the victims come to see the authorities trying to rescue them as the enemy. See the *Washington Post,* April 25, 1993, p. C3. This condition has been offered as a partial explanation, aside from the effects of ritual abuse, for why Patty Hearst took part alongside her former captors in the Hibernia Bank robbery, a crime for which she was tried and convicted in 1976. See ritual abuse syndrome discussed above.

SUPER BOWL SUNDAY SYNDROME Several women's advocates maintain that there is a direct correlation between watching the Super Bowl and violence against women. These feminists rely on data that they claim support the assertion that Super Bowl Sunday is "the biggest day of the year for violence against women." One cited study indicated a 40 percent increase in such violence after games won by the Washington Redskins. According to the *Boston Globe,* women's shelters and hotlines are "flooded with more calls from victims [on Super Bowl Sunday] than any day of the year." As it turns out, every study linking football to violence against women proved unreliable.

SUPERJOCK SYNDROME This term was coined by Dr. Susan Forward, the therapist who treated Nicole Simpson and then proceeded to disclose confidential communications to the press. She describes the syndrome as athletes who become prone to violence when frustrated. "These guys become conditioned to all this wealth, prestige and power. They begin to think they can do no wrong and are above the law." No respected psychological organization recognizes this as a valid syndrome.

TELEVISION DEFENSE This defense contends that repeated exposure to violent programs on television can lead an individual to commit violent acts. The case that brought this defense to the nation's attention was the trial of Ronney Zamora, a fifteen-year-old Florida youth who was tried and convicted of the murder of eighty-two-year-old Elinor Haggart. The jury found Mr. Zamora guilty of murdering Ms. Haggart despite his claim that the violent programs that he watched on television served as his "instructor, his brainwasher, his hypnotizer." It is somewhat ironic that Zamora's trial was covered from start to finish by Miami's public television station. See the *Washington Post*, October 2, 1977, p. A10.

TWINKIE DEFENSE This excuse was made famous by the Dan White case in San Francisco, California, during the late 1970s. Mr. White, a former police officer, was found guilty of involuntary manslaughter, not first-degree murder, for the killing of San Francisco Mayor George Moscone and Supervisor Harvey Milk. The jury accepted Mr. White's claim that he had become mentally incapacitated at the time of the killings in part because of his consumption of junk foods, a claim that has since become known as the "Twinkie defense." See the *Los Angeles Times*, May 3, 1992, p. A26.

UFO SURVIVOR SYNDROME According to John Mack, a professor of psychiatry at Harvard Medical School and author of a recent book, *Human Encounters with Aliens*, hundreds of thousands of Americans believe that they have had encounters with aliens or have seen unidentified flying objects (UFOs). Although Dr. Mack found that each individual's experience with aliens was unique in some way, he identifies a number of symptoms that many of the survivors have shared, including dreams of UFOs or alien encounters, anxiety, frequent and inexplicable nosebleeds, physical scarring, and other bodily sensations. Perhaps the most interesting point about Mack's treatise on alien encounters is that he has been unable to identify a psychiatric illness, or a common set of psychological or emotional conditions, that could account for his patients' memories of their abduction. See the *New York Times*, May 1, 1994, p. 13.

UNHAPPY GAY SAILOR SYNDROME This condition is designed to reflect the frustration and anger that gay and lesbian sailors experience while being forced to serve out their tour of duty "in the closet" because of the U.S. Navy's prohibition against openly gay sailors. However, this syndrome has most often been invoked to foster feelings of prejudice against gays and lesbians in the navy. For example, after forty-seven sailors were killed when a gun turret exploded aboard the USS *Iowa*, some critics attempted to place the blame for that tragedy on the gay and lesbian members of the ship's crew, who they believed conspired to cause the disaster. See *Esquire*, December 1993, p. 101.

URBAN SURVIVAL SYNDROME This syndrome was first used as a legal defense in the Texas murder trial of Daimian Osby, who was accused of murdering Marcus Brooks and Willie Brooks. Osby's defense lawyers raised urban survival syndrome as a defense, claiming that the violent conditions in Osby's neighborhood helped justify the shooting of the two men. The jury who heard Osby's case eventually split 11–1 on the verdict, which resulted in the judge declaring a mistrial. See the *Fort Worth Star-Telegram*, April 20, 1994, p. 17.

VIETNAM SYNDROME A variation of posttraumatic stress disorder, Vietnam syndrome is characterized by symptoms that involve recurring and intrusive recollections of military combat, avoidance of stimuli associated with the war, diminished responsiveness to the outside world (referred to as "psychic numbing" or "emotional anesthesia"), and increased arousal (including insomnia and hypervigilance). According to the *Diagnostic and Statistical Manual of Mental Disorders*, Version III (revised), "the person commonly makes deliberate efforts to avoid thoughts or feelings about the traumatic event." Many defendants have invoked this syndrome as an excuse for being incapable of distinguishing right from wrong. In a 1982 case, a Vietnam veteran was convicted of first-degree murder of his aunt's husband. Prior to the assault, the defendant was rejected by his wife and assaulted by her relatives. Acting in a "state of primitive rage" based on "survival instinct," the defendant became increasingly violent, eventually killing his aunt's husband. During the trial, one psychiatrist argued that the defendant "resorted to survival tactics, just striking out blindly, and not knowing what he was doing wrong." See *State v. Kenneth J. Sharp, Jr.*, 418 So. 2d 1344 (Louisiana Sup. Ct., 1982).